Daily

GRADE
4

Fundamentals

Writing: Teera Safi
Content Editing: Lisa Vitarisi Mathews
Kathleen Jorgensen
Copy Editing: Cathy Harber
Art Direction: Yuki Meyer
Design/Production: Jessica Onken
Susan Lovell
Paula Acojido

EMC 3244

Evan-Moor.™

Visit
teaching-standards.com
to view a correlation
of this book.
This is a free service.

**Correlated to
Current Standards**

**Congratulations on your purchase of some of the
finest teaching materials in the world.**

*Photocopying the pages in this book
is permitted for <u>single-classroom use only</u>.
Making photocopies for additional classes
or schools is prohibited.*

CPSIA: McNaughton & Gunn, Saline, MI USA [5/2021]

CONTENTS

What's Inside?

Daily Fundamentals has 30 weeks of cross-curricular skills practice. Each week provides targeted practice with language, math, and reading skills. The focused daily tasks progress in difficulty as students move from Day 1 tasks to Day 5 tasks. Item types range from multiple choice and matching to constructed response and open-ended questions.

Language items practice grammar, mechanics, spelling, and vocabulary.

Math items practice number and operations, algebraic thinking, geometry, measurement and data, and problem solving.

Reading items practice core reading comprehension skills such as inference, prediction, author's purpose, main idea and details, summarizing, fact or opinion, nonfiction text features, and literary analysis.

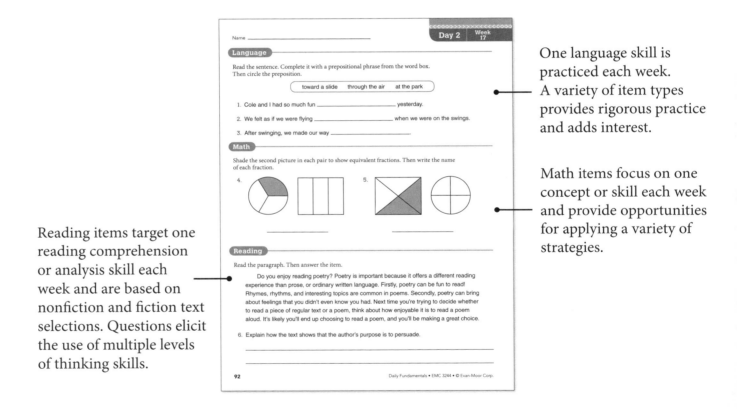

One language skill is practiced each week. A variety of item types provides rigorous practice and adds interest.

Math items focus on one concept or skill each week and provide opportunities for applying a variety of strategies.

Reading items target one reading comprehension or analysis skill each week and are based on nonfiction and fiction text selections. Questions elicit the use of multiple levels of thinking skills.

Answer Key

Correct or exemplar responses are shown on a reduced version of the actual page. An *
is used to indicate an open-ended item or an item with many ways to word the answer.
Accept any reasonable response.

Daily Fundamentals • EMC 3244 • © Evan-Moor Corp.

How to Use This Book

Using *Daily Fundamentals* as morning work or bell ringers

Have the daily practice activity on students' desks when they arrive in the morning, after recess, or during a transitional period. Have students complete the assignment independently. Then have them share their answers and the strategy or approach they used. Encourage discussion about each item so students can share their thinking and provide support and insights to one another. These discussions may also provide you with teachable moments and information to guide your instruction.

Using *Daily Fundamentals* for homework

Assign one weekly unit at the beginning of each week. Students will have the autonomy to manage their time to complete the assignment, and they will benefit from the focused practice of language, math, and reading comprehension skills. At the end of the week, display the answer key and allow students to correct their own work. Facilitate a class discussion about the items and allow students to share their answers. Encourage students to model how to solve problems or answer items that their classmates may have struggled with.

Using *Daily Fundamentals* as an informal assessment

You may wish to use the weekly lessons as an informal assessment of students' competencies. Because each week's practice focuses on a particular skill or concept, the tasks provide you with a detailed view of each student's level of mastery.

Skills Scope and Sequence

Use the scope and sequence chart to identify the specific skills that students are practicing.

Student Progress Chart

Students can monitor their own progress by recording their daily scores and thinking about their success with different skills. Reproduce and distribute the progress chart to students at the beginning of each week. For older students, you may wish to have them write the number correct out of the total number of items.

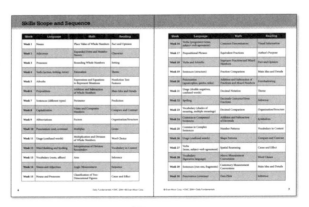

Student Record Sheet

Record students' scores on the record sheet. This form will provide you with a snapshot of each student's skills mastery in language, math, and reading and serve as a resource to track students' progress throughout the year.

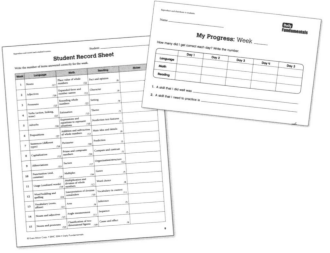

Skills Scope and Sequence

Week	Language	Math	Reading
Week 1	Nouns	Place Value of Whole Numbers	Fact and Opinion
Week 2	Adjectives	Expanded Form and Number Names	Character
Week 3	Pronouns	Rounding Whole Numbers	Setting
Week 4	Verbs (action, linking, tense)	Estimation	Theme
Week 5	Adverbs	Expressions and Equations to Represent Situations	Nonfiction Text Features
Week 6	Prepositions	Addition and Subtraction of Whole Numbers	Main Idea and Details
Week 7	Sentences (different types)	Perimeter	Prediction
Week 8	Capitalization	Prime and Composite Numbers	Compare and Contrast
Week 9	Abbreviations	Factors	Organization/Structure
Week 10	Punctuation (end, commas)	Multiples	Genre
Week 11	Usage (confused words)	Multiplication and Division of Whole Numbers	Word Choice
Week 12	Word Building and Spelling	Interpretation of Division Remainders	Vocabulary in Context
Week 13	Vocabulary (roots, affixes)	Area	Inference
Week 14	Nouns and Adjectives	Angle Measurement	Sequence
Week 15	Nouns and Pronouns	Classification of Two-Dimensional Figures	Cause and Effect

Daily Fundamentals • EMC 3244 • © Evan-Moor Corp.

Week	Language	Math	Reading
Week 16	Verbs (progressive tense, subject-verb agreement)	Common Denominators	Visual Information
Week 17	Prepositional Phrases	Equivalent Fractions	Author's Purpose
Week 18	Verbs and Adverbs	Improper Fractions and Mixed Numbers	Fact and Opinion
Week 19	Sentences (structure)	Fraction Comparison	Main Idea and Details
Week 20	Punctuation (apostrophes, quotes, titles)	Addition and Subtraction of Fractions and Mixed Numbers	Foreshadowing
Week 21	Usage (double negatives, confused words)	Decimal Notation	Theme
Week 22	Spelling	Decimals Converted from Fractions	Inference
Week 23	Vocabulary (shades of meaning, multiple meanings)	Decimal Comparison	Organization/Structure
Week 24	Commas in Compound Sentences	Addition and Subtraction of Decimals	Symbolism
Week 25	Commas in Complex Sentences	Number Patterns	Vocabulary in Context
Week 26	Usage (confused words)	Shape Patterns	Compare and Contrast
Week 27	Verbs (tense, subject-verb agreement)	Spatial Reasoning	Cause and Effect
Week 28	Vocabulary (figurative language)	Metric Measurement Conversions	Word Choice
Week 29	Sentences (run-ons, fragments)	Customary Measurement Conversions	Main Idea and Details
Week 30	Punctuation (commas)	Data Plots	Inference

Name _____

My Progress: Week _____

How many did I get correct each day? Write the number.

	Day 1	Day 2	Day 3	Day 4	Day 5
Language					
Math					
Reading					

1. A skill that I did well was _____.

2. A skill that I need to practice is _____.

- ✂

Name _____

My Progress: Week _____

How many did I get correct each day? Write the number.

	Day 1	Day 2	Day 3	Day 4	Day 5
Language					
Math					
Reading					

1. A skill that I did well was _____.

2. A skill that I need to practice is _____.

Student: _____

Student Record Sheet

Write the number of items answered correctly for the week.

Week	Language	Math	Reading	Notes
1	Nouns /17	Place value of whole numbers /22	Fact and opinion /8	
2	Adjectives /16	Expanded form and number names /12	Character /9	
3	Pronouns /23	Rounding whole numbers /22	Setting /9	
4	Verbs (action, linking, tense) /23	Estimation /13	Theme /5	
5	Adverbs /16	Expressions and equations to represent situations /10	Nonfiction text features /5	
6	Prepositions /27	Addition and subtraction of whole numbers /13	Main idea and details /9	
7	Sentences (different types) /16	Perimeter /10	Prediction /5	
8	Capitalization /12	Prime and composite numbers /24	Compare and contrast /5	
9	Abbreviations /33	Factors /17	Organization/structure /12	
10	Punctuation (end, commas) /18	Multiples /16	Genre /5	
11	Usage (confused words) /19	Multiplication and division of whole numbers /12	Word choice /8	
12	Word building and spelling /24	Interpretation of division remainders /10	Vocabulary in context /11	
13	Vocabulary (roots, affixes) /23	Area /9	Inference /5	
14	Nouns and adjectives /13	Angle measurement /11	Sequence /5	
15	Nouns and pronouns /23	Classification of two-dimensional figures /19	Cause and effect /9	

Student Record Sheet, *continued*

Week	Language	Math	Reading	Notes
16	Verbs (progressive tense, subject-verb agreement) /18	Common denominators /23	Visual information /6	
17	Prepositional phrases /15	Equivalent fractions /14	Author's purpose /5	
18	Verbs and adverbs /22	Improper fractions and mixed numbers /21	Fact and opinion /9	
19	Sentences (structure) /14	Fraction comparison /12	Main idea and details /5	
20	Punctuation (apostrophes, quotes, titles) /11	Addition and subtraction of fractions and mixed numbers /18	Foreshadowing /5	
21	Usage (double negatives, confused words) /14	Decimal notation /15	Theme /11	
22	Spelling /23	Decimals converted from fractions /20	Inference /5	
23	Vocabulary (shades of meaning, multiple meanings) /14	Decimal comparison /14	Organization/structure /5	
24	Commas in compound sentences /13	Addition and subtraction of decimals /14	Symbolism /11	
25	Commas in complex sentences /16	Number patterns /6	Vocabulary in context /9	
26	Usage (confused words) /12	Shape patterns /6	Compare and contrast /5	
27	Verbs (tense, subject-verb agreement) /13	Spatial reasoning /6	Cause and effect /10	
28	Vocabulary (figurative language) /12	Metric measurement conversions /11	Word choice /7	
29	Sentences (run-ons, fragments) /14	Customary measurement conversions /14	Main idea and details /5	
30	Punctuation (commas) /17	Data plots /7	Inference /12	

Daily Fundamentals • EMC 3244 • © Evan-Moor Corp.

Language

Read the sentence. Circle the possessive pronoun.

1. The purple backpack used to be mine.

2. My cousin wanted it, so now it's his.

3. Shelly has one, and hers is newer.

4. Ours are kept in the garage.

5. The Craig twins use theirs for camping.

6. Yours would be great for camping, too.

7. Its size and shape make it seem huge.

Math

Round the whole number to the value of the underlined digit.

8. 54,624 _____

9. 128,762 _____

10. 929,304 _____

11. 827,218 _____

12. 198,077 _____

13. 483,600 _____

14. 398,111 _____

15. 782,684 _____

Reading

Read the paragraph. Then answer the items.

Once there was a troll who lived under a dark, grubby bridge. There always seemed to be a dark cloud over the bridge. The troll tried not to disturb the animals who lived in the sunny, green, lush meadow nearby. He slept all day and stayed awake all night. Everyone thought he was wicked because of the hideous bridge. Actually, he was rather polite.

16. Why would the troll's home make others assume the troll was wicked?
    Ⓐ It appears dark, so it seems like nobody is ever home.
    Ⓑ It appears dark, so it seems like an appropriate place for dark deeds.
    Ⓒ It's next to a sunny meadow, so it seems like a nice bridge.
    Ⓓ Most people think all bridges are wicked places.

17. Does the bridge's closeness to the meadow make it seem more or less dark? Why?

_____

_____

Language

Read the sentence. Write a pronoun from the word box that agrees with the bold noun or nouns.

> she   it   they

1. Jamal passed the **soccer ball** to Phil,

   who kicked _____ to Tim.

2. **Ava** ran around the track until

   _____ felt tired.

3. Tory tried to use the **treadmill** and the

   bike, but _____ were being used.

Math

Answer the item.

4. Gia and Ted both rounded the number **61,709**. Gia ended up with 62,000, and Ted ended up with 61,700. Is Gia or Ted correct? Explain why.

   _____

   _____

   _____

5. If Gia and Ted rounded the original number to the tens place, what number would they get?

   _____

Reading

Read the paragraph. Then answer the items.

   Chas was a poor college student who lived in a tiny apartment above a pasta restaurant. One evening he had friends visiting. They were overcome with hunger when a scent drifted into the apartment through a floor vent. At first they were all crushed. Then Chas formed a plan. He boiled plain pasta. The friends ate it while sniffing the pasta sauce scent at the vent. "And it's free!" Chas said happily. They were all pleased because they could almost taste the sauce.

6. How did the setting of the story influence the characters' actions? Use details to explain.

   _____

   _____

7. How would the story be different with a different setting?

   _____

   _____

Language

Read the sentence. Write *who* or *whom* to complete it.

1. Marcy is the person _____ wanted to buy potatoes.

2. Leah, _____ Marcy is making a vegetable soup for, has a cold.

3. Kyle might ask _____ the soup is being made for.

4. He is the person _____ likes to eat every kind of food imaginable.

Math

This chart shows how many families in Clara County prefer certain yogurt flavors. Use the chart to answer the items.

Favorite Yogurt Flavors	
Strawberry	16,194
Vanilla	16,619
Plain	11,826

5. Round each number to the nearest thousand. Then write the flavor preferred by most families.

   _____

6. Round each number to the nearest hundred. Then add the rounded numbers. Write the total for an estimate of how many families took the survey.

   _____

Reading

Read the paragraph and look at the picture. Then answer the item.

The five friends sat inside the small wooden shed in Ricardo's backyard. Without windows, the shed, with its cracked door and bare walls, was very dim. The children sat on the rough, splintery floor because there were no chairs. "It's freezing in here!" exclaimed Sophia. "And sad!"

7. Explain why the friends are in the shed. Then explain why Sophia says it feels "sad."

_____

_____

_____

3/25

Language

Read the sentence. Underline the verb. Then circle *action verb* or *linking verb*.

1. Carmen's lunch smells fresh and fruity.   **action verb**   **linking verb**

2. Chang stirs his bowl of pasta.   **action verb**   **linking verb**

3. Kingsley pours salad dressing onto his tomato.   **action verb**   **linking verb**

4. Pearl appears hungrier than usual.   **action verb**   **linking verb**

Math

Round the numbers to the nearest hundred, and then add. Show your work.
Write the estimated sum on the line.

5.   521
    + 411

6.   389
    + 132

7.   8,207
    +   663

8.   2,445
    + 1,796

_____   _____   _____   _____

Reading

Read the paragraph. Then answer the item.

     Joe lived near a small petting zoo. One day, he rode his bike there, wanting to see the animals. But the zoo was closed and the gates were locked. He decided to climb over the fence. He thought the owners wouldn't mind because his mom knew them. Inside, he saw the owners, and they were furious when they saw him. They told him that the animals were sick, and that the zoo was closed for the animals' safety.

9. One possible theme of this text is that _____.
   Ⓐ trespassing is never acceptable
   Ⓑ trespassing is acceptable
   Ⓒ knowing someone means you can treat them poorly
   Ⓓ living near a place means you can go there anytime

Language

Read the sentence. Circle the helping verb. Then underline the main verb.

1. Dory has trimmed the bushes in the yard.

2. Mom does push the mower on occasion.

3. Dad is repairing the lawn furniture.

4. He will build a fence this summer.

Math

Round the numbers to the nearest thousand, and then subtract. Show your work. Write the estimated difference on the line.

5. $\begin{array}{r} 8,394 \\ -6,728 \end{array}$

6. $\begin{array}{r} 9,837 \\ -9,086 \end{array}$

7. $\begin{array}{r} 1,571 \\ -849 \end{array}$

8. $\begin{array}{r} 6,482 \\ -3,940 \end{array}$

_____   _____   _____   _____

Reading

Read the paragraph. Then answer the item.

Dinner was ruined! As I was cooking, the new fridge magnets kept sliding across the counter and sticking to the frying pan. Wind from the open window blew napkins all around. And, annoyingly, the gravy kept sinking to the bottom of the jar.

9. Explain how the theme of natural forces (magnetism, wind, and gravity) is explored in the text.

_____

_____

_____

Language

Read the sentence. Underline the verb or verb phrase. Then circle *past, present,* or *future* to name the verb tense.

1. Tyson painted a portrait of his grandmother.   past   present   future

2. Belinda will study art history.   past   present   future

3. Forrest sketches images he finds in nature.   past   present   future

4. Vera designed a colorful picture frame.   past   present   future

Math

Solve the problem. Show your work.

5. Zari flew on two airplanes to visit her family overseas. Her first flight carried her 2,434 miles. Her second flight carried her 5,539 miles. Estimate the total distance Zari flew by rounding to the nearest ten and adding.

   _____

6. Ayako planned to travel 6,738 miles to visit her family. Then her family said they'd travel 5,355 miles in her direction to meet her in between. Estimate the total distance Ayako now has to travel by rounding to the nearest hundred and subtracting.

   _____

Reading

Read the paragraph. Then answer the item.

   Long ago, a young Native American boy named Fast One joined the older tribesmen on his first deer hunt. His mom asked him to bring home any parts of the deer that the others didn't take. But Fast One thought the remaining parts were useless scraps. He ignored his mom's request. "Son," she said, "now we have less food and clothing." Fast One tried to explain that it was only scraps, but his mom explained their value.

7. Was Fast One justified in not doing what his mom requested? Explain why or why not.

_____

_____

_____

Language

Write the past tense of the verb.

1. keep _____

2. do _____

3. speak _____

4. take _____

5. leave _____

6. wear _____

7. write _____

8. see _____

Math

Solve the problem. Use models, numbers, or words to show your thinking.

9. Bruno planned to pay $891 for a new bike. But when he got to the store, it was on sale for $567. Round to the nearest ten and subtract to estimate how much Bruno saved.

_____

10. A family of six is going on vacation. They spent $2,386 per person for plane tickets. Round to the nearest hundred and multiply to estimate how much the family spent on plane tickets.

_____

Reading

Read the paragraph. Then answer the item.

This trip back to the Louisiana coast is different from earlier visits. The hurricane changed it all. Grampa and I won't have fun fishing, and Gramma won't bake cookies. This visit we'll help Grampa and Gramma fix their house. We'll clear out their soaked rugs, replace warped wallboards, paint walls, and install new carpet. Gramma wants to replant the destroyed flowers. "First we have to replant ourselves," says Grampa.

11. Explain how the theme of people's adaptation to Earth is discussed in the text. Use examples.

_____

_____

3/28

Language

Rewrite the phrase using the present progressive form of the verb.
Remember to use the helping verb *am, is,* or *are.*

Simple Present Tense	**Present Progressive Tense**
1. we climb	_____
2. he swims	_____
3. I cheer	_____

Math

Use the chart to answer the item.

4. Students were asked to estimate the answer to the
   following math problem: **18,775 + 21,648.** The chart
   shows that each student got a different answer.
   Explain how that's possible.

   _____

   _____

   _____

Student Estimation Answers	
Student	**Answer**
Miranda	40,430
Summer	40,400
Tyrese	41,000
Lincoln	40,000

Reading

Read the paragraph. Then answer the item.

     Emmet's family started a farm. At first, Emmet didn't think that his family's small
farm would make a difference in the town. But after some time, he realized that people
in the community appreciated the eggs, vegetables, and grains that his family provided.
Locals trusted his family to grow healthful foods that were safe to eat. And the money
spent by locals at the farm stayed within the community, benefiting the local economy.

5. Write one of the themes being explored in the text. Explain how you identified this theme.

   _____

   _____

Name _____

Language

Read the sentence. Circle the adverb(s).

1. Moby firmly presses the elevator button.
2. Matilda energetically parks her bike.
3. Gina grips the railing tightly as she slowly walks up the stairs.
4. Preston suddenly sits on the bench and stubbornly refuses to get up.

Math

Read the problem. Then circle *a* or *b* to show the correct expression to solve it.

5. Jason can save 30 dollars of allowance every month. He hopes to save 270 dollars to buy a new bike helmet. How many months will it take Jason to save enough money?

   a. 270×30 b. $270 \div 30$

6. Rosario swam 18,422 yards in a single year. If she continues to swim at this rate, how many total yards will she have swum in fifteen years?

   a. $18,422 \times 15$ b. $18,422 \div 15$

Reading

Read the text. Then answer the item.

Meteorologists study and predict the weather. They use tools and technology to obtain information. Each tool measures something specific.
- A *thermometer* measures air temperature.
- An *anemometer* measures wind speed.
- A *rain gauge* measures rainfall.

7. Each bullet point _____.
   Ⓐ explains how meteorologists work
   Ⓑ represents weather data
   Ⓒ indicates a separate item in a list
   Ⓓ indicates a new paragraph

Language

Read the sentence. Complete it with an adverb from the word box.

(rarely   slightly   quite)

1. Greta was _____ hungry, so she ate only part of her dinner.

2. Maria was very thirsty, so the amount of water she drank was _____ large.

3. Paula is _____ cold because she often wears a jacket.

Math

Read the problem. Then write an equation or expression to solve it.

4. Jolene and her mom are baking cookies together for a family party. Each batch contains 36 cookies. They made 3 batches on Wednesday, 4 batches on Thursday, and 6 batches on Friday. How many cookies did they make for the party?

   equation: _____   answer: _____

5. Paolo and his dad walk 2 miles every weekend. If they continue doing this, how many miles will each person have walked after 5 years?

   equation: _____   answer: _____

Reading

Read the text. Then answer the item.

Where Snakes Live
Snakes live on almost every continent. Sometimes they stay underground. They like warm environments.

How Snakes Eat
Snakes swallow their prey whole. Their jawbones separate. Their mouths open wide.

6. Explain how each bold heading relates to the text below it. Use examples.

   _____

   _____

Language

Read the sentence. Complete it with a negative adverb from the word box.

> never   nowhere   not

1. Dodi could find his sunglasses _____.

2. He looked in many places, but he _____ checked his pocket.

3. Luckily, his old pair was _____ damaged.

Math

Read the problem. Circle *a* or *b* to show the correct expression to solve it. Then answer the item.

4. Trevor eats 8 ounces of vegetables with each meal. He eats 3 meals a day. Which expression would help you figure out how many ounces of vegetables Trevor eats in a given number of days? The variable *y* represents the number of days.

   a. $y \times 8 \times 3$ **b.** $y + 8 + 3$

5. Use the expression you just chose to calculate how many ounces of vegetables Trevor eats in a week. Solve the problem by using the formula $y = 7$.

   _____

Reading

Read the text. Then answer the item.

Hydroelectric Power Plants
Some power plants use falling water to spin a machine called a *turbine*. The turbine moves a coil of wire between magnets. This creates an electric current.

Transformers
The current goes through a *transformer*. It increases the power so it can travel long distances.

6. Explain how headings can be useful when trying to quickly find specific information.

_____

_____

Language

Read the sentence. Underline the comparative or superlative adverb.
Then write *comparative* or *superlative*.

1. Danny types quicker than his little sister, Jess.   _____

2. Jake jumps the highest when his class does fitness testing.   _____

3. Desmond dives deeper than his friend at the pool.   _____

Math

Read the problem. Then write and solve an equation. Use *a* for the number of boxes.

4. Perla works at a pretzel shop. A customer wants to buy 48 pretzels. There are 8 pretzels in a box. How many boxes should Perla sell to her customer?

   equation: _____   answer: _____

5. If a different customer wants to buy 264 pretzels, what would the equation be?

   equation: _____

Reading

Look at the photo and read the caption. Then answer the item.

These tall towers hold up transmission lines. Transmission lines carry electricity from power plants to cities and towns.

6. What kind of information does the caption provide? Explain how it helps you better understand the photo.

   _____

   _____

   _____

   _____

   _____

Language

Read the sentence. Complete it with a relative adverb from the word box.

when	why	where

1. Melissa filled her water bottle _____ she had a chance.

2. The water was really warm, but she didn't understand _____.

3. We like to buy the water _____ they sell it cold.

Math

Read the problem and look at the chart. Then write and solve an equation. Use *a* for the cost.

4. Yoshi needs a deck cleaned, which takes 3 hours. How much will it cost?

   equation: _____ $a =$ _____

5. How much will it cost for 4 hours of patio washing?

   equation: _____ $a =$ _____

Costs of Services	
Service	Cost Per Hour
Car Washing	$12
Deck Washing	$17
Patio Washing	$19

Reading

Read the table of contents. Then answer the item.

Contents

6. Explain how much information this table of contents provides.

   _____

   _____

Language

Read the sentence. Circle the preposition.

1. Dan gave a speech before the bell rang.

2. Dolly sang with the choir.

3. Pritty glanced at the camera.

4. Logan spoke to the audience.

5. Miguel sneaked behind the curtain.

6. Abe walked toward the stage.

7. Vanna sat beside the statue.

8. Roland threw a rose over Vanna's head.

Math

Add. Use regrouping if needed.

9.
```
  9,167
+   843
```

10.
```
  5,932
+   462
```

11.
```
  2,419
+ 6,534
```

12.
```
  8,768
+ 1,627
```

Reading

Read the paragraph. Then answer the items.

Papua New Guinea occupies half an island in the Pacific Ocean. Its economy depends on crops that it grows. This country grows coffee, cocoa bean, tea, coconut, vanilla, and more. It grows so many crops because its climate and soil are perfect for growing plants. Many people in Papua New Guinea eat the crops grown there.

13. The main idea of the text is that Papua New Guinea _____.

    Ⓐ is on an island
    Ⓑ sells coffee
    Ⓒ grows vanilla
    Ⓓ grows many crops

14. Write one sentence from the text that supports the main idea.

    _____

    _____

Daily Fundamentals • EMC 3244 • © Evan-Moor Corp.

Language

Read the sentence. Complete it with a preposition from the word box.

> between   on   under

1. Eric observed the moss growing

   _____ the rock.

2. Stella squinted from the sunlight beaming

   _____ a tree's leaves.

3. Jane rested in the shade she found

   _____ the forest canopy.

Math

Read the problem. Draw a model to help you solve it.

4. Juliet has been part of Crew Club for three years. She helps set up the stage before school concerts and musicals. Her first year, she helped a total of 235 hours. Her second year, she helped 292 hours. Her third year, she helped 198 hours. How many total hours has Juliet helped on Crew Club?

   _____

Reading

Read the paragraph. Then answer the items.

Flossing is an easy way to care for teeth. It clears out plaque and pieces of food stuck between teeth that were missed when brushing, which can lead to cavities. In addition to preventing cavities, flossing regularly can help prevent tooth decay and gum disease. To floss, simply wrap floss tightly around one finger on each hand, and slide the floss up and down along each side of each tooth. It doesn't take long at all.

5. The main idea of the text is that flossing _____.
   Ⓐ is difficult but guarantees tooth health
   Ⓑ is an easy way to care for teeth
   Ⓒ can lead to tooth decay
   Ⓓ takes a long time but is worth it

6. Write one sentence from the text that supports the main idea.

   _____

   _____

Language

Read the sentence. Underline the prepositional phrase. Circle the noun it describes.

1. There are assigned seats in the classroom.

2. Boyd sits beside the window.

3. Mrs. Roper sits under the ceiling fan.

4. Lucy sits between Lou and Miguel.

5. Aishwarya's desk is at the window.

6. Trish's desk stands behind the table.

7. Kareena's seat is near the bookshelf.

Math

Subtract. Use regrouping if needed.

8.
$$
\begin{array}{r}
7{,}865 \\
-\ \ \ 504 \\
\hline
\end{array}
$$

9.
$$
\begin{array}{r}
9{,}348 \\
-\ \ \ 133 \\
\hline
\end{array}
$$

10.
$$
\begin{array}{r}
6{,}276 \\
-\ 3{,}148 \\
\hline
\end{array}
$$

11.
$$
\begin{array}{r}
5{,}469 \\
-\ 1{,}557 \\
\hline
\end{array}
$$

Reading

Read the paragraph. Then answer the items.

One way to be an active citizen is to vote in elections. Voting is a way to exercise the right to have input in what happens around you. When you vote, you are basically saying that you care about yourself, your neighbors, and your community. Adults vote for presidents, governors, mayors, and other officials. Sometimes, students can also vote to elect leaders in school government, teams, and clubs. The purpose of voting is to allow your voice to be heard and participate in the community. If you value your own opinion, voting is for you!

12. Write the main idea of the text in your own words.

_____

_____

13. Write one sentence from the text that supports the main idea.

_____

_____

Language

Read the sentence. Underline the prepositional phrase. Circle the object of the preposition.

1. Riley places flowers inside a vase.

2. Mack hangs a photo above the window.

3. Rita drives by the pink house.

4. Brett pushes a toy car along the sidewalk.

5. Sam pulls thread through a needle's hole.

6. Vince crawls under the bed.

7. Chad sprays water toward his muddy bike.

Math

Read the problem. Draw a model to help you solve it.

8. Roya has a large ant farm. She started with 2,984 ants. Her cousin wanted to start his own ant farm, so Roya gave him 545 of her ants. Then her little brother removed 326 of Roya's ants to observe them in the yard, and he forgot to bring them back. How many ants does Roya have now?

_____

Reading

Read the paragraph. Then answer the items.

Roald Dahl was a creative author with an adventurous, humorous personality. Can you imagine riding in a huge peach with a group of magical insects? How about touring the world's most amazing chocolate factory? Well, master storyteller Roald Dahl could. He wrote many fantastical children's stories between the years of 1943 and 1990. Some of his books, including *James and the Giant Peach* and *The Witches,* are so famous they were made into films.

9. Write one sentence from the text that contains the main idea.

_____

_____

10. Explain how the details in the text support the main idea.

_____

_____

Language

Read the sentence. Then rewrite it, adding a prepositional phrase.

1. Zach read the book.

   _____

   _____

   _____

2. Bertha ate.

   _____

   _____

   _____

Math

Add or subtract. Use regrouping if needed. Then solve the problem.

3. $\begin{array}{r} 8,427 \\ + 9,362 \\ \hline \end{array}$

4. $\begin{array}{r} 6,984 \\ - 3,596 \\ \hline \end{array}$

5. Bess had $589. She spent $327 on a new skateboard. Then her mom paid her $50 for her monthly chores. Bess spent $68 on knee pads. How much money does Bess have now?

   _____

Reading

Read the paragraph. Then answer the item.

The theory of *continental drift* suggests that Earth's surface used to be very different from how we know it today. In 1912, a German scientist named Alfred Wegener developed the theory. It suggests that all of Earth's continents were joined together about 250 million years ago, forming one giant continent called *Pangaea*. Then Pangaea broke up. The continents slowly drifted apart and became the seven separate ones we know today. In the 1960s, other scientists developed the theory of *plate tectonics,* which explains how continents can move. Plate tectonics doesn't oppose the theory of continental drift.

6. Circle the main idea of the text. Then write your own paragraph about a topic you're familiar with. Circle the main idea in your paragraph. Use details to support your main idea.

   _____

   _____

   _____

   _____

 Daily Fundamentals • EMC 3244 • © Evan-Moor Corp.

Language

Read the question. Then write a declarative sentence to answer it.

1. What is your favorite color to wear?

_____

2. Where do you enjoy spending time when you're not studying?

_____

Math

Explain the steps for how someone would find the perimeter of the figure.

3. _____

_____

_____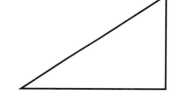

_____

_____

_____

Reading

Read the paragraph. Then answer the item.

    Jay had been looking forward to camping with his dad again since they went last
summer. He thought about how they roasted hot dogs on sticks because they forgot
the wire skewers. He thought of the bug bites they had gotten because they forgot
bug repellent. He thought about setting up the tent in the dark. His alarm went off.

4. Predict what will happen on Jay's camping trip. Explain your thinking.

_____

_____

_____

Language

Read the answer. Then write an interrogative sentence to go with the answer.

1. Answer: Every day the experts feed the sea otters once an hour between noon and midnight.

   Question: _____

2. Answer: There are two experts who work here: Dr. Mitchell and Ms. Patel.

   Question: _____

Math

Find the perimeter of the figure using the grid squares as units of measurement.

3.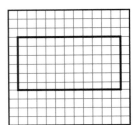

4.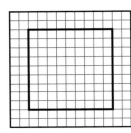

_____   _____

Reading

Read the paragraph. Then answer the item.

As Joe rushed out the door, his mom reminded him to put on a raincoat. The cool autumn air was getting stronger daily, and there were dark clouds in the sky. "I'll be fine, Mom!" Joe hollered, stepping out. The cold, damp air was impossible to ignore. "Maybe I *should* get a raincoat," Joe thought to himself. He wasn't worried about being cold. He just didn't want to get wet. But he didn't go back to get a raincoat.

5. Write two different predictions for what could happen to Joe later in the story.

   a. _____

   b. _____

Language

Read the given topic. Write an exclamatory sentence about the topic.

1. **sharks** _____

2. **bears** _____

3. **rats** _____

4. **bees** _____

Math

Find the perimeter of the figure. Include the unit in your answer.

5.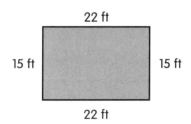

_____

6.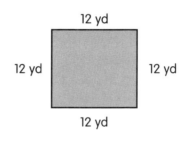

_____

Reading

Read the paragraph. Then answer the item.

   Anna was worried. She borrowed her friend Tom's book a few weeks ago, and now she can't find it anywhere. She lost it. She asked her friend Macy what to do. Macy told Anna to come up with a story of how the book was stolen. Anna asked her brother for advice. He said to buy the same book and pass it off as the original copy. Anna didn't feel right about being dishonest with Tom. She questioned the advice.

7. Write two different predictions for what could happen if Anna follows other people's advice.

   a. _____

   b. _____

Language

Write two imperative sentences a parent might say to a child.

1. _____

2. _____

Write two imperative sentences a basketball coach might say to the whole team before a game.

3. _____

4. _____

Math

Solve the problem. Include the unit of measurement in your answer.

5. Joey will paint the fence that surrounds his shed. He needs to buy the right amount of paint. What is the perimeter of the fence?

   _____

6. Next, Joey will clean the outside of the shed. What is the perimeter of the shed?

   _____

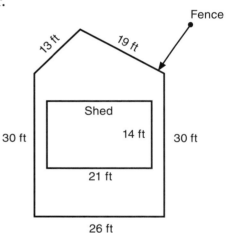

Fence

13 ft   19 ft

Shed

30 ft   14 ft   30 ft

21 ft

26 ft

Reading

Look at the picture. Then answer the item.

7. Write two predictions for what might happen next or later in the story.

   a. _____

   _____

   _____

   b. _____

   _____

Language

Read the sentence. Draw one line under the subject and two lines under the predicate.

1. The roller coaster with the cave has the most comfortable seats.

2. Janice and Tawanda prefer the haunted house to the rides.

3. Passengers on the water ride experience a huge splash at the bottom.

4. The whole family bought ice cream, pretzels, and hot dogs.

Math

Find the perimeter of the figure.

5.

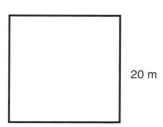

6.

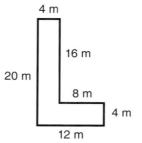

7.

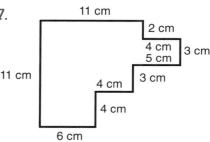

_____   _____   _____

Reading

Read the paragraph. Then answer the item.

After closing the pet store, Mike went to the shipping office to pick up his shipment of guinea pigs. He was excited until he found out the company was charging him six thousand dollars for them. "Well, pigs are large livestock, sir," said the office clerk. "It's expensive to ship livestock." Mike was shocked. He tried to explain that pigs are very different from guinea pigs. But the clerk kept saying the phrase "pigs is pigs" over and over again.

8. Write a prediction for how Mike will deal with this misunderstanding.

_____

_____

Language

Draw three lines under the first letter of the word that needs to be capitalized.

1. my sister must fold the laundry before she puts it away.

2. the clothing line is in the backyard.

3. call the repair business to fix the machines in the laundry room.

4. if the repair expert can't come today, we can schedule it for another day.

Math

Write all of the multiplication expressions that are equal to the given composite number.

5. **6**   expressions: _____

6. **8**   expressions: _____

7. **10**   expressions: _____

8. **16**   expressions: _____

9. **9**   expressions: _____

Reading

Read the paragraph. Then answer the item.

 In the early 1600s, colonists from Europe started settling in what is now the United States. At first, they got along with the Native Americans living there already. But the two groups' attitudes toward land tore a divide between them. Native Americans believed that land should be shared and didn't belong to anyone. Europeans believed that people should own land. A war broke out, and it lasted for years.

10. Write two differences between the European colonists and the Native Americans.

 a. _____

 b. _____

Language

Read the sentence. Rewrite the sentence using correct capitalization.

1. Bristol has soccer on tuesday and guitar lessons on friday.

   _____

2. Jermaine's grandma will visit in july and again in october.

   _____

Math

Answer the item.

3. The number 18 has six different factors: 1, 18, 2, 9, 3, and 6.
   Do you think 18 is a prime or composite number? Explain your answer.

   _____

4. Do you think the number 19 is a prime or composite number? Explain your answer.

   _____

Reading

Read the paragraph. Then answer the item.

   Marie and Lila are twins. Lila loves wearing dresses, while Marie prefers to wear shorts. Marie plays soccer, and Lila sings in the choir. The girls love going to the movies together, although they usually argue over which movie to see. Marie loves sports films, but Lila chooses horror films. They always get movie theater snacks. At home, they disagree on which games to play. Marie likes cards, and Lila likes video games.

5. Write two similarities between Marie and Lila, other than the fact that they are twins.

   a. _____

   b. _____

Language

Read the sentence. Rewrite the sentence using correct capitalization.

1. Dayton participated in a school musical on presidents' day.

_____

2. Teresa's family celebrates independence day with a party.

_____

Math

Write whether the given number is *prime* or *composite*.

3. **17** _____

4. **20** _____

5. **10** _____

6. **30** _____

7. **11** _____

8. **22** _____

9. **13** _____

10. **21** _____

11. **23** _____

12. **24** _____

Reading

Read the paragraph. Then answer the item.

> Weather tools help us prepare for storms and other weather events. Anemometers, for example, measure wind speed. This is related to how fast a storm approaches. Barometers measure atmospheric pressure. High pressure is associated with traditionally pleasant weather. Low pressure is related to storms.

13. Write one similarity and one difference between anemometers and barometers.

_____

_____

_____

Language

Read the sentence. Then write to explain why each letter, except the first letter of the sentence, is capitalized.

1. I know that Mr. Sharp's dog, Bessie, loves going for long walks.

   _____

2. My favorite book to read is *Treasure Island*.

   _____

Math

Answer the item.

3. Write all of the prime numbers from 2 to 32.

   _____

4. Write all of the composite numbers from 35 to 50.

   _____

Reading

Read the paragraph. Then answer the item.

   Toads are so much like frogs that scientists often classify toads as frogs. But toads are not frogs! Even though toads and frogs are both amphibians, toads are wider and heavier than most frogs. Toads have shorter hind legs, so they can't hop as far as frogs can. Toads have bumpy skin and frogs have smooth skin. Neither frogs nor toads drink water. They both absorb moisture through their skin.

5. Based on the text, do toads and frogs have more similarities or differences? Give examples.

   _____

   _____

Language

Write two sentences. Include the name of a monument, a person, and a holiday at least once.

1. _____

_____

2. _____

_____

Math

Write all the factors of the given number. Then circle the number if it is prime.

3. **48** _____

4. **47** _____

5. **32** _____

6. **31** _____

7. **54** _____

Reading

Read the paragraph. Then answer the item.

Have you heard of silkworms? Farmers raise them to get the special fibers they produce. We use the fibers for clothing and household items. These fibers have been used for thousands of years. You may be wondering how silkworms are different from common earthworms. Silkworms aren't actually worms—they're caterpillars. Earthworms consume soil and help keep soil healthy for crops and plants. Without earthworms, materials wouldn't decompose.

8. Do you think silkworms help people more than earthworms? Explain why or why not.

_____

_____

Language

Draw a line to match each word or phrase with its abbreviation.

1. orange juice ●   ● Jr.

2. Junior ●   ● mph

3. television ●   ● UN

4. teaspoon ●   ● FYI

5. miles per hour ●   ● TV

6. for your
   information ●   ● tsp

7. United Nations ●   ● oj

Math

Complete the table.

8.

Multiply 9 by the given factor	Result
1	
2	
3	
4	
5	
6	
7	
8	
9	

Reading

Read the text. Then answer the items.

What is a hydroelectric power plant? A hydroelectric plant uses falling water and a spinning turbine, which is a special machine, to move a coil of wire between magnets. This creates an electric current in the wire. The electric current moves constantly.

Where does the electric current go? After leaving the plant, the electric current passes through transmission lines to pieces of equipment called *transformers*.

Why are transformers important? Transformers increase power, allowing it to travel far.

How do we get electricity in our homes? The current travels through switches and outlets.

9. What is the organization of this text?

   Ⓐ compare and contrast
   Ⓑ question and answer
   Ⓒ main idea and details
   Ⓓ time sequence

10. The main idea of the text is that _____.

   Ⓐ electricity is generated at a power plant and travels long distances
   Ⓑ power plants have turbines
   Ⓒ transformers are helpful but not necessary
   Ⓓ electricity is generated in our homes

4/30

Language

Write the correct abbreviation for each day of the week. Use a period in the abbreviation.

1. Monday   _____

2. Tuesday   _____

3. Wednesday   _____

4. Thursday   _____

5. Friday   _____

6. Saturday   _____

7. Sunday   _____

Math

Circle the numbers that are factors in the equation.

8. $16 \times 5 = 80$

9. $11 \times 20 = 220$

10. $9 \times 7 = 63$

11. $8 \times 23 = 184$

12. $6 \times 42 = 252$

13. $12 \times 56 = 672$

14. $13 \times 21 = 273$

Reading

Read the paragraph. Then answer the items.

Julia Morgan was born in 1872 in San Francisco, California. While in her teens, she became interested in architecture and decided to pursue her dream. In 1906, there was a devastating earthquake in San Francisco. Many buildings were destroyed, but one designed by Julia was left standing. She designed over 700 buildings in her lifetime. Julia passed away in 1957. In 2008, she was accepted into the California Hall of Fame.

15. What is the organization of this text?
   Ⓐ compare and contrast
   Ⓑ question and answer
   Ⓒ cause and effect
   Ⓓ time sequence

16. Which graphic could best support the text?
   Ⓐ a photo
   Ⓑ a timeline
   Ⓒ a diagram
   Ⓓ a graph

17. How did Julia's teenage decision leave an imprint on the world?

_____

_____

Language

Complete the sentence with the correct title:
Ms., Mrs., Mr., or *Dr.*

1. _____ Forsythe is a married woman.

2. _____ Shawl is the kind of doctor who works with feet.

3. Toby asked _____ Russo if she'd like to get married one day.

4. She is an unmarried woman named

   _____ Furlong.

5. The local farmer, _____ Gregory, bought his tractor last summer.

Math

Write all the factors of the given number.

6. **21** _____

7. **7** _____

8. **28** _____

9. **32** _____

Reading

Read the paragraph. Then answer the items.

Many forces on Earth are invisible, but they can cause things to move. Magnetism and air currents are examples. Magnets push away from each other and make objects vibrate and move. Magnetism leads to sound vibrations, such as the music you hear through earbuds. And air can be strong enough to move sailboats, kites, and clouds. Has wind ever moved the strands of your hair? That is an effect of an invisible force.

10. What is the organization of this text?

    Ⓐ compare and contrast

    Ⓑ cause and effect

    Ⓒ time sequence

    Ⓓ question and answer

11. Draw an image to support the text.

12. Describe one cause-and-effect relationship from the text that you have seen yourself.

    _____

    _____

Language

Draw a line to match each type of street or road with its abbreviation.

1. Highway   •   • Ct.

2. Court   •   • Blvd.

3. Drive   •   • Cir.

4. Circle   •   • Ave.

5. Lane   •   • Hwy.

6. Avenue   •   • Dr.

7. Boulevard •   • Ln.

Math

Write all of the multiplication expressions that are equal to the given product to find its factors.

8. **12**

_____

9. **15**

_____

10. **30**

_____

Reading

Read the text. Then answer the items.

How Ravens and Crows Are Similar

Both birds are dark black in color. They can have a purple tint on their wings. Ravens and crows are both highly intelligent. They are both widespread with high numbers in North America.

How Ravens and Crows Are Different

Ravens usually travel in pairs, but crows travel in large groups. Crows make a cawing sound, and ravens produce a low croak. Crows are frequently in urban areas, but ravens are in the wild.

11. What is the organizational structure of the text? Explain how you know.

_____

_____

12. Write another title for each of the paragraphs.

a. _____

b. _____

Language

Write the abbreviation for each measurement and time word. **Hint:** All of the abbreviations have periods.

1. inch _____

2. foot _____

3. ounce _____

4. pound _____

5. second _____

6. minute _____

7. hour _____

Math

Answer the item.

8. Is 7 a factor of 64? Explain why or why not.

_____

_____

_____

9. Is 10 a factor of 90? Explain why or why not.

_____

_____

_____

Reading

Read the paragraph. Then answer the items.

Some people believe it's important to help others. Dana Dakin is one of those people. In 2003, she was a successful woman in the U.S. She traveled to Ghana, Africa, and helped women start businesses so they could pull themselves out of poverty. Her efforts were a success in the village of Pokuase. So Dana returned to the U.S. and brought together retired business leaders who could also help. Today, Dana has an organization called WomensTrust. They've helped over 1,000 women in Ghana with healthcare and education.

10. What is the main idea of this text?

_____

11. Explain how the author uses details to support the main idea.

_____

_____

_____

Language

Read the pair of sentences. Write the correct end punctuation for each sentence.

1. Cory plays the violin___ Did Cory play the saxophone in the past___

2. Aretha, you did such a great job___ Did you feel nervous when you were onstage___

3. Quickly grab your drumsticks___ Antonio and Yosef want to have a jam session___

4. I need to buy a new clarinet reed___ Run to the car as fast as you can___

Math

Complete the table. Then answer the item.

5.

Factor	Factor	Product
6	5	
6	10	
6	11	
6	20	

6. The products are all multiples

of _____.

Reading

Read the paragraph. Then answer the item.

It was just a regular morning, and Corbin was making himself a snack at home. As he unpeeled his banana, out burst a purple cloud. It floated above his head and grew bigger. Then it spoke! "Corbin, I'll grant you three wishes," the cloud said. "Use your wishes wisely." Corbin was overjoyed. His first wish was to become human and stop being a monkey. He was tired of living in a tree! He wanted to live in a house and go to school.

7. Explain why this text would **not** be considered realistic fiction.

_____

_____

Language

Read the sentence. Rewrite it correctly by inserting comma(s) where they are needed.

1. Romeo ask your sister if she has completed her homework.

   _____

2. If you can rake the leaves Dennis I can put them in bags.

   _____

Math

Answer the item.

3. Explain why 15 is a multiple of 5. _____

   _____

4. Is 99 a multiple of 11? Explain why or why not.

   _____

   _____

Reading

Read the paragraph. Then answer the item.

> "Let's take a galaxy cab!" exclaimed Rory. "We'll get there much faster." Rory's friends agreed. The cab driver asked what planet the youngsters wanted to go to. They wanted to go to a particular park in the Whirlpool Galaxy. On the ride there, they passed people riding their space horses and walking their pet stars.

5. Write two sentences from the text that shows it is science fiction.

   a. _____

   b. _____

   _____

5|8 **Day 3** | **Week 10**

Language

Read the sentence. Insert commas to separate the items in the series.

1. Madison used a pencil stapler pen and crayon to complete her project.

2. Matt invited Ignacio Bill Scott and Brandon to his birthday party.

3. Joon-woo adds fruit nuts honey seeds and yogurt to his bowl of oatmeal.

4. Steven considers hummus granola fruit and crackers to be nutritious snacks.

Math

Write all the multiples up to 100 for the given number.

5. **8** _____

6. **10** _____

7. **15** _____

8. **20** _____

9. **25** _____

Reading

Read the paragraph. Then answer the item.

    Gina tried to stop trembling and stand completely still. She didn't want to make a peep. The entire house was dark. She decided that she wouldn't leave the closet until her parents came back home. Suddenly, she heard a crash downstairs. Then footsteps slowly climbing up the stairs. She could see the large, shadowy figure through the crack of the closet door. She could hear the creature snarl. Gina shut her eyes tightly.

10. Write two reasons that support the idea that this text is from a horror story.

    a. _____

    b. _____

Language

Read the compound sentence. Insert a comma where it is needed.

1. Jayden was watching a funny movie and he laughed so hard that his cheeks hurt.

2. Vanessa warned Nick that the film was scary so he decided not to watch it after all.

3. Sasha loves documentaries but she doesn't have much time to watch them.

4. Morgan may choose to go to the theater or he may decide to stay home tonight.

Math

Answer the item.

5. Explain how factors and multiples are related to multiplication.

_____

_____

6. Explain how factors and multiples are related to each other.

_____

_____

Reading

Read the paragraph. Then answer the item.

Keira and Rob had an agreement. They'd race, and the person who didn't win could say only one word for a whole day: "ouchy." Keira won, and Rob was dreading the next day. At school, Mrs. Thu called on him to answer a math question. As he opened his mouth, he saw Keira shaking her head. "Ouchy," Rob said. Everyone laughed. Later, he told the lunch lady that he wanted "ouchy" for lunch. He was being a good sport!

7. Is this text a comedy or a tragedy? Explain your answer.

_____

_____

Language

Read the complex sentence. Insert a comma if one is needed.

1. While he listened to the radio Eddie was able to get his chores done.

2. Terrence will arrive at the stadium before the players run onto the field.

3. Unless he has an umbrella Bob's clothes will get soaked in the rain.

4. Joel remembers his first day of school whenever he hears classical music.

Math

Answer the item.

5. Write the first seven multiples of **4**. _____

6. Write the first ten multiples of **11**. _____

7. Write the first eight multiples of **7**. _____

8. Write the first six multiples of **12**. _____

9. Write the first nine multiples of **10**. _____

Reading

Read the paragraph. Then answer the item.

"Son, jump out of the wagon and help me set up the family's camp for tonight," hollered Pa. "We'll eat the rest of that buffalo meat and potatoes for supper." Jeffrey helped his dad. The family of eight were headed west to California. They had a covered wagon, two horses, and two oxen. Some of them were walking on foot. They had months of travel ahead of them. The biggest threats were cholera and exhaustion.

10. Is this fictional text set in the present, past, or future? Explain why.

_____

_____

Name _____

5/13

Day 1 | **Week 11**

Language

Read the sentence. Circle the article or articles and underline the word or words being introduced.

1. Amelia walked to the store and bought an air conditioner.

2. A puppy pawed at an orange that rolled across the floor.

3. If Aaron has a headache, he should lay his head on a pillow.

4. Roger used a phone to call the movie theater.

Math

Multiply. Use models if needed. Show your work.

5. $7 \times 89 =$ _____

6. $9 \times 625 =$ _____

Reading

Read the paragraph. Then answer the item.

The pounding at the door continued as he tried to sit up, but he simply couldn't. He struggled to stay calm. Finally, he was able to speak. He croaked, "I'm up, Mom." But as he tried to move, his body felt like cement and he writhed in pain. He heard himself groan. "What's happening to me?" he thought.

7. Write the words that help you understand how the characters are feeling.

_____

_____

_____

Language

Read the sentence. Underline the article. Then circle *definite* or *indefinite* to show the kind of article you underlined.

1. A zebra roams Africa's plains.	**definite**	**indefinite**
2. The giraffe calmly chews on leaves.	**definite**	**indefinite**
3. Countless lion prides survive in the grassland.	**definite**	**indefinite**
4. Tourists spot an elephant drinking water.	**definite**	**indefinite**

Math

Solve the problem. Show your work.

5. Darla bought 31 packages of erasers. Each package has 25 erasers in it. How many erasers did Darla buy?

6. Each student in Mr. Bee's class has a box of colored pencils. Each box has 64 pencils, and there are 27 students in the class. What is the total number of colored pencils?

Reading

Read the paragraph. Then answer the item.

Mike's mom left an urgent voice message. "Hon, you better get home quick," she said in a worried tone. "Your rabbits are multiplying." Mike was astounded. He couldn't take care of more rabbits! He already had five. He was really worried and didn't know what to do. He was even more shocked when he got home. His rabbits were sitting at the table with pencils and paper. They were actually solving multiplication problems!

7. Explain the misunderstanding in the text. How did the word choice make the text funny?

_____

_____

5|15

Language

Read the sentence. Complete it with the correct word from the word box.

> they're   there   their

1. Hal will leave here at noon and arrive _____ at midnight.

2. James and Ernie made _____ dog a birthday cake.

3. If the party is this Saturday, _____ not going to be able to make it.

Math

Divide. Show your work.

4. $964 \div 4 =$ _____

5. $768 \div 8 =$ _____

Reading

Read the paragraph. Then answer the items.

You've seen Br'er Lizard. He's been runnin' 'round and standin' on all fours in the yard. But I'm a-guessin' you've never seen him sittin'. He used to sit on a lily pad, jus' like his pal, ol' Br'er Frog. They did some swimmin' and pushin' and squeezin' through fences. Then everything changed. Poor ol' Br'er Lizard got himself a-flattened.

6. Explain how the text uses nontraditional spelling.

_____

7. How would the text be different using more traditional spelling of the words?

_____

Language

Read the sentence. Write *good* or *well* to complete the sentence.

1. Bertha knows the scenes of this movie _____.

2. Carl thought the book was _____, even though he disliked the ending.

3. Although Peggy normally cooks _____, the dinner she made tonight was odd.

4. Rob is a _____ friend because he is always there when I need him.

Math

Solve the problem. Show your work.

5. Maria has downloaded 856 songs. She has them evenly categorized in 8 different playlists. How many songs does Maria have in each playlist?

    _____

6. Mom bought a big basket that contained 435 strawberries. She divided them equally among 5 relatives. How many strawberries did each relative get?

    _____

Reading

Read the paragraph. Then answer the items.

   Dina, Amy, and Yoko were hanging out in Amy's room. Amy left the room briefly. As she was returning, she overheard Dina saying, "Amy's nice but also extreme and forceful." This hurt Amy's feelings a little. She always thought of herself as energetic and lively. Amy knew Dina was a good friend. She'd ask her about it later.

7. How did Amy react to Dina's word choice?

   _____

8. Write two words that have a similar meaning to *extreme* and *forceful*.

   _____

5/17

Language

Read the sentence. Write *bad* or *badly* to complete the sentence.

1. The park ranger saw litter on the trail, which was a _____ sign.

2. Dave's room is still messy because he cleaned it _____.

3. Paul got sprayed by a skunk, so now he smells _____.

4. Louisa washes dishes _____ because she doesn't use enough soap.

Math

Multiply or divide. Show your work.

5. 65 × 17 = _____

6. 93 × 52 = _____

7. 38 ÷ 2 = _____

8. 388 ÷ 4 = _____

Reading

Read the paragraph. Then answer the items.

Forests can give us a continuous supply of raw materials. In order to stay healthy and productive, forests must be managed carefully. This means making sure that trees are not cut down faster than they can be replanted. Some companies cut down numerous trees in order to sell more tree products and make higher profits. All around the world, the demand for goods from trees is high.

9. Is the vocabulary in the text serious and formal, or fun and informal? Explain why.

_____

10. Underline the words in the text that support your answer for number 9.

5|20

Language

Draw a line to match the base word to the same word with an affix.

1. luck •   • hopeful

2. appear •   • rewrite

3. build •   • undo

4. heat •   • lucky

5. write •   • buildable

6. do •   • preheat

7. hope •   • disappear

Math

Solve the problem. Show your work.

8. There are 290 people in line to ride the roller coaster. The roller coaster takes up to 12 riders at a time. How many times will the roller coaster have to run to allow everyone to ride?

_____

9. How many riders will be on the last run?

_____

Reading

Read the paragraph. Then answer the items.

   Gordon planned to sneak into the zoo after the zookeepers left for the night. When he had his chance, he crept in and had the whole zoo to himself! First, he ate the monkeys' bananas and left a trail of peels around the zoo. He spread mud on the glass of several exhibits. He broke the penguin slide. Then he swam in the hippo pool and left his clothes scattered nearby. The zookeepers returned to find their zoo vandalized by Gordon.

10. The word *vandalized* means _____.

   Ⓐ destroyed or ruined
   Ⓑ improved or repaired
   Ⓒ padlocked or secured
   Ⓓ maintained or cared for

11. Which word best describes Gordon?

   Ⓐ innovative
   Ⓑ careful
   Ⓒ destructive
   Ⓓ curious

12. Write some examples from the text explaining how Gordon *vandalized* the zoo.

_____

_____

Language

Write the new word made from the base word and affix.

1. sub + way = _____

2. nation + al = _____

3. mis + guide = _____

4. non + sense = _____

5. under + sea = _____

6. pre + heat = _____

7. pain + less = _____

Math

Solve the problem. Think about the remainder and how it affects the answer.

8. Max needs 262 feet of wood. The wooden boards at the store are 8 feet long. How many full wooden boards should he buy to make sure he has enough?

_____

9. Will Max have to cut any boards to have exactly 262 feet?

_____

Reading

Read the paragraph. Then answer the items.

Green Jacket, a Shawnee tribe leader, was disturbed by what he saw. The land that was once so green and lush was now gray and unhealthy. The land was unsightly now because of the British settlers. They didn't care about the land itself. All they cared about was cutting down trees to build houses on it. Before, there were flowers, trees, and wide stretches of green grass. Now, Green Jacket saw only lifeless tree stumps and dry land.

10. The word *unsightly* means _____.
   Ⓐ interesting to look at
   Ⓑ having lots of open space
   Ⓒ unusually cold
   Ⓓ unpleasant to look at

11. Write an antonym for *unsightly*.

   _____

12. Write an explanation to contrast how the land was before and after it became unsightly.

   _____

   _____

5/22

Language

Choose a prefix to complete the word in the sentence.

> over   mis   under   mid

1. Mom warned me not to _____load the shelf with heavy books.

2. Their dog will _____go tests at the veterinarian's office.

3. Most people believe that it's wrong to

   _____treat animals.

4. Jay's flight arrives at _____night on Monday.

Math

Divide. Show your work.

5. 478 ÷ 5 = _____

6. 551 ÷ 8 = _____

Reading

Read the paragraph. Then answer the item.

Like all countries, Papua New Guinea and Japan must decide how to make and spend their money. This is what countries do to manage their economies. It's common for a country to send goods to other countries in exchange for different goods or money. Papua New Guinea sends crops to other countries, and Japan sends machinery. When they export these goods, they receive valuable things in return. Sometimes, Papua New Guinea and Japan take in goods from other countries. When a country imports goods like this, it usually tries to get items that it can't grow or make on its own. Many countries have strong economic relationships with others.

7. Explain what the words *import* and *export* mean. Use details and examples from the text.

_____

_____

_____

_____

Language

Choose a suffix to complete the word in the sentence.

> less   ful   ation   ment

1. Sara needs some relax_____ after her long school day.

2. Barb is looking forward to the quiz because she is hope_____ she'll do well.

3. Tim is naturally good at sports and finds baseball effort_____.

4. There is a lot of excite_____ when De visits her cousins.

Math

Solve the problem.

5. Margo has 93 lemons. She'll give each of her 9 friends 10 lemons. How many lemons will she have left?

   _____

6. Tran ate 365 bowls of cereal last year. Each box of cereal contained enough cereal for 9 bowls. How many full boxes of cereal did Tran eat last year?

   _____

Reading

Read the paragraph. Then answer the items.

In the early 1600s, European colonists began settling what is now the United States. A Native American chief named Massasoit maintained peaceful relations with the colonists for decades. But tensions grew after Massasoit's death. His son believed the colonists wanted to rid the land of his people entirely. He formed an alliance with other Native American tribes. As a result of the alliance, different groups of Native Americans combined their efforts for the common goal of wiping out the colonists. They wanted to prevent the colonists from driving away all of the Native Americans from their homes. The tribes started a war in 1675.

7. Explain what an *alliance* is.

   _____

8. How did the alliance mentioned in the text affect history?

   _____

   _____

Language

Read the sentence. Rewrite the sentence using the correct spelling of the misspelled word.

1. Jackson polightly asked for a glass of water.

   _____

   _____

2. The ice cubes floted to the top of the glass.

   _____

   _____

Math

Solve the problem. Show your work.

3. The school has 837 students. For the school assembly, the teachers are setting up the auditorium to have rows of 25 seats each. How many rows will be completely full of students seated at the assembly?

   _____

4. How many students will be seated in a row that is not full?

   _____

Reading

Read the paragraph. Then answer the items.

Kal and Max's dad took them on a hike. They were walking a trail they'd never been on before. The boys' dad was always enthusiastic about nature. "Dad, do we really have to stop and examine every single plant we see?" asked Max. Max had his headphones on and wasn't really listening to his dad's informative remarks. He wasn't even looking when his dad would point to certain trees or flowers. Unlike Max, Kal was being very attentive toward his dad and the information being shared. He loved nature, too. He ended up learning a lot from the hike. At the end, the boys' dad thanked them for the fun day. He winked at Kal as he did so.

5. Based on the text, what do you think the word *attentive* means?

   _____

6. Explain how Max was not being attentive during the hike.

   _____

Language

Read the bold word roots and their definitions in the word box. Then explain how each word below gets its meaning from its root.

> **form** = shape   **aqua** = water   **tech** = skill

1. aquarium: _____

2. technical: _____

3. uniform: _____

Math

Find the area of the figure.

4.

12 in.

4 in.

_____

5.

17 ft

_____

6.

21 ft

_____

Reading

Read the paragraph. Then answer the item.

 Snakes eat mice, rats, and other animals that humans consider pests. Without snakes, those animals would multiply beyond balanced levels. Snakes help keep nature in balance in another way, too. Their predators, including foxes, raccoons, large birds, and coyotes, would have less food to eat if snakes disappeared.

7. Which of the following statements do you think the author would agree with? Circle *a* or *b*.

   a. Most humans wouldn't be affected if snakes were to completely disappear.

   b. Snakes have a big impact on their ecosystems and on humans.

Language

Match the prefix to a base word to create a new word. Write the new word on the same line as the prefix it has.

1. tele •   • virus   _____

2. multi •   • view   _____

3. anti •   • vision   _____

4. inter •   • millionaire   _____

Math

Find the area of the figure.

5.

11 ft

6 ft

_____

6.

13 ft

_____

Reading

Read the paragraph. Then answer the item.

It felt to Greg as though he'd just closed his eyes when he was awakened by barking. He cracked open one eye and looked at the clock. "8:15! I'm so late!" Greg jumped out of bed and frantically looked for his running shoes and the leash. Before he even opened his bedroom door, he heard his mom shouting at Pugsy. "Who would have thought weekdays would be easier than weekends?" Greg muttered to himself.

7. What problem is Greg having in the text? Explain how you know.

_____

_____

Daily Fundamentals • EMC 3244 • © Evan-Moor Corp.

Language

Match the base word to a suffix to create a new word. Write the new word on the same line as the suffix it has.

1. entertain •   • ive   _____

2. decorate •   • ity   _____

3. quick   •   • ment _____

4. personal •   • en   _____

Math

Solve the problem. Show your work.

5. Alf and his dad want to know how much room their pool takes up in the backyard. They measure the pool. Its length is 44 feet, and its width is 24 feet. What is the area of the pool?

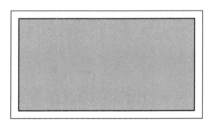

24 ft

44 ft

_____

Reading

Read the paragraph. Then answer the item.

Every day, Wilbur sat at the back door of the factory. He would sit and wait for hours, sighing deeply. The workers who entered the building greeted Wilbur with a pat on the head and said, "That's a good boy, Wilbur." Wilbur would look at them with sad eyes and whimper as they went in. They knew that Wilbur would sit in that spot until five o'clock when his owner would swing open the door and say, "I'll race you home, boy!"

6. How does Wilbur feel about his owner going to work every day? Explain how you know.

_____

_____

Language

Underline the affix in the word. Then write the base word.

1. strengthen _____

2. interstate _____

3. multipurpose _____

4. attachment _____

5. telephone _____

6. antifreeze _____

7. expressive _____

8. electricity _____

Math

Solve the problem. Show your work.

9. Charity's mom is ordering a new dresser online. She wants to figure out how much floor space to clear to make room for it, so she needs to calculate the dresser's area. The website states that the dresser is 4 ft long and 2 ft wide. What is the area of the floor space that Charity's mom should clear?

_____

10. Patsy has a toy chest that is 72 in. long and 42 in. wide. What is its area?

_____

Reading

Read the paragraph. Then answer the item.

After the sun sets in Tasmania, the Tasmanian devils wake up. These scavengers are one of nature's important garbage collectors. They feed on dead animals. In fact, their favorite food is rotten meat. Their sharp teeth can crush the toughest foods. They even swallow bones. And the poisons and germs they eat don't seem to harm them. Their eating habits actually stop bacteria and disease from spreading to other animals.

11. What relationship does the Tasmanian devil have with other animals?

_____

_____

Language

Explain how the affix changes the meaning of the base word.

1. **recalculate** _____

2. **politely** _____

3. **sensitivity** _____

4. **interact** _____

Math

Solve the problem. Show your work.

5. Edwin is planting a big cabbage garden. The garden will have 16 rows of 13 heads of cabbage. Each head of cabbage has its own square-shaped growth area that is 14 in. wide. What will be the total area of Edwin's cabbage garden?

_____

Reading

Read the paragraph. Then answer the item.

Emmet changed into comfortable clothes so he could do his chores. He was in charge of the chickens, which meant he had to feed them, collect and wash their eggs, and keep the chickens and their pens clean. His dad fertilized the crops with compost from the pile that Mom tended. Everyone helped harvest the crops as they ripened, and all spare time was spent pulling weeds and eliminating pests.

6. Where does Emmet live? Explain your thinking.

_____

_____

Language

Read the sentence. Underline the adjective. Then circle the noun the adjective is describing.

1. Craig is a fan of snacks, especially stinky cheese.

2. His favorite thing about it is the salty flavor.

3. He once received an exotic collection of cheeses from overseas.

4. Sometimes he uses cheese to create a delicious meal.

Math

Answer the item.

5. This circle has been divided into equal parts. What is the measure of each angle formed? Explain how you know.

Angle measure: _____

_____
_____
_____

Reading

Read the paragraph. Then answer the item.

An electric toaster is not as simple as it looks. When you push the lever down on a toaster, a switch completes a circuit. This sends electric current flowing through the toaster. Electric current flowing through a circuit can turn into heat. Inventors had a hard time figuring out how to make a toaster that wouldn't catch fire! They knew that electricity flows through conductors, such as metal. They also knew that some metals were not as good at conducting heat as others. Those metals are called *resistors*.

6. List the key words in the process of electricity flowing through a toaster.

_____
_____

Language

Read the sentence. Complete it with an adjective from the word box.
Then underline the noun that the adjective is describing.

> calm   talented   strong

1. Ryan is a _____ kayaker.

2. He uses _____ paddles to move the kayak in the water.

3. Ryan especially loves kayaking on days when the water is _____.

Math

Shade part of the circle to match the given angle measurement.

4. 90°

6. 360°

5. 270°

7. 180°

Reading

Read the paragraph. Then answer the item.

Granny shared her simple recipe for making homemade noodles. They're the best noodles I've ever tasted! First, she whisked together flour and eggs to form a dough. Second, she boiled a pot of water. Next, she tested a small amount of dough in the water. Then she boiled the rest of the dough in teaspoon-sized chunks. When they were all cooked, she took them out of the water and covered them in butter.

8. In your own words, write two steps in Granny's process for making homemade noodles.

_____

_____

Language

Read the paragraph. Write your own adjectives to complete it.

1.   Joe used a _____ ladder to reach the _____ bowl on the

top shelf. He wanted to use it to mix _____ berries with _____

granola. This day was going to be _____, so Joe wanted to have a

_____ breakfast. He felt extra _____ this morning.

Math

Write the measurement of the angle that is marked. Then explain how you found it.

2.   _____

_____

_____

3.   _____

_____

_____

Reading

Read the text. Then answer the item.

Follow these steps each day while I am out of town:
   1) Pour fresh filtered water into Sparkle's red bowl.
   2) Fill Sparkle's yellow bowl with 2 cups of dry dog food.
   3) Go outside with Sparkle, on leash, for a 20-minute walk.
   4) Throw the ball for Sparkle for 10 minutes.

4. What kind of process does the list describe? Who is the author of this text?

_____

_____

Language

Write three sentences using the adjectives from the word box.

| stylish   confusing   brave |

1. _____

2. _____

3. _____

Math

Find the unknown angle measure without measuring.

4.

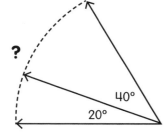

_____

5.

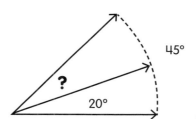

_____

Reading

Read the text. Then answer the item.

　　　Suzy and her dad wanted to eat more healthfully. They asked a nutritionist for some tips to make a nutritious version of their favorite foods. The nutritionist's first tip was to determine whether a particular snack is sweet or savory. The next tip was to replace an ingredient with a more nutritious one that has a similar flavor or texture. For example, one might replace ice cream with yogurt, or chips with cucumbers.

6. Based on the text, describe how you would make one of your favorite snacks more nutritious.

_____

_____

Language

Answer the item.

1. Explain why adjectives are important when describing nouns.

_____

_____

2. List four adjectives that you enjoy using in your writing.

_____

Math

Draw a figure that has the given angle or angles. Then circle the angle or angles.

3. a triangle with a right angle

4. a parallelogram with two acute angles

Reading

Read the text. Then answer the item.

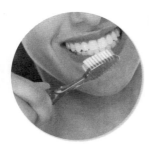

Here are some tips on proper brushing:
1) Hold your toothbrush at a 45-degree angle at the gumline.
   Brush gently in short strokes from the gumline to the chewing surface.
2) Hold your toothbrush in a vertical position, and clean the inner surfaces.
3) Gently brush your tongue and the roof of your mouth to remove bacteria.

5. How did the author help you understand that this text is about a process or procedure?

_____

_____

Language

Write the subject pronoun that replaces the given word or words.

1. Sheila and Don _____

2. Carlos _____

3. a dog and cat _____

4. Gloria _____

5. you and Paul _____

6. Ari and I _____

7. the bike _____

Math

Write *perpendicular, intersecting,* or *parallel* to describe the pair of lines.

8. _____

9. _____

10. _____

11. _____

Reading

Read the paragraph. Then answer the items.

Mia was nervous. This was the day that she had to tell her best friend, Tay, that she didn't want to play soccer anymore. Mia and Tay had played soccer together every year since second grade. But Mia recently tried a new sport that she liked even better. She wanted to play golf. She wouldn't have enough time to do both sports. Mia was worried about how Tay would take the news because Tay was obsessed with soccer. It's all she ever talked about. But Mia just planned to be honest.

12. What caused Mia to feel nervous?

_____

_____

13. What is one possible reaction that Tay may have when she finds out the news?

_____

_____

Language

Write the object pronoun that replaces the given word or words.

1. Dory and Luis   _____

2. Pablo   _____

3. the pencil   _____

4. Cory and me   _____

5. you and Rita   _____

6. Ramona   _____

7. a leaf and a twig _____

Math

Write *obtuse, right, acute,* or *straight* to describe the angle.

8. _____

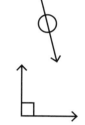

9. _____

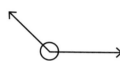

10. _____

11. _____

Reading

Look at the picture and read the caption. Then answer the items.

The whole neighborhood pitched in after the hurricane.

12. What is being shown in the picture?

_____

_____

_____

_____

_____

_____

13. What led to the activities shown in the picture?

_____

_____

Language

Read the sentence. Rewrite the sentence and replace all of the nouns with correct pronouns.

1. Jack remembers the movie.

   _____

2. Mom gave the cellphone to Lily and Nina.

   _____

3. You and Pete will see Yolanda and me.

   _____

Math

Write *scalene, equilateral, isosceles,* or *right* to describe the triangle.

4. _____

5. _____

6. _____

7. _____

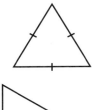

Reading

Read the paragraph. Then answer the items.

     Scientists sometimes talk about light as a ray, or a thin beam. Light rays move from place to place in a straight line. You see an object when light rays bounce off the object and travel to your eyes. Light rays pass through a transparent object, such as a window. Translucent objects let some light pass through, but not all. For example, sunglasses and tinted car windows are translucent.

8. How are light rays part of a cause-and-effect relationship?

   _____

   _____

9. How are light rays affected by a translucent object?

   _____

   _____

Language

Answer the item.

1. Explain how the use of pronouns could improve the following sentence:

   Vera heard a song, and Vera loved the song.

   _____
   _____
   _____
   _____
   _____
   _____

Math

Write an *S* if the figure is symmetrical.

2.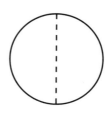
   _____

3.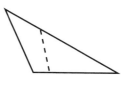
   _____

4.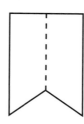
   _____

5.
   _____

Reading

Read the paragraph and look at the photo. Then answer the items.

A wind surfer sails across the water.

An air current is an invisible force that can move objects. It's caused by changes in temperature and air pressure. Warm air rises, and the cooler air around it moves in to take its place. This air movement, or wind, causes tree branches to sway, flags to flap, and clouds to move.

6. Explain what causes a wind surfer to be able to move across the water.

   _____
   _____

7. Explain how wind is formed.

   _____
   _____

Language

Read the sentence. Write *who* or *whom* to complete it.

1. Maya, _____ included me in the activities, is very thoughtful.

2. Terry, _____ we invited to the concert, is always cheerful.

3. Bella lent a dollar to Sal, _____ spent it on a bottle of water.

4. Blake is _____ the award was given to.

5. Please contact Gill, _____ we ordered the book for.

Math

Answer the items about the figure.

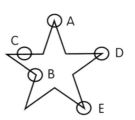

6. Which labeled angles in this figure are acute?

   _____

7. What kind of angle is angle C?

   _____

8. Is the figure symmetrical?

   _____

Reading

Read the text and look at the chart. Then answer the item.

Forests provide people with many raw materials. People must manage forest resources carefully in order to keep forests healthy and productive.

Forest Resources and Their Uses

Forest resources	Used for
cocoa beans, vanilla beans, coffee beans, tapioca, bananas	food or drink
timber trees	construction, floors, furniture, paper
kapok tree fibers	furniture fabric, pillows, life preservers
vines	clothing fibers

9. Explain what the chart shows. Then explain what the result would be for the forest and for humans if we overused any of the resources in the chart.

   _____

   _____

   _____

Language

Write a sentence using the present progressive tense of the given verb.

1. **study** _____

2. **visit** _____

3. **request** _____

4. **read** _____

Math

Circle the pair of fractions if they are written with a common denominator.

5. $\frac{2}{3}$, $\frac{2}{5}$

6. $\frac{5}{9}$, $\frac{0}{9}$

7. $\frac{6}{7}$, $\frac{7}{10}$

8. $\frac{9}{10}$, $\frac{1}{10}$

9. $\frac{8}{11}$, $\frac{1}{11}$

10. $\frac{21}{22}$, $\frac{3}{22}$

11. $\frac{3}{11}$, $\frac{3}{8}$

12. $\frac{1}{6}$, $\frac{2}{12}$

13. $\frac{4}{5}$, $\frac{3}{5}$

Reading

Look at the photo and read the caption. Then answer the item.

Snakes' jawbones are able to separate in order to fit rodents and other small animals.

14. What does a snake look like when its jaws separate? How does this help the snake eat?

_____

_____

_____

_____

_____

Language

Rewrite the phrase using the past progressive form of the verb.

Simple Present Tense	**Past Progressive Tense**
1. we wonder	_____
2. she imagines	_____
3. you decide	_____
4. I pretend	_____

Math

Circle *yes* or *no* to answer the item.

5. Can 12 be a common denominator for $\frac{1}{3}$ and $\frac{1}{6}$?   **yes**   **no**

6. Can 6 be a common denominator for $\frac{1}{2}$ and $\frac{3}{4}$?   **yes**   **no**

7. Can 15 be a common denominator for $\frac{5}{10}$ and $\frac{2}{3}$?   **yes**   **no**

8. Can 10 be a common denominator for $\frac{8}{10}$ and $\frac{2}{5}$?   **yes**   **no**

Reading

Read the chart. Then answer the item.

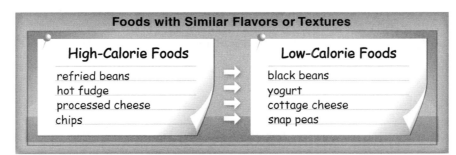

Foods with Similar Flavors or Textures

High-Calorie Foods	Low-Calorie Foods
refried beans	black beans
hot fudge	yogurt
processed cheese	cottage cheese
chips	snap peas

9. Who would probably be interested in reading the information shown in the chart?

_____

_____

Language

Rewrite the phrase using the future progressive form of the verb.

Simple Present Tense	Future Progressive Tense
1. they kick	_____
2. I sing	_____
3. he jogs	_____
4. it shines	_____

Math

Skip count by each denominator to find a common denominator for each pair of fractions.

5. $\frac{2}{7}$, $\frac{1}{2}$

_____ is a common denominator because 7 goes into it and 2 goes into it.

6. $\frac{4}{9}$, $\frac{3}{5}$

_____ is a common denominator because 9 goes into it and 5 goes into it.

Reading

Read the paragraph. Then answer the item.

Magnetism is an invisible force that can move objects. It's all around us. The center of Earth itself is actually a big magnet. It creates a protective barrier around the planet like a fence. Dangerous particles from the sun are always rushing toward Earth and can strip away our atmosphere. But Earth's magnetic barrier pushes most of the particles away.

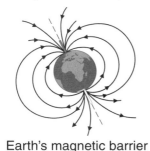

Earth's magnetic barrier

7. How does the image help you better understand the text?

_____

_____

_____

Language

Read the sentence. Circle the verb. Then write the correct form of the verb.

1. Jerome and Carlton fixes the bike tire.   _____

2. The dog jump over the fence.   _____

3. Callie appear tired and thirsty.   _____

4. Annette are moving to Australia soon.   _____

Math

Write a common denominator for each pair of fractions.

5. $\frac{1}{10}$, $\frac{1}{2}$ _____

8. $\frac{5}{6}$, $\frac{3}{4}$ _____

6. $\frac{8}{15}$, $\frac{3}{5}$ _____

9. $\frac{4}{5}$, $\frac{13}{20}$ _____

7. $\frac{1}{3}$, $\frac{4}{9}$ _____

10. $\frac{5}{8}$, $\frac{2}{3}$ _____

Reading

Look at the map and read the caption. Then answer the item.

South America Africa

Researchers believe that South America and Africa were once a part of one large continent called Pangaea.

11. Explain how the map is different from a map that shows Earth's surface today.

_____

_____

_____

_____

_____

Language

Answer the item.

1. Is the following sentence complete? Explain why or why not.

    Carlos the best player on the team.

    _____

2. Does a subject need to agree in number with the verb? Explain your answer.

    _____

Math

Answer the item.

3. Explain what a common denominator is.

    _____

4. Explain what an equivalent fraction is.

    _____

    _____

Reading

Look at the photo and read the caption. Then answer the items.

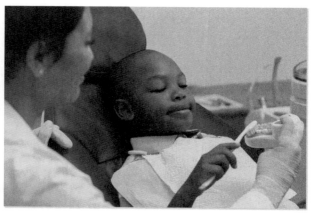

Regular visits to the dentist keep your teeth healthy.

5. Does the caption explicitly describe what is shown in the photo? Or, does it give general information related to the photo? Explain your thinking.

    _____

    _____

6. Write a caption that gives explicit information.

    _____

    _____

Language

Read the sentence. Circle the preposition. Then underline the noun that it is describing a location for.

1. A fence stands around the schoolyard.

2. The bus is parked along a sidewalk.

3. Their house faces toward the lake.

4. A swing hangs from the tree's branches.

Math

Write *equivalent* if the pair of shaded figures show equivalent fractions or *no* if not.

5.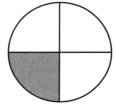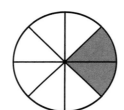

_____

6.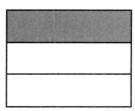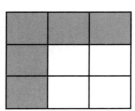

_____

Reading

Read the paragraph. Then answer the item.

      In 1803, the United States of America was much smaller than it is today. That year, the U.S. government bought a large area of land known as the "Louisiana Territory" from France. It stretched from the Mississippi River to the Rocky Mountains. Explorers traveled through it to map it out. Years later, the state of Louisiana was formed using part of this new land. It was the 18th U.S. state.

7. What was the author's purpose for writing this text?
   Ⓐ to entertain with a story
   Ⓑ to inform with facts
   Ⓒ to persuade with an argument
   Ⓓ to teach with a process

Language

Read the sentence. Complete it with a prepositional phrase from the word box.
Then circle the preposition.

> toward a slide   through the air   at the park

1. Cole and I had so much fun _____ yesterday.

2. We felt as if we were flying _____ when we were on the swings.

3. After swinging, we made our way _____ .

Math

Shade the second picture in each pair to show equivalent fractions. Then write the name of each fraction.

4.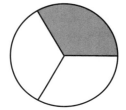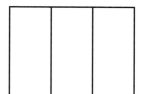

_____

5.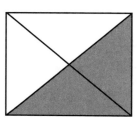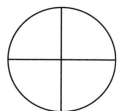

_____

Reading

Read the paragraph. Then answer the item.

Do you enjoy reading poetry? Poetry is important because it offers a different reading experience than prose, or ordinary written language. Firstly, poetry can be fun to read! Rhymes, rhythms, and interesting topics are common in poems. Secondly, poetry can bring about feelings that you didn't even know you had. Next time you're trying to decide whether to read a piece of regular text or a poem, think about how enjoyable it is to read a poem aloud. It's likely you'll end up choosing to read a poem, and you'll be making a great choice.

6. Explain how the text shows that the author's purpose is to persuade.

_____

_____

Language

Read the sentence. Rewrite it, replacing the underlined prepositional phrase with a new one.

1. Judy left her glasses <u>beside her book</u>.

_____

2. Rohan shook the saltshaker <u>over his food</u>.

_____

Math

Find and label the fractions on the number lines. Then circle *yes* or *no* to answer the item.

3. Is $\frac{2}{5}$ equivalent to $\frac{4}{10}$? **yes** **no**

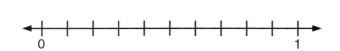

4. Is $\frac{1}{3}$ equivalent to $\frac{3}{12}$? **yes** **no**

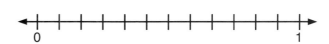

Reading

Read the paragraph. Then answer the item.

It would be excellent to know a few basics before trying to ice-skate for the first time. First, make sure the skates fit snugly but not too tightly. Next, step onto the ice very slowly. When you want to move, remember to move your feet to the side. Keep your feet underneath your body most of the time, even when you are moving forward. It is important to keep your legs bent slightly at all times. Finally, brake by bending your knees even more and raising your arms out to the side for additional balance.

5. Explain how the text shows that the author's purpose is to teach.

_____

_____

Language

Read the sentence. Underline the prepositional phrase. Then circle the object of the preposition.

1. There are hundreds of geese by the pond.

2. We can see a huge flock from the bike trail.

3. We like to ride our bikes through the park.

4. We pass ducks when we cross over the bridge.

Math

Write an equivalent fraction.

5. $\frac{4}{5}$ _____

6. $\frac{9}{12}$ _____

7. $\frac{9}{10}$ _____

8. $\frac{1}{6}$ _____

9. $\frac{1}{2}$ _____

10. $\frac{13}{26}$ _____

Reading

Read the paragraph. Then answer the item.

Boom! Crash! Splat! "Oops!" exclaimed Jaya. "There goes another dozen eggs," she thought to herself. Jaya's visit to her aunt's egg ranch had been a disaster so far. In a short two hours, Jaya had managed to break two dozen eggs. Luckily, her aunt was so kind and patient. Aunt Dolma suggested that Jaya take a break from helping out. Jaya thought that was an excellent idea. She felt flustered. She got herself a glass of lemonade and went to sit down. But as soon as she sat, she heard a loud "crunch!" Oh well. There went another dozen!

11. Explain how the text shows that the author's purpose is to entertain.

_____

_____

Language

Answer the item.

1. What information do prepositions give about nouns in a sentence? Explain your answer.

_____

_____

2. Write a sentence that contains a prepositional phrase. Then circle it.

_____

Math

Read the math story and answer the item.

Pam and Michelle each made a 10-inch pizza. Pam cut hers into 8 slices and ate 3 of them.

3. What fraction of her pizza did Pam eat? _____

Michelle ate the same amount of pizza as Pam, but her pizza was cut into 16 slices.

4. What fraction of her pizza did Michelle eat? _____

Reading

Read the paragraph. Then answer the item.

Milton Hershey was born in 1857 in rural Pennsylvania. As a young man, Hershey worked for a candy maker who taught him many things. In 1893, Hershey was able to start his own business, the Hershey Chocolate Company, on a dairy farm. For years, he experimented with combinations of sugar, milk, and cocoa. As a result of hard work, Hershey finally came up with his famous chocolate bar. After some success, Hershey wanted to do good in the world. He and his wife established a school for orphans in 1909 named the Hershey Industrial School.

5. What is the author's purpose for writing this text? Explain your thinking.

_____

_____

Language

Read the sentence. Circle the adverb.
Then underline the verb it's describing.

1. Tom quickly makes a sandwich.

2. Jenny selfishly eats the last cookie.

3. Fa-Chen quietly reads her book.

4. Aleeya rudely replies to an email.

5. Shanice cautiously pours a cup of tea.

6. Shaquille gently waters the flowers.

7. Reagan kindly holds the door open for me.

Math

Write a mixed number to show what part
is shaded.

8. 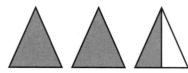 _____

9. 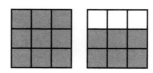 _____

10. 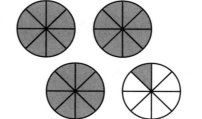 _____

Reading

Read the paragraph. Then answer the items.

Oprah Winfrey is a television personality. She has her own TV show, and she has also acted in movies. Although Oprah is very wealthy now, she grew up poor in Mississippi. After becoming successful, she decided that she wanted to do good things to help other people. She established Oprah's Angel Network in 1998 to fund many of her good works. In 2007, she built a school in South Africa. It's called the Oprah Winfrey Leadership Academy for Girls. The academy teaches the values of respect, honor, service to others, and compassion.

11. Is it a fact or opinion that Oprah Winfrey built a school in South Africa? Explain your thinking.

_____

_____

12. Is it a fact or opinion that Oprah Winfrey's show and acting are good? Explain your thinking.

_____

_____

Language

Read the sentence. Rewrite it, replacing the adverb with a new one.

1. The movie is unexpectedly funny.

_____

_____

2. Josh is cheerfully doing his chores.

_____

_____

Math

Write an improper fraction to show what part is shaded.

3. 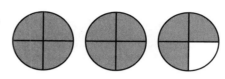 _____

4.  _____

5. 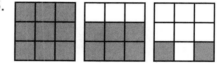 _____

Reading

Read the paragraph. Then answer the items.

India is a country with many religions. Each religion has holy days and festivals, so the people of India have a lot of holidays. Festivals and holidays are fun! Muslims, Sikhs, Buddhists, Christians, Hindus, and Jains celebrate their own holidays throughout the year. These different religions also celebrate national holidays and other special days together. The best part about celebrations is that people get together and eat food and enjoy each other's company.

6. Is it a fact or opinion that India is a country with many religions? Tell how you know.

_____

_____

7. Is it a fact or opinion that festivals and holidays are fun? Explain your thinking.

_____

_____

Language

Write an adverb to describe the given verb.

1. sings _____

2. speaks _____

3. _____ tiptoes

4. dances _____

5. _____ searches

6. _____ examines

7. _____ forgets

8. _____ disagrees

Math

Convert the improper fraction to a mixed number.

9. $\frac{16}{5}$ _____

10. $\frac{22}{5}$ _____

11. $\frac{17}{4}$ _____

12. $\frac{19}{6}$ _____

13. $\frac{9}{2}$ _____

14. $\frac{13}{3}$ _____

15. $\frac{11}{3}$ _____

Reading

Read the paragraph. Then answer the items.

Exercise benefits people of all ages. There are many different ways to exercise. Some exercises, such as those using weights, focus on strengthening muscles. Other exercises are cardiovascular, which means they focus on getting the heart pumping. Some cardiovascular exercises include jogging and doing jumping jacks. Some people prefer to exercise privately in their homes, while others enjoy taking fitness classes and going to the gym. There are also different exercise disciplines, such as yoga, Pilates, and martial arts.

16. Write your own opinion about the text.

_____

17. Write one additional fact that you know about exercise. Then list any additional types of exercise that you know about.

_____

_____

Language

Write three sentences using the adverbs from the word box.

| rapidly   mysteriously   easily |

1. _____

_____

2. _____

_____

3. _____

_____

Math

Convert the mixed number to an improper fraction.

4. $4\frac{3}{5}$ _____

5. $2\frac{5}{8}$ _____

6. $10\frac{8}{9}$ _____

7. $6\frac{3}{7}$ _____

8. $8\frac{1}{6}$ _____

9. $5\frac{2}{3}$ _____

10. $7\frac{3}{4}$ _____

Reading

Read the text. Then answer the item.

Belinda and Maury were disagreeing. Mom told them they could go to any restaurant Friday night, as long as they agreed on where to go. They both had different opinions.

"I want pizza on Friday," declared Maury. "You know I only like cheesy foods."

"Well, that's your problem," said Belinda. "I think you need to be open to different options sometimes. I want to go to the salad bar. My opinion is that salad tastes better than pizza."

Maury had a comeback ready. "I think food should be eaten only if enjoyed, and I don't enjoy salads or vegetables," he said. "If you don't give pizza a chance, then you're not open to other options, either." Maury thought he'd made a good point, and Belinda would have to agree.

"Well, I usually don't give in to others," sighed Belinda, "but I will try it your way this time."

"Sweet," said Maury. "Next time, I'll try salad. Maybe my opinion about it will change."

11. Explain how opinions play a role in this text.

_____

_____

_____

Language

Answer the item.

1. Explain the difference between verbs and adverbs.

   _____

   _____

   _____

2. Write a sentence that contains the negative *never*.

   _____

   _____

   _____

Math

Answer the item.

3. Explain how to convert a mixed number to an improper fraction.

   _____

   _____

   _____

   _____

   _____

   _____

   _____

Reading

Read the paragraph. Then answer the items.

   We all know that when something gets tossed into the air, it ends up coming back down again. Actually, it's because of the invisible force called *gravity*. Gravity pulls us, and everything else on the planet, to the ground. Because of gravity, we don't fly away every time we take a step. Gravity even holds the air we breathe down where we need it. Basically, gravity is a force of attraction between objects. Smaller objects are naturally drawn to larger objects. Because Earth is the biggest object that humans are ever close to, we are all drawn to it. Gravity exists everywhere in the universe, including in outer space.

4. Explain how facts play a role in the text.

   _____

   _____

5. Are science texts made up mostly of facts or opinions? Explain your thinking.

   _____

   _____

Language

Read the sentence. Circle the coordinating conjunction.

1. Georgette may go to math camp, or she may go to science camp.

2. Erin has friends in California and Illinois.

3. Dax enjoys baseball, but his favorite sport is rugby.

4. Gina thought it was going to rain, yet the sun was shining brightly.

Math

Compare the fractions. Write **>**, **<**, or **=** in the ◯.

5.

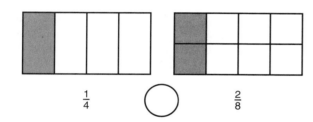

$\frac{1}{4}$ ◯ $\frac{2}{8}$

6.

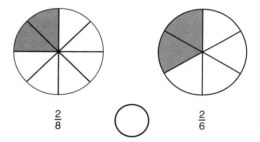

$\frac{2}{8}$ ◯ $\frac{2}{6}$

Reading

Read the paragraph. Then answer the item.

A thick band of air, called the *atmosphere,* surrounds Earth. It consists of layers of invisible gases. The atmosphere extends hundreds of miles into the sky. The lowest layer—the *troposphere*—is only about 6 to 9 miles (10 to 15 km) thick. The troposphere is where Earth's weather happens because this layer of air contains the most water. You usually can't see this water because it's in the form of an invisible gas, or *water vapor.*

7. Write the main idea of the text in your own words. Explain your thinking.

_____

_____

Language

Read the sentence. Circle the subordinating conjunction.

1. Francisco can't concentrate on his book because the television is on.

2. Whenever Ursula reads, she becomes sleepy.

3. Betsy takes a book with her wherever she goes.

4. Unless Kurt has a library card, he won't be able to borrow the book.

Math

Shade each figure so it matches the given fraction. Then compare the fractions.
Write **>**, **<**, or **=** in the ◯.

5.

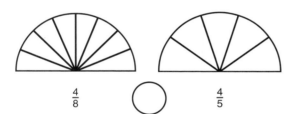

$\frac{4}{8}$ ◯ $\frac{4}{5}$

6.

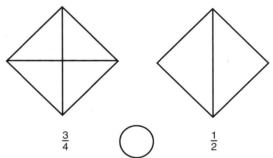

$\frac{3}{4}$ ◯ $\frac{1}{2}$

Reading

Read the paragraph. Then answer the item.

Sounds affect our lives in many ways every day. *Acoustics* is the study of sound. People may make acoustics their life's work if they are interested in how sound affects us. For example, some scientists study how to make the world quieter for people by making machines less noisy. Other scientists teach the dangers of loud sounds to people's hearing.

7. Write a sentence from the text that supports the main idea.

_____

_____

Language

Read the sentence fragment. Rewrite it as a complete sentence.

1. The boat on the other side of the marina.

_____

2. Rose and her dog, Moose.

_____

Math

Compare the fractions. Write **>**, **<**, or **=** in the ◯.

3. $\frac{3}{5}$ ◯ $\frac{6}{10}$

4. $\frac{15}{20}$ ◯ $\frac{2}{5}$

5. $\frac{1}{7}$ ◯ $\frac{1}{6}$

6. $\frac{4}{16}$ ◯ $\frac{1}{4}$

7. $\frac{25}{100}$ ◯ $\frac{2}{3}$

8. $\frac{5}{6}$ ◯ $\frac{5}{8}$

Reading

Read the paragraph. Then answer the item.

Alnwick Treehouse

     Some people think treehouses are just for children, but they're not. Some treehouses are very large, and adults live in them. Living in a treehouse is private and peaceful. Treehouse living also uses less energy, so it's good for the environment. People like to live in treehouses because treehouses cope well in heat, cold, and in other environmental conditions.

9. Write the main idea of the text in your own words. Write one supporting detail from the text.

_____

_____

Language

Read the run-on sentence. Correct it by dividing it into two simple sentences. Write the new sentences.

1. Drew is taking a kickboxing class he goes one day a week.

_____

2. Evan visits his grandma in Wyoming she is 92 years old.

_____

Math

Compare the fractions and write them in order from smallest to largest.

3. $\frac{4}{5}$ $\frac{1}{2}$ $\frac{25}{100}$ $\frac{7}{10}$

_____   _____   _____   _____

Reading

Read the paragraph. Then answer the item.

Two Degrees Food is a company that fights to end worldwide hunger while selling a healthy product. Lauren Walters and Will Hauser started the company in 2011. They wanted to create a healthy energy bar, not a candy bar. Their bar is made of fruit, nuts, and seeds. For every bar sold, Two Degrees Food donates a meal to a hungry child in a developing country in Asia or Africa.

4. Explain how the details in the text support the main idea.

_____

_____

Language

Read the pair of sentences. Combine them into one sentence by moving words or phrases.
Hint: You may need to add or remove words.

1. Ray ordered a calculator online. The calculator is red.

   _____

2. Imad gave his brother a bike. It was Imad's old bike.

   _____

Math

Compare the fractions. Write **>**, **<**, or **=** in the $\bigcirc$. Then explain your thinking.

3. $\frac{9}{10}$ $\bigcirc$ $\frac{18}{20}$

   _____

   _____

   _____

Reading

Read the paragraph. Then answer the item.

   Forest agriculture provides many people with jobs. Let's take cocoa beans, for example. Forest laborers are paid to harvest the raw materials, cacao pods, which contain cocoa beans. Then a chocolate factory buys the beans, and workers put them through a process to manufacture chocolate bars and cocoa powder. Bakeries buy these products and make treats with them. We buy the chocolate treats.

4. Write the main idea of the text. Explain how the author supports it.

   _____

   _____

Language

Read the sentence. Rewrite it, making the underlined noun possessive.

1. The <u>squirrel</u> burrow went deep into the ground.

    _____

2. The <u>student</u> lunch was packed in a red bag.

    _____

Math

First, write each fraction as a sum of unit fractions. Then write the sum in a different way.

3. $\frac{5}{6} =$ _____ $\frac{5}{6} =$ _____

4. $\frac{3}{4} =$ _____ $\frac{3}{4} =$ _____

Reading

Read the paragraph. Then answer the item.

 Claire sat in her backyard, enjoying the sunny afternoon. She often hung out there so she could be alone. She listened to the birds singing. She admired the colorful wildflowers. Suddenly, she heard her little brother, Jack, yelling in the distance. He was always so loud. Just then, gray clouds moved in front of the sun, covering the yard in a cold, dark shadow. Jack came around the corner, yelling, stick in hand.

5. How do the sun and clouds relate to what happened in the text? Explain your thinking.

    _____

    _____

Name _____

Language

Read the sentence. Insert a comma where it is needed.

1. The label on the sleeping bag reads "Keep away from fire and heat."

2. Gia read the first sentence of the paragraph, which said "Some days are truly memorable."

3. The sign by the pool cautioned "Running or jogging near the pool is prohibited."

4. The food label reads "This product contains milk and peanuts."

Math

Find two different ways to write the given number as a sum of fractions.
Draw a model to help you.

5. Write 1 as a sum of fifths.

_____   _____

6. Write 2 as a sum of thirds.

_____   _____

Reading

Read the paragraph. Then answer the item.

Ted whistled to himself as he carried the trash bags out to the garbage cans. He was so glad that he had trash duty instead of basement duty. That dark, dank basement gave him the creeps. He looked up at the blue sky, put on his bike helmet, and checked his pocket for his mom's grocery list. All of a sudden, he heard his dad calling his name from the web-covered basement. "Ted, there's a leak down here, can you help me?"

7. Did the text give a clue that Ted would end up going into the basement? Explain your answer.

_____

_____

Language

Read the sentence. Rewrite it to correct the punctuation errors.

1. How "can I find the information I need"? Maya asked.

   _____

2. This game is complicated, Craig stated.

   _____

Math

Find a common denominator for the pair of fractions. Then add the fractions. Show your work.

3. $\frac{2}{5} + \frac{8}{15} =$ _____

4. $\frac{1}{3} + \frac{1}{2} =$ _____

5. $\frac{5}{12} + \frac{2}{6} =$ _____

6. $\frac{3}{4} + \frac{1}{20} =$ _____

Reading

Read the paragraph. Then answer the item.

It was a dark, cloudy day. Tyler was nervous about his first day at the new school. "Why did we have to move?" he thought. He felt invisible as he entered the school. He walked alone through a stuffy, dim hallway, looking for his classroom. Then he saw a brightly lit, colorfully decorated room. He wondered if this was his class and walked faster. As he got closer, he saw a poster on the door that said, "Welcome, Tyler!"

7. How does lighting relate to what happened in the text? Explain your thinking.

   _____

   _____

Language

Read the sentence. Rewrite it using quotation marks where they are needed.

1. Becca can play Buffalo Gals very well on the piano.

   _____

2. Tory loves the rhymes in The Walrus and the Carpenter.

   _____

Math

Find a common denominator for the pair of fractions, and then subtract. Show your work.

3. $\frac{3}{4} - \frac{5}{16} =$ _____

4. $\frac{3}{5} - \frac{1}{2} =$ _____

5. $\frac{8}{9} - \frac{2}{3} =$ _____

6. $\frac{11}{14} - \frac{3}{7} =$ _____

Reading

Read the paragraph. Then answer the item.

     Walking to school, Tara thought she saw her grandma's dog, Sputnik, across the street. "No, can't be," she thought. "Sputnik lives with Grandma four hours away." Later, Tara thought she saw Sputnik outside her classroom window. She knew she was imagining things. On her walk home, a car stopped at a stop sign. Inside the car, she saw Sputnik. Tara raced home. To her surprise, Grandma and Sputnik were visiting!

7. Is there foreshadowing in the text? Explain your thinking.

   _____

   _____

Language

Read the paragraph. Underline the titles of books, movies, plays, television shows, newspapers, and magazines.

1.   Jen and Tuck were going to the movie theater to see Woman of Mystery. It was based on a book called Lady Spy. The movie was getting great reviews in the New City Times. Jen had read an article in Entertainment Magazine that gave behind-the-scenes details about making the movie. It made her want to see the movie even more. Tuck was also willing to see the movie Fun Class.

Math

Add or subtract. Write the answer as a whole number or a mixed number.

2. $2\frac{2}{3}$
     $+ 4\frac{1}{3}$

4. $9\frac{6}{8}$
     $+ 7\frac{1}{8}$

6. $5\frac{3}{12}$
     $+ 1\frac{5}{12}$

3. $9\frac{5}{7}$
     $- 3\frac{2}{7}$

5. $10\frac{5}{6}$
     $- 4\frac{5}{6}$

7. $11\frac{10}{11}$
     $- 5\frac{8}{11}$

Reading

Read the paragraph. Then answer the item.

   "We can't be late," Mom said for the hundredth time. Our whole family was in the van on our way to the airport. All five of us were flying to Oregon for vacation. The fog was thick and the traffic was bad. "We can't miss the flight," Mom said. Dad was driving, and he sighed deeply. The van was barely inching along. An hour later, we arrived at the airport. To our surprise, planes were sitting on the runway, delayed because of fog.

8. Did foreshadowing make the text more or less suspenseful? Explain your thinking.

_____

_____

Language

Read the sentence. Rewrite the sentence so it does not have a double negative.

1. Pam can't have no dessert until after dinner.

   _____

   _____

2. Alex did not find his gym shorts nowhere.

   _____

   _____

Math

Write the decimal in word form.

3. **0.6** _____

4. **0.04** _____

5. **0.7** _____

6. **1.2** _____

7. **9.9** _____

8. **0.03** _____

9. **4.01** _____

10. **0.26** _____

Reading

Read the paragraph. Then answer the items.

Mrs. Reed asked the students to bring their science articles to the carpet. They were going to discuss what they'd read. Everyone but Meg had an article. She had forgotten hers at home. She was new to the class and didn't know anyone well enough to ask to share. Meg felt her stomach tense up as Lila looked at her empty hands. Lila smiled and sat next to Meg. She put her copy of the article between them so they could both see it.

11. One possible theme of this text is _____.
    Ⓐ good versus evil
    Ⓑ kindness
    Ⓒ honesty
    Ⓓ perseverance

12. Which word best describes Lila?
    Ⓐ funny
    Ⓑ smart
    Ⓒ cranky
    Ⓓ generous

13. Explain how the theme was demonstrated in the text. Use examples.

    _____

    _____

Language

Read the sentence. Write the correct word from the word box to complete it.

> you're   your

1. I might need to borrow _____ umbrella tomorrow.

2. May I use the umbrella if _____ not using it?

3. You can wear _____ raincoat to school if it starts raining.

Math

Change the word form to decimal notation.

4. thirty-two hundredths

   _____

5. eight tenths

   _____

6. seven hundredths

   _____

7. five and two hundredths

   _____

Reading

Read the paragraph. Then answer the items.

   Cruz's friend, Max, was in the hospital. "I know we have to visit Max," Cruz told his mom, "but I don't like hospitals. They're boring." Cruz's mom listened to her son's feelings. Then she reminded Cruz of who visited him at the hospital when he hurt his leg. Cruz remembered other times, like when Max helped him shovel snow off the driveway. Max often lent Cruz comic books. "Max is a good friend," thought Cruz. He put down his video game and got dressed.

8. Explain how the theme of friendship is shown in the text.

   _____

   _____

9. Do you think Max has been a good friend to Cruz? Explain your thinking.

   _____

   _____

Language

Read the sentence. Write the correct word from the word box to complete it.

(bye   buy   by)

1. Tyrese said _____ to his teacher on the last day of school.

2. Charity put her backpack on the floor _____ the rocking chair.

3. Cora's mom gave her money to _____ lunch at school today.

Math

Write information about the model in the table. Then write it in decimal notation.

4.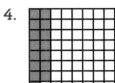

ones	.	tenths	hundredths

decimal: _____

Reading

Read the paragraph. Then answer the items.

It was fourth grade's Competition Day at Foster Elementary. The school had set up lots of games and activities for the day. The two classes, 4A and 4B, were going to compete in a game of tug of war. Class 4B was really excited. They had won most of the games so far. They worked together well as a team. Some of the students in 4A didn't feel like participating. "I know you can do it!" Mr. Johnson, 4A's teacher, yelled from the bleachers. "Just work together, and you'll do great!" he shouted. Suddenly, 4A was just as excited as 4B.

5. What is a possible theme of this text? Explain your thinking.

_____

_____

6. Why do you think 4B had won most of the games on Competition Day?

_____

_____

Language

Read the sentence. Write the correct word from the word box to complete it.

(hear   here)

1. Bill said he rang the doorbell, but I didn't

   _____ it ring.

2. Let me know when all of the guests get

   _____ .

3. Thanks for inviting me to your house, but

   I think I'll stay _____ instead.

Math

Explain what the digits and decimal point mean in the given number.

4. **7.84**

   _____

   _____

   _____

   _____

   _____

   _____

Reading

Read the paragraph. Then answer the items.

Br'er Frog and Br'er Lizard loved sittin', standin', restin', and swimmin', all day, every day. But one day, Br'er Frog got the idea stuck in his head that he was wantin' to see what was outside the swamp. Br'er Lizard didn't have the same idea. "I'm happy in this ol' swamp," he said, "and I don't want to leave." Br'er Frog figured that Br'er Lizard was afraid to leave. But he convinced Br'er Lizard that they needed to be brave. Br'er Frog was scared, too. But he wanted to have new experiences and see new places beyond the same ol' swamp.

5. Describe what a *theme* is.

   _____

   _____

6. Describe a possible theme of this text. Explain why you think it's a possible theme.

   _____

   _____

Language

Read the sentence. Write the correct word from the word box to complete it.

(where   wear)

1. Pablo can't decide whether to

   _____ his blue or black jeans.

2. Dave is trying to figure out _____ his friends are sitting at the assembly.

3. Kate will choose _____ her birthday celebration will be.

Math

Solve the problem.

4. Tam, Doug, and Molly are friends. Tam is 4.25 feet tall. Doug is 4.05 feet tall. Molly is 4.5 feet tall. Who of the friends is tallest? Who is shortest? Explain your thinking.

   _____

   _____

   _____

   _____

   _____

   _____

Reading

Read the paragraph. Then answer the items.

Patty felt a huge pit in her stomach. She was so nervous to tell her parents that she had ruined the dining room table. She accidentally left her art project (wet from paint) on the table, and it got stained. She knew her parents would be frustrated. For a second, Patty considered blaming it on her little sister, who was only 3 years old. But Patty wouldn't be able to look herself in the mirror ever again if she did that. When she finally told her parents about it, they weren't mad at all. They said, "Mistakes happen. Thanks for being honest."

5. Explain the main theme of the text. Explain how you know this is the main theme.

   _____

   _____

6. Do themes in stories relate to things that happen in the real world? Explain your thinking.

   _____

   _____

Language

Form a noun by adding a suffix to the word.

> ment   er   ness

1. write   _____
2. kind   _____
3. enjoy   _____

4. accomplish   _____
5. sick   _____
6. report   _____

Math

Write the fraction as a decimal and in words.

7. $\frac{2}{10}$ _____   _____

8. $\frac{9}{10}$ _____   _____

9. $\frac{31}{100}$ _____   _____

10. $\frac{67}{100}$ _____   _____

11. $\frac{5}{100}$ _____   _____

Reading

Read the paragraph. Then answer the item.

The bones in our body are made of hard tissue. Hard tissue protects parts of the body and provides support. For example, the bones of your rib cage protect your lungs and heart. Your femur, or thighbone, provides support for the muscles in your upper leg. Bones and cartilage are two types of hard tissue in humans. Some animals have other types of hard tissue such as antlers or shells.

12. Which of the following statements do you think the author would agree with? Circle *a* or *b*.

   a. Humans should have more hard tissue in their bodies.

   b. Humans need hard tissue to have a body that functions well.

Language

Form a new word by adding a prefix to the word.

$$\boxed{\text{re} \quad \text{dis} \quad \text{un}}$$

1. hydrate _____

2. acceptable _____

3. continue _____

4. wash _____

5. obey _____

6. alike _____

Math

Complete the chart with information about the model. Write a decimal and a fraction for the model.

7.

ones	.	tenths	hundredths

_____ _____

8.

ones	.	tenths	hundredths

_____ _____

Reading

Read the paragraph. Then answer the item.

Josh was helping his parents get ready for the neighborhood party they were hosting at their house. Josh's jobs were to vacuum the living room and put out paper plates. His sister was putting out the food. The guests were arriving soon, and Josh realized that he hadn't had lunch. When he reached for a handful of peanuts, his sister said, "Josh, those are for the guests, get your own food!" He just walked out of the room.

9. How did Josh feel when his sister snapped at him? Explain your thinking.

_____

_____

Language

Read the sentence. If the bold word is spelled correctly, circle *correct*.
If it is not spelled correctly, circle *incorrect* and rewrite the sentence.

1. Cole can't wait for his birthday party on **Wedsday**.   **correct**   **incorrect**

_____

2. After running, we got a drink from the water **fowntain**.   **correct**   **incorrect**

_____

Math

Write the decimal in fraction form.

3. 0.75 _____   7. 0.99 _____   11. 0.28 _____

4. 0.08 _____   8. 0.01 _____   12. 0.7 _____

5. 0.4 _____   9. 0.35 _____

6. 0.1 _____   10. 0.46 _____

Reading

Read the paragraph. Then answer the item.

Aziza was making homemade yogurt for the first time. She had been trying to make more foods at home. She followed the recipe's steps exactly. After allowing the yogurt to set for six hours, it was time to check the container. Unfortunately, the yogurt was too watery, but it smelled fine. Aziza wasn't sure how to fix it. She thought about it while she followed the recipe for a homemade smoothie. Hey, she could use the yogurt!

13. Was Aziza's attempt to make more foods at home successful? Explain your answer.

_____

_____

Language

Write the misspelled word correctly.

1. apropriyate _____

2. freekwent _____

3. karefree _____

4. generositee _____

5. rekognize _____

6. fronteer _____

7. plentyfull _____

8. furryous _____

Math

Answer the item.

9. Explain how these numbers are related: **0.3** $\frac{3}{10}$

_____

_____

10. Draw a model to represent the pair of numbers.

Reading

Read the paragraph. Then answer the item.

   Fibers from silkworms are useful for more than just clothing and household items. Doctors use silk fiber to sew up the wounds of some patients. Scientists are working on ways to use silk to repair ligaments and bones. Other scientists are experimenting with silk to create new skin for burn victims. Another group of scientists hopes to use silk, or to develop similar materials, to make protective armor, car parts, and other items.

11. What will happen if the scientists successfully find other uses for silkworms' fibers?

_____

_____

Language

Read the paragraph. Cross out any word that is spelled incorrectly.
Rewrite the word correctly above it.

1. Marie had a diffikult day. First, she woke up late and almost missed the school bus. At school,

she found math chalinjing. She just figurred that she needed more praktise with desimalz. But the

worst part of Marie's day was when she realized that she'd forgawtin her lunch. She had to go to

the school awfice to call her mom to bring lunch. Lukkilee, Marie's day got better after lunch.

Math

Solve the problem. Write the answer as a mixed number. Then convert it to decimal notation.

2. Mrs. Royple made lasagna for a dinner party. In addition to herself, her husband, her three kids, and her sister, Mrs. Royple invited the Hendersons, a family of five, and the Turlocks, a family of three. Each person ate $\frac{25}{100}$ of one tray of lasagna. How many trays of lasagna did they eat in all?

mixed number: _____   decimal: _____

Reading

Read the paragraph. Then answer the item.

The Onondaga cave ecosystem in Missouri is home to many species. The bats there feed on insects. Salamanders and cavefish are predators that feed on tiny organisms. Cave spiders eat insects. Millipedes, centipedes, and crustaceans feed on tiny organisms and funguses. Cave beetles eat the eggs of cave crickets. The cave food web is also sometimes called a *cave food pyramid*. Decomposers are at the bottom.

3. How would the Onondaga cave ecosystem be different if all the tiny organisms disappeared?

_____

_____

Language

Read the sentence. Write a synonym for the bold word.

1. Bette keeps her room and her belongings very **tidy**. _____

2. Frita owns the **complete** encyclopedia series. _____

3. Luis feels **terror** when he sees a snake. _____

4. Paula **communicates** with her friends using technology. _____

Math

Compare the decimals in each pair. Circle the greater decimal.

5. 0.06   0.6

6. 0.98   0.89

7. 0.34   0.31

8. 0.9   0.99

Reading

Read the paragraph. Then answer the item.

Seeds are planted in the ground, and the outcome is a beautiful plant. How does it happen? First, seeds, which have energy inside, are planted. They form roots that take hold underground. This causes a small plant to start growing. The plant absorbs sunlight, water, and nutrients. This absorption allows the plant to make food, which leads to the plant growing healthier, bigger, and stronger as a result.

9. Explain why this text is organized with a cause-and-effect structure.

_____

_____

Language

Read the sentence. Write an antonym of the bold word.

1. Jaya's performance made her feel **disappointed**.   _____

2. Betsy found the book to be **outstanding**.   _____

3. After the assembly, Rick felt **discouraged**.   _____

4. Today I feel particularly **exhausted**.   _____

Math

Compare the numbers and write them in order from least to greatest.

5.   **48.29**   **50.1**   **48.8**   **49.02**

_____   _____   _____   _____

Reading

Read the paragraph. Then answer the item.

Abraham Lincoln was born in 1809 in Kentucky. His family moved to Indiana in 1816. He moved to Illinois in 1830. During the 1830s, Lincoln became involved in politics. He was elected to the U.S. House of Representatives in 1846. He continued to work in politics, eventually becoming the U.S. president. He was inaugurated in 1861. President Lincoln served as U.S. president until his tragic death in 1865.

6. How are the facts in this text organized?

_____

_____

Language

Write two sentences, each using a different meaning of the word *shake*.

1. _____

_____

2. _____

_____

Math

Shade the grids to match the decimals. Then circle the greater decimal in each pair.

3.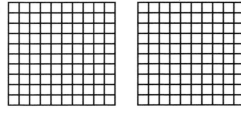

0.98   0.89

4.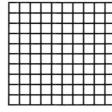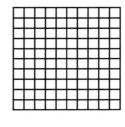

0.6   0.9

Reading

Read the paragraphs. Then answer the item.

Todd and Kurt are brothers. Todd plays chess, but Kurt likes football. Kurt's favorite food is cereal, and Todd's favorite is pasta. Todd spends a lot of free time reading, while Kurt spends most of his free time playing his guitar. Kurt wears a hat, and Todd doesn't.

Both Todd and Kurt love scary movies. The brothers also enjoy playing harmless pranks on their sister. They both love hiking and fishing. They like similar music, too.

5. How is the first paragraph different from the second paragraph?

_____

_____

Language

Read the sentence. Think about what the bold word means to you.
Then use that word in a sentence about your own life.

1. Jon doesn't always **recognize** the ingredients listed on food labels.

   _____

2. Mr. Furlow wasn't trying to **confuse** his students.

   _____

Math

Compare the decimals. Write **>**, **<**, or **=** in the ◯.

3. 0.87 ◯ 8.7

4. 0.24 ◯ 0.42

5. 6.5 ◯ 6.1

6. 0.08 ◯ 0.03

7. 1.9 ◯ 1.90

8. 0.78 ◯ 0.72

Reading

Read the text. Then answer the item.

How to Wash a Bike

   1) Fill a bucket with warm, soapy water and a sponge.
   2) Use the soapy sponge to scrub the bike from top to bottom.
   3) Rinse the bike with clean water.
   4) Use rags or towels to dry the bike.

9. Is the organization of the text helpful? Explain your thinking.

   _____

   _____

Language

Arrange the words from weakest to strongest.

1. spoke, shouted, whispered

   _____

2. demand, ask, insist

   _____

Math

Compare the decimals. Write **>**, **<**, or **=** in the ◯. Then explain your answer.

3. 0.38 0.04

   _____

   _____

   _____

   _____

Reading

Read the paragraph. Then answer the item.

Exercise has different effects on the body. People usually gain muscle, strength, and improved cardiovascular endurance (the body's ability to do physical activity for longer periods of time) as a result of exercise. Regular exercise often leads to a body that feels better, with fewer aches and pains. Exercise also causes most people to feel more energetic. Other results of exercise could be intentional weight loss or gain.

4. Explain how the text is organized and why its organization makes sense.

   _____

   _____

Name _____

Language

Read the sentence. Insert a comma where it is needed.

1. Ron plays golf and he plays the flute.

2. Sean likes jogging but he dislikes running laps.

3. Jada rides the bus every morning and she walks home every afternoon.

4. Yoshi wants a new bike yet the bike he has now works fine.

5. Maria is interested in trains so she plans to visit the train museum soon.

Math

Add.

6. $\begin{array}{r} 2.46 \\ +0.23 \\ \hline \end{array}$

7. $\begin{array}{r} 0.89 \\ +0.45 \\ \hline \end{array}$

8. $\begin{array}{r} 0.74 \\ +0.94 \\ \hline \end{array}$

9. $\begin{array}{r} 3.25 \\ +4.61 \\ \hline \end{array}$

Reading

Read the paragraph. Then answer the items.

Kimani had always longed to live near the ocean. Unfortunately, she happened to grow up in a hot desert town. Because Kimani loved the ocean so much, she painted her bedroom walls, including the ceiling, blue. Her bedsheets and blankets were blue. She wore at least one piece of blue clothing every day. Almost everything she owned was blue, too.

10. What does the color blue symbolize to Kimani?
Ⓐ the desert
Ⓑ the ocean
Ⓒ a town
Ⓓ her bedroom

11. What can you infer about Kimani?
Ⓐ She is very certain of what she likes.
Ⓑ She does not have any interests.
Ⓒ Her goal is to be settled in the desert.
Ⓓ Comfort is her biggest concern.

12. Explain why Kimani surrounded herself with blue items, and how a color could be a symbol.

_____

_____

Language

Read the paragraph. Insert commas where they are needed.

1.　　　Guanyu plays an instrument and she is a member of the school's orchestra. She plays the oboe but she used to play the clarinet. The orchestra needed an oboe player so Guanyu decided to try something new. She ended up liking the oboe yet she still plays her old clarinet just for fun.

Math

Subtract.

2.　　$\begin{array}{r} 0.86 \\ -\ 0.24 \\ \hline \end{array}$

3.　　$\begin{array}{r} 0.57 \\ -\ 0.12 \\ \hline \end{array}$

4.　　$\begin{array}{r} 6.19 \\ -\ 0.32 \\ \hline \end{array}$

5.　　$\begin{array}{r} 7.74 \\ -\ 5.31 \\ \hline \end{array}$

Reading

Read the paragraph. Then answer the items.

　　　Brett was in the back seat on his way to the city with his parents. His parents had errands and office stuff to do, and Brett knew it'd be more fun than staying home in his quiet room. "Thanks for bringing me with you!" he said. He enjoyed sitting in the back seat with his sketch pad. There was so much to see in the city. Brett stared out the window at all the people in the city park. He noticed a squirrel poking its head out of its quiet burrow to look around. The squirrel watched the people in the park. Brett felt like the squirrel.

6. What does the burrow symbolize? What does the squirrel symbolize? Explain your thinking.

_____

_____

_____

7. Explain what a *symbol* in a story is.

_____

Language

Read the pair of sentences. Then rewrite them as a compound sentence, using correct punctuation.

1. Mal loves fiction. He enjoys different genres.

   _____

   _____

2. Leah loves puppies. She is not a fan of kittens.

   _____

   _____

Math

Add or subtract. Then solve the problem.

3. $\begin{array}{r} 5.63 \\ + 1.12 \\ \hline \end{array}$

4. $\begin{array}{r} 4.93 \\ - 0.45 \\ \hline \end{array}$

5. Vera wants to buy some golf clubs that cost $123.97. Her dad said that if she used her saved allowance, he'd pay the rest. Vera has $52.41 saved. How much will her dad pay?

   _____

Reading

Read the paragraph. Then answer the items.

If only Chul Young could get his famous cousin to come visit, he'd be so happy. He'd love to introduce everyone to "Seven-foot Seth." The neighborhood kids will finally believe that he knows an NBA player. He would be the most popular kid in the neighborhood. Everyone would want to come over to his house and hang out. He could probably get away with telling other kids what to do because they'd be so eager to be his friend. Chul Young daydreamed as he waited for his mom to come in and tell him where they decided to hold the family reunion.

6. What does "Seven-foot Seth" symbolize to Chul Young?

   _____

   _____

7. Does Chul Young want to visit with his cousin, or does he want what his cousin symbolizes?

   _____

   _____

Daily Fundamentals • EMC 3244 • © Evan-Moor Corp.

Language

Write three compound sentences.

1. _____

_____

_____

2. _____

_____

_____

3. _____

_____

_____

Math

Read the math story. Then answer the items.

Pam is collecting small shells to decorate the border of a picture. She is laying them end to end in lines. So far, she has one line of shells that is 15.39 centimeters long and another that is 8.62 centimeters long.

4. How many centimeters around the picture could she decorate right now?

_____

5. The picture's border is 50 centimeters long. How many more centimeters of shells does she need?

_____

Reading

Read the paragraph. Then answer the items.

My brother, Jeb, graduated from middle school last week. Grampa Ed gave Jeb a unique pen as a graduation gift. Apparently, it is a very good-quality pen. Grampa Ed said he gave one to Dad and Aunt Sue when they were about to enter high school. He also said that I'd get one of those nice pens when I graduate middle school. Grampa Ed says it's a big step in one's life, moving on to high school. I can't wait to make Grampa Ed proud and to get one of those pens!

6. What does the pen symbolize to the narrator of the text?

_____

_____

7. What information do you know about the narrator from the text?

_____

_____

Language

Explain whether or not the sentence needs a comma inserted.

1. Alejandro uses his calculator frequently so he protects it with a plastic case.

   _____

   _____

   _____

2. Deanie made a veggie sandwich but left it on the school bus by mistake.

   _____

   _____

   _____

Math

Explain the process for solving the addition problem.

3. **5.5 + 1.06**

   _____

   _____

   _____

   _____

   _____

   _____

Reading

Read the paragraph. Then answer the items.

Gloria was so upset about the rain. It wasn't letting up, and it had been continuously pouring for days. Gloria's mom, on the other hand, was extremely happy about it. "We really needed this rain," her mom said. "The garden will become green and healthy again." In Gloria's opinion, the rain was a big mop, soaking up all her fun time. It stopped her from being able to go outside, and it made the ground sloppy and muddy. To Gloria's mom, it was an energizing potion for nature.

4. Explain the metaphor in the text that describes Gloria's view of the rain.

   _____

   _____

5. What did the rain symbolize to Gloria's mom?

   _____

   _____

Language

Read the sentence. Insert a comma where it is needed.

1. Before Darla uses mouthwash she brushes her teeth.

2. Wherever Gerard goes the dog follows him.

3. Because the cat is orange you can't miss him.

4. Until Amelia returns we will wait to have dinner.

Math

Solve the problem.

5. Maisy started out with 7 gems in her collection. Every week, she got 5 more gems. How many gems did she have at the end of week 4?   _____

   Week 1: $7 + 5 =$ _____

   Week 2: $7 +$ _____ $+$ _____ $=$ _____

   Week 3: $7 +$ _____ $+$ _____ $+$ _____ $=$ _____

   Week 4: $7 +$ _____ $+$ _____ $+$ _____ $+$ _____ $=$ _____

Reading

Read the paragraph. Then answer the item.

     Chanel always has a role in the annual school plays. Last year, when she was in third grade, she played a wicked witch. This year's play is about a pirate ship. Chanel is playing a seamstress who lives on the ship. Because the play is annual, Chanel is already thinking about what kind of role she wants to have in next year's play. She's likely to play a superhero or a historical character.

6. Which of the following sentences uses *annual* in the same way as the text? Circle *a* or *b*.

   a. Trisha's annual friend is a kind and patient animal lover.

   b. Veronica's annual birthday party is always exciting.

Language

Read the sentence. Correct the comma error by either crossing out the comma or inserting a comma.

1. Beth pulls the weeds, while Taylor trims the hedges.

2. Jason will wait patiently, until his laundry is finished drying.

3. Unless she has moved Bess is in her room.

4. Charity gets excited, whenever she hears the doorbell ring.

Math

Read the problem. Then write the rule and fill in the chart. Use it to write the answer.

5. Sean jogged for 10 minutes one day. Each day after the first day, he jogged for 9 minutes longer than he did the previous day.

Rule: _____

Start	Day 1	Day 2	Day 3	Day 4

How many minutes did Sean jog on Day 4? _____

Reading

Read the paragraph. Notice how the words in the word box are used. Then complete the items.

Valerie assists Mia with her project by taping photos on paper as Mia writes captions. Using tape instead of glue benefits the project because tape is less messy. If Mia completes the project early, she will have time to do other things.

> completes   assists   benefits

6. Danielle's skill in volleyball _____ her performance in other sports.

7. Dinah usually _____ her homework before dinner.

8. Cole _____ his mom with dinner by washing the vegetables.

Language

Write a complex sentence using the given dependent clause. Use correct punctuation.

1. if she has a tummy ache

_____

2. because the mall is closed

_____

Math

Read the problem. Then answer the item.

3. Pritty says that if you start with 8 and follow the rule "Add 6," every number in the pattern will be even. Complete the pattern to find out.

8									

Is Pritty correct? _____ Why do you think you got the results you did? _____

_____

Reading

Read the paragraph. Then answer the items.

Jolie went to the comic book fair with her cousin Mario. She was envious when Mario bought a T-shirt with a picture of her favorite comic book hero. She wished that she could afford to buy a shirt. But when she counted her money, she confirmed that she didn't have enough. To her surprise, Mario bought a shirt for her!

4. Explain what the word *envious* means.

_____

5. Explain what the word *afford* means.

_____

Language

Write four complex sentences using correct punctuation.

1. _____

2. _____

3. _____

4. _____

Math

Use the rule to complete the number pattern. Then answer the item.

5. **Rule:** Start with 4. Add 5.

4, 9, _____, _____, _____, _____, _____, _____, _____, _____

What would the 20th number in the pattern be? _____ How can you find out without writing all the numbers?

_____

_____

Reading

Read the paragraph. Then answer the items.

Jorge always motivates his friends to try new things. He often makes comments such as, "You can do it!" He also says, "It will be fun!" He has motivated his friends to try new foods and activities, and even to join school clubs. Last year, Jorge persuaded his friends to join Chess Club so they would have a new experience.

6. Explain what the word *motivate* means.

_____

7. Write a sentence using the word *motivate*.

_____

Language

Explain whether or not the sentence needs a comma inserted. If it does, correctly insert it.

1. After dinosaurs roamed the earth the presence of humans increased.

   _____

2. Classes have been full since the school opened in August.

   _____

Math

Start with an odd number greater than 40 and follow the rule "Subtract 4."
Fill in the chart to show your results. Then answer the items.

3. Did you get all even numbers, all odd numbers, or both? _____

4. Why do you think you got the results you did? _____

   _____

Reading

Read the paragraph. Then answer the item.

   Amal's older brother, Rob, constantly claims that she can't do various things. But Amal protests, saying, "I am capable of doing that, Rob." Once, Rob claimed that Amal was not capable of bringing bricks from their dad's truck to the backyard when they were building a patio. Amal proved she was capable. She helped to carry many bricks.

5. Explain what *capable* means. Then explain how the text gives clues about its meaning.

   _____

   _____

   _____

Language

Read the sentence. Write the correct word from the word box to complete it.

(worst   bad   worse)

1. Joann made the _____ sandwich because it was soggy.

2. Pearl's sandwich was _____ than Ray's sandwich.

3. Ray made a _____ sandwich because its bread was stale.

Math

Answer the item.

4. Continue this shape pattern until there are 10 shapes in all.

Describe the pattern. _____

What will the 15th shape be? _____

Reading

Read the paragraph. Then answer the item.

   In the American Civil War, the North and South fought against each other. Each side had different advantages. The North had more people, money, factories, and railroads. They had better supplies and weapons. The South had experienced military generals. Southern soldiers were more physically fit because of the demands of farm work. Most of the battles occurred on southern land, so the southern troops knew the land well.

5. Would you have preferred to have the advantages of the North or the South? Explain.

_____

_____

Language

Read the sentence. Write the correct word from the word box to complete it.

better   best   good

1. Farida's song was _____.

2. Danica played her instrument _____ than her sister did.

3. Of everyone in the choir, Agatha sang _____.

Math

Answer the item.

4. Continue this shape pattern until there are 10 shapes in all.

○ △ ○ □ ○ △

Describe the pattern. _____

What will the 16th shape be? _____

Reading

Read the paragraph. Then answer the item.

People start businesses to meet a need and to make money. Some business owners use their money to help other people. For example, the Hershey Company started a boarding school for orphans in 1909. Milton Hershey also built a town for his employees to live in. Another company called Two Degrees Food sells healthy energy bars and uses their profits to donate meals to hungry children in Asia and Africa.

5. Explain how the Hershey Company and Two Degrees Food are similar. Give examples.

_____

_____

Language

Write two sentences using the words from the word box correctly.

than   then

1. _____

2. _____

Math

Answer the item.

3. Continue this shape pattern until there are 10 shapes in all.

□ △ △ □ ○ ○

Describe the pattern. _____

What will the 21st shape be? _____

Reading

Read the paragraph. Then answer the item.

Birds and bats may seem similar. They both have wings and feet, and both fly. Birds eat insects, and some types of bats do, too. Both birds and bats may live in or on buildings or trees. However, in some ways, birds and bats are different. Birds are not mammals (birds hatch from eggs.) Bats sleep upside down. Birds have feathers, and bats have fur. Bats drink milk, and birds do not.

4. Explain why someone might mistake a bat for a bird.

_____

_____

Language

Write two sentences using the words from the word box correctly.

(sit   set)

1. _____

2. _____

Math

Look at the shape pattern. Continue the pattern three times by drawing in the boxes.

3.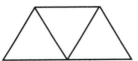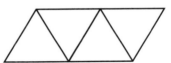

Reading

Read the paragraph. Then answer the item.

Different types of pets require different kinds of care. Some pets, such as dogs, cats, and turtles, can spend a lot of time outdoors. Other pets, such as fish, birds, and hamsters, must remain inside most if not all of the time. Snakes require live food, which may be a challenge for some pet owners. Energetic pets may cause damage to furniture or outdoor landscaping if left unattended. Some exotic pets require a city permit to own.

4. What considerations should be made before choosing a pet?

_____

_____

Language

Write two sentences using the words from the word box correctly.

(raise   rise)

1. _____

2. _____

Math

Look at the shape pattern. Then answer the item.

3. Draw the fourth shape in the pattern.

first

second

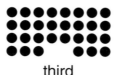
third

fourth

4. How did you figure out how to draw the fourth shape? _____

_____

Reading

Read the paragraph. Then answer the item.

   We use books and movies for entertainment. Often, movies are created based on books. Less often, books are created based on movies. One benefit of movies is that it takes less time to watch a story than to read one. A disadvantage is that movies aren't always accurate representations of books. Books allow us to read an author's words directly and use our imaginations. Movies are someone else's interpretation.

5. In your opinion, what are the advantages and disadvantages of movies versus books?

_____

_____

_____

Language

Write a sentence using the irregular past tense of the given verb.

1. **wear**

_____

_____

_____

2. **know**

_____

_____

_____

Math

Answer the item.

3. How many squares are in the figure?
   Hint: Some squares may have other squares within them.

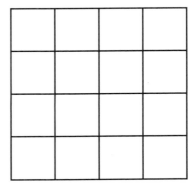

_____

Reading

Read the paragraph. Then answer the items.

Pat was getting on his bike to ride to school as his dad approached. "Son, let me take a look at your bike before you head out. I noticed it needs a few repairs," his dad said. Pat didn't want to be delayed. He was in a rush to get to school this morning because he had woken up late. Plus, he couldn't find the cover to his calculator and spent time looking for it in his room. He asked his dad to repair the bike after school. His dad hesitantly agreed, and Pat left. Unfortunately, he didn't realize that his front basket was loose. As Pat rode, his calculator fell out and broke, and his books got torn under the tires.

4. What events led to Pat's calculator breaking?

_____

_____

5. Could the calculator accident have been prevented?

_____

Language

Read the sentence. Complete it using a verb that agrees with the subject.

1. Marie and Tia _____ poems together.

2. Shelly _____ oatmeal with maple syrup, raisins, and nuts.

3. Dad and I _____ the map to figure out which direction to travel in.

4. You often _____ when your favorite sports team is winning.

5. Mr. and Mrs. Carter _____ at the school that I attend.

Math

Answer the item.

6. Circle the letter that is backwards.

7. Circle the figure that is different.

Reading

Read the paragraph. Then answer the items.

Many inventions, including the simplest ones, have made the world better. The wheel, for example, was invented when people were still living in caves. They figured out that a wheel could help transport things more easily. The paper and pen is another invention that is still being used today. The ancient Egyptians created symbols on papyrus. These symbols shared information, similar to writing today. The steam engine and automobiles are inventions that have improved people's lives. They helped us travel greater distances more quickly and comfortably.

8. What do you think causes people to invent new things? Explain your thinking.

_____

_____

9. List some other inventions that have made your own life easier.

_____

Language

Write a sentence using the present progressive tense of the given verb.

1. **perform**

_____

_____

_____

2. **study**

_____

_____

_____

Math

Answer the item.

3. Draw how the figure would look upside down.

Reading

Read the paragraph. Then answer the items.

      Janie is a member of the student council at her school. At the last student council meeting, she and the other members talked about how they could improve students' attitudes. It seemed like the students weren't happy to be at school. So they came up with a plan to try to change this. One idea was to place a "compliment jar" in every classroom. Students could write compliments to their classmates. Another idea was to have whole-class lunches once a month or to have a "snack shack" that students could help run. Janie felt certain that these ideas would lead to a happier group of students.

4. Do you agree with Janie that these ideas could have good results? Explain your thinking.

_____

_____

5. List some other ideas that could lead to positive results for the students.

_____

Name ______________________________

Language

Write a sentence using the past progressive tense of the given verb.

1. **smile**

____

____

____

2. **swim**

____

____

____

Math

Answer the item.

3. How many 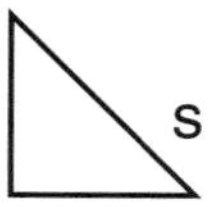 s will fit in the rectangle?

____

Reading

Read the paragraph. Then answer the items.

Various things cause climate change. Historically, climate change has been a result of natural causes, such as changes in the sun's energy being absorbed by Earth's atmosphere. Volcanic eruptions can affect climate change by releasing particles and gases into the air. These particles can make Earth cooler by reflecting sunlight away from the planet. Some factors in climate change are related to human activities. Factories and vehicles add carbon dioxide and other harmful gases into the air. The outcome is that Earth retains heat. This has become a larger problem in recent years.

4. Are humans making climate change better or worse? Explain your thinking.

____

____

5. What is a possible outcome if Earth continues to retain heat?

____

Language

Write a sentence using the future progressive tense of the given verb.

1. **grow**

_____

_____

_____

2. **find**

_____

_____

_____

Math

Answer the item.

3. Is this figure symmetrical? Explain why or why not.

_____

_____

_____

_____

Reading

Read the paragraph. Then answer the items.

Does playing music for plants help them grow? Some scientists believe that it does. In a study done at a university, scientists grew four plants in four different controlled environments. The plants that "listened to music" grew more quickly than those that did not. However, many scientists believe it's unlikely that music helps a plant grow. These scientists believe that light, minerals, and water are the most important factors that result in a healthy plant. Interestingly, another study seems to suggest that plants prefer classical music to rock 'n' roll.

4. Do you believe that music is as important as other factors in healthy plant growth?

_____

_____

5. If music really does help plants grow, what considerations should be made when planting?

_____

Language

Read the sentence. Circle the simile.

1. Hua is as strong as an ox.

Write two sentences that each contain a simile.

2. _____

3. _____

Math

Complete the tables by converting the measurements. The first one of each table has been done for you.

4.

Meters	Centimeters
1	100
2	
3	
4	

5.

Centimeters	Millimeters
1	10
2	
3	
4	

6.

Kilometers	Meters
1	1,000
2	
3	
4	

Reading

Read the paragraph. Then answer the item.

The perfectly dressed lady held herself upright and tall, like a statue, as she walked to the counter at the bank. She wore fancy gloves, high-heeled shoes, a long coat, and shiny jewelry. She also wore a sour expression on her face. She didn't appear angry, but she seemed terribly unhappy. When she got to the counter, the clerk smiled at her. But she didn't return the smile. She squinted as if she was suspicious of the friendly employee.

7. Explain how the vocabulary in the text creates a strong image of the lady.

_____

_____

Language

Read the sentence. Circle the metaphor.

1. My family is the sun in my sky.

Write two sentences that each contain a metaphor.

2. _____

3. _____

Math

Complete the tables by converting the measurements. Then answer the item.

4.

Meters	Centimeters
5	500
7	
8	

5.

Centimeters	Millimeters
6	60
9	
11	

6.

Kilometers	Meters
2	2,000
5	
7	

7. Explain how you converted kilometers to meters.

_____

Reading

Read the paragraph. Then answer the items.

Once upon a time in a land far away, three brothers lived in a magical kingdom ruled by animals. The animals were kind to the human brothers. A legend told of an evil wizard who would one day arrive at the kingdom and try to take over. But the brothers had a powerful family amulet that would protect the kingdom and all of the animals in it. And the brothers, although not originally from this kingdom, loved it with all their hearts.

8. What do you think is the genre of this story? Explain why.

_____

9. Underline the words in the text that support your answer for number 8.

Language

Write two sentences that each use a different meaning of the word *club*.

1. _____

2. _____

List any other words you know that have more than one meaning.

3. _____

Math

Solve the problem.

4. Lia is collecting twigs to make a wreath. She found a twig that was 0.25 meter long. She found a branch that was 0.9 meter long. And she found another twig that was 30 millimeters long. Write the lengths in order from the shortest to the longest.

_____ , _____ , _____

Explain your thinking. _____

_____

Reading

Read the paragraph. Then answer the item.

Corbin was hanging out with his little sister, Cassie, who is in kindergarten. They were playing a board game, when Corbin said the phrase, "piece of cake." Cassie immediately thought there was cake in the house. Corbin laughed, and they kept playing. A short while later, Corbin said, "The ball is in your court, Cass." Cassie was confused, and she protested that this wasn't a game that had a ball in it.

5. Explain why Cassie was confused by the words Corbin was using.

_____

_____

Language

Explain what the idiom means in your own words.

1. Actions speak louder than words.

_____

2. This is the best thing since sliced bread.

_____

Math

Complete the table by converting the measurements. Then answer the item.

3.

Liters	Milliliters
5	5,000
7	
8	

4. Explain how you converted liters to milliliters.

_____

Reading

Read the paragraph carefully. Then read it again. Answer the item.

     A man walked up to the hotel counter and said to the clerk, "Ineida Frank." The hotel clerk politely told the man that nobody named "Frank" worked there. "No, Ineida Frank," the man said again. The clerk was confused. "Fine, try Ima Frank," said the man. The clerk then became very confused. The man tried again, "Kenya Dance"? Eventually, the man realized that he needed to explain to the clerk that these were names of hotel guests.

5. Explain why word choice plays an important role in this text.

_____

_____

Language

Read the proverb. Then explain what you think it means.

1. The early bird catches the worm.

_____

_____

_____

Math

Solve the problem. Show your work.

2. For a birthday party, Jody's mom bought 5 bottles that each contained 2 liters of lemonade. How many milliliters of lemonade were bought for the party?

> 1 liter = 1,000 milliliters

_____

Reading

Read the paragraph. Then answer the items.

> Dr. Akers gave me the high honor of allowing me to introduce him at the Doctors and Medical Professionals' Conference last autumn. I was flattered that he asked me to perform this duty. He was the guest of honor at this respectable event.

3. Does the word choice used give this text a formal or informal tone? Explain your answer.

_____

4. Explain how different word choices could give it a different tone.

_____

Language

Fix the run-on sentence by rewriting it as a compound sentence.

1. Hye Joon enjoys hiking she hasn't seen the trails here.

_____

2. Peter made a mess in the kitchen he's cleaning it now.

_____

Math

Complete the tables by converting the measurements.

3.

Feet	Inches
1	12
2	
3	
4	
5	

4.

Yards	Feet
1	3
2	
3	
4	
5	

5.

Yards	Inches
1	36
2	
3	
4	
5	

Reading

Read the paragraph. Then answer the item.

Mount Kilimanjaro is a unique mountain. Known as the "roof of Africa," it's the highest point in Africa and the tallest lone mountain in the world. Kilimanjaro is 19,341 ft (5,895 m) high. Many people try to reach its summit every year. The mountain is known worldwide for its beauty and surrounding African wildlife. It contains different ecosystems: rainforest, heath, alpine desert, arctic summit, and more.

6. Circle the main idea of the text. Then write one detail that supports the main idea.

_____

_____

Language

Fix the run-on sentence by rewriting it as two complete sentences.

1. Liza is learning American Sign Language she practices daily.

   _____

2. Dubaku is a fan of hockey he wants to go to a game.

   _____

Math

Complete the tables by converting the measurements. Then answer the item.

3.
Feet	Inches
2	24
5	
10	

4.
Yards	Feet
3	9
4	
7	

5.
Yards	Inches
4	144
5	
6	

6. Explain how you converted yards to inches.

   _____

Reading

Read the paragraph. Then answer the item.

> Thomas Jefferson and John Adams were two U.S. presidents with some surprising similarities. Both of the men were patriots who helped gain independence during the American Revolution. They both helped to draft the U.S. Constitution, and both served as vice president before being elected as president. Astonishingly, they died on the same day, the 50th anniversary of the signing of the Declaration of Independence.

7. Circle the main idea of the text. Then explain how the details support the main idea.

   _____

   _____

Language

Read the sentence. Write whether the sentence is a *run-on*, a *fragment*, or is *complete*.

1. Pedro and his family.   _____

2. We joined a book club last month.   _____

3. The cat's collar is tight she needs a new one. _____

4. Our friends who live in Florida.   _____

Math

Solve the problem.

5. Jedidiah can jump as high as 36 inches. Callie can jump as high as 2 feet. Manuel can jump as high as 0.5 yard. Write the heights in order from shortest to highest.

_____, _____, _____

Explain your thinking. _____

_____

Reading

Read the paragraph. Then answer the item.

     The blobfish is a rare species of fish that has an unusual appearance. Its features resemble a human face. It has no skeleton and very few muscles, so its face droops downward. It doesn't even have teeth to eat with! Many people consider the blobfish to be ugly because its body seems to have the texture of jelly. It lives deep in the ocean where the water pressure is very high.

6. Underline the details in the text. Then explain how they helped you better understand the main idea.

_____

_____

Language

Circle *fragment* if the sentence is a fragment. Circle *complete* if it is a complete sentence. Then explain why you chose that answer.

1. When Bazul walks through the door.   **fragment**   **complete**

_____

2. The new shopping mall will open next week.   **fragment**   **complete**

_____

Math

Complete the tables by converting the measurements.

3.
Pints	Cups
1	2
2	
3	
4	

4.
Quarts	Cups
1	4
2	
3	
4	

5.
Gallons	Quarts
1	4
2	
3	
4	

Reading

Read the paragraph. Then answer the item.

Magnetism is at work all around us. When you use a compass, the needle shows you where north is by lining up with a magnetic force. But where is this force? It is in the middle of the planet—the center of Earth itself is actually a big magnet! Think of a giant bar magnet running from the North Pole to the South Pole. Its magnetic force extends through the poles thousands of kilometers into space, forming a barrier around Earth.

6. Explain the main idea of the text in your own words.

_____

_____

Language

Write four sentences. Circle the complete subject and underline the complete predicate.

1. _____

2. _____

3. _____

4. _____

Math

Complete the tables by converting the measurements.

5.

Quarts	Pints
1	2
2	
3	
4	

6.

Gallons	Cups
1	16
2	
3	
4	

7.

Gallons	Pints
1	8
2	
3	
4	

Reading

Read the paragraph. Then answer the item.

Objects make sounds by vibrating, or moving quickly back and forth. These vibrations produce sound waves that move just like ripples in water. The highness or lowness of a sound is called the *pitch*. The faster an object vibrates, the higher the pitch of the sound. The slower an object vibrates, the lower the pitch of the sound. People can hear a wide range of sounds—from a low, deep drum to a high-pitched whistle.

8. Explain the main idea of the text in your own words.

_____

_____

Language

Read the sentence. Insert commas to correctly punctuate the series in the sentence.

1. Ashley got stickers pens and erasers as her birthday gifts.

2. Dharma enjoys math English and science.

3. Rafael has seen goats cows pigs and horses.

4. Eleanor is afraid of mice bugs and reptiles.

5. Bruce's best friends are Carol Gina and Nat.

6. Chris collects rocks stamps coins and books.

Math

Read the problem. Then plot the data from the table on the line plot.

7. The table shows how many plants a nursery sold at specific prices on a given day.

Prices of Plants Sold at Nursery		
$5.00	$10.00	$15.00
8	6	4

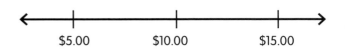

$5.00 $10.00 $15.00

Reading

Read the paragraph. Then answer the items.

Dana Dakin spent many years building a career in finance. Then she heard about the idea of living life in thirds. The idea is that each third of life has a different goal: to learn, to earn, and to return. In other words, the first third of life is devoted to school and learning. The second third is devoted to earning a living. And the final third is devoted to returning, or giving back, to help others. In 2003, when Dakin reached the age of 60, she decided it was time to start giving back. She started helping women in Africa.

8. Based on the text, which of the following is likely true?
   Ⓐ Dana Dakin wasn't very successful in finance.
   Ⓑ Dana Dakin's career in finance was successful.
   Ⓒ Dana Dakin didn't attend school.
   Ⓓ Dana Dakin was not able to live life in thirds.

9. What led to Dakin's decision to help women in Africa?

_____

Language

Write three sentences that each contain a series. Use correct punctuation.

1. _____

_____

2. _____

_____

3. _____

_____

Math

Use the line plot to answer the items.

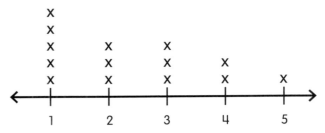

Number of Instruments Students Play

4. How many students play 3 or more instruments? _____

5. How many students play only 1 instrument? _____

Reading

Read the paragraph. Then answer the items.

Paul and his mom are eating breakfast. They're discussing what they have to do today. They are going to put on their walking shoes and head down in the elevator as usual. They are deciding whether to take a taxi cab or walk to the bus stop. Because they have so many errands to run today, they are leaning toward taking the bus. The local buses will take them wherever they need to go. Tonight, they may go to the movie theater.

6. Paul and his mom most likely live in a _____.

Ⓐ campsite

Ⓑ rural area

Ⓒ suburb

Ⓓ city

7. Why would they take a bus or taxi cab?

Ⓐ They dislike all automobiles.

Ⓑ They walk everywhere.

Ⓒ They don't need a car where they live.

Ⓓ It's a rare treat for them.

8. How do Paul and his mom feel about where they live? Explain your thinking.

_____

_____

Language

Read the letter. Insert commas to punctuate the letter correctly.

1. Dear Nyari

   Thank you for your interest in our school. We are always happy to hear from students at other schools. We like learning about how our schools are similar and different. Please write to us again in the future.

   Sincerely

   Mrs. Delaney

Math

Use the line plot to solve the problem.

2. A health food store has 12 packages of granola left. Mr. Tomlin needs to buy 5 pounds of granola. The line plot shows how much the packages weigh in pounds. Write one way Mr. Tomlin can combine the packages to get how much he needs.

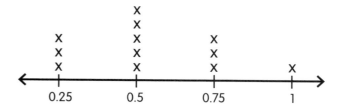

_____

_____

_____

Reading

Read the paragraph. Then answer the items.

   Carrie woke up extra early to say goodbye to her dad before he left for work. She usually tried to wake up early enough to see him go, but sometimes she was too tired. Sometimes she made him toast before he left for the day. She watched him put on his uniform jacket and hat. His badge gleamed in the room's dim light. She thought he appeared very official. "I'm sure you'll get lots of bad guys today, Dad!" she said as she waved goodbye.

3. Why does Carrie wake up to see her dad off?
   Ⓐ He won't leave unless she wakes up.
   Ⓑ She can't sleep.
   Ⓒ She loves her dad.
   Ⓓ He asks her to do that.

4. Which words best describe Carrie?
   Ⓐ sweet and caring
   Ⓑ smart and funny
   Ⓒ tired and sleepy
   Ⓓ hungry and cranky

5. What do you think Carrie's dad does for a living? Explain your thinking.

_____

_____

Language

Read the sentence. Insert comma(s) where they are needed.

1. Whenever Sung-Young sees a rainbow she smiles.

2. The sun is shining yet it's cold outside.

3. We are having chicken peas and potatoes for dinner tonight.

4. To get to Chicago, we'll take a train a bus and a plane.

5. Steve reads his book until the bus arrives.

Math

Use the line plot to solve the problem. Show your work.

6. Ms. Farrah wants to buy origami paper. She collected prices from stores. The line plot shows how many stores sell origami paper at each price. How many stores sell origami paper for $6.99?

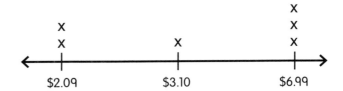

_____

Reading

Read the paragraph. Then answer the items.

Brad rolled his eyes as he arrived at soccer practice. As he stepped onto the field with his teammates, he couldn't help but think of all the stuff he wanted to do at that moment: read his book, walk his dog, or ride his bike with Josh. The soccer players did their usual practice warm-ups, then they practiced dribbling and other soccer moves. "Watch your footwork!" yelled the coach. Once again, Brad rolled his eyes. He wondered what time it was. After a few minutes more of practice, he asked the coach if he could sit on the bench.

7. How does Brad feel about soccer? Use details from the text to explain.

_____

_____

8. How does Brad feel about doing physical activities in general? Explain your thinking.

_____

_____

Language

Read the sentence. Then rewrite it to correct the punctuation error.

1. Malik is allergic to nuts so he doesn't eat them.

   _____

   _____

Is the punctuation in the sentence correct or incorrect? Explain your thinking.

2. Tilda is happy because it's the weekend.

   _____

   _____

Math

Answer the item.

3. Explain what kind of information you can get from a line plot.

   _____

   _____

   _____

4. Write a specific example of something you might learn from a line plot.

   _____

   _____

   _____

Reading

Read the paragraph. Then answer the items.

Valencia was excited to go to the new restaurant with her family. It was Saturday night, and the family had been planning this dinner outing for over a week. She guessed that her brother would order the fettucini alfredo. She assumed her sister would order the lasagna. Her parents were both fans of chicken parmesan. And she would order the pasta marinara. Valencia daydreamed about the restaurant's pasta dishes the entire day. But when everyone was seated and looked at their menus, there was not a single pasta dish!

5. How did Valencia probably feel about the menu at the restaurant? Explain your thinking.

   _____

   _____

6. How attentive is Valencia to what her family members like? Explain your thinking.

   _____

   _____

Answer Key

✳ These answers will vary. Examples are given.

Page 11

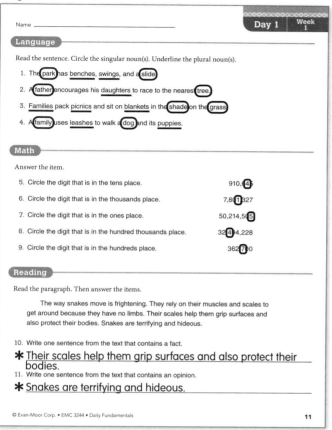

Name _____

Day 1 | Week 1

Language

Read the sentence. Circle the singular noun(s). Underline the plural noun(s).

1. The (park) has benches, swings, and a (slide)
2. A (father) encourages his daughters to race to the nearest (tree)
3. Families pack picnics and sit on blankets in the (shade) on the (grass)
4. A (family) uses leashes to walk a (dog) and its puppies.

Math

Answer the item.

5. Circle the digit that is in the tens place.   910,0(4)6
6. Circle the digit that is in the thousands place.   7,8(1)327
7. Circle the digit that is in the ones place.   50,214,5(5)
8. Circle the digit that is in the hundred thousands place. 32(4)4,228
9. Circle the digit that is in the hundreds place.   362(7)00

Reading

Read the paragraph. Then answer the items.

The way snakes move is frightening. They rely on their muscles and scales to get around because they have no limbs. Their scales help them grip surfaces and also protect their bodies. Snakes are terrifying and hideous.

10. Write one sentence from the text that contains a fact.

✳ Their scales help them grip surfaces and also protect their bodies.

11. Write one sentence from the text that contains an opinion.

✳ Snakes are terrifying and hideous.

© Evan-Moor Corp. • EMC 3244 • Daily Fundamentals   11

Page 12

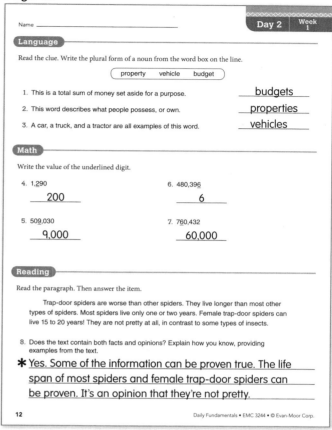

Name _____

Day 2 | Week 1

Language

Read the clue. Write the plural form of a noun from the word box on the line.

| property   vehicle   budget |

1. This is a total sum of money set aside for a purpose.   budgets
2. This word describes what people possess, or own.   properties
3. A car, a truck, and a tractor are all examples of this word.   vehicles

Math

Write the value of the underlined digit.

4. 1,290   6. 480,396
   200   6

5. 509,030   7. 760,432
   9,000   60,000

Reading

Read the paragraph. Then answer the item.

Trap-door spiders are worse than other spiders. They live longer than most other types of spiders. Most spiders live only one or two years. Female trap-door spiders can live 15 to 20 years! They are not pretty at all, in contrast to some types of insects.

8. Does the text contain both facts and opinions? Explain how you know, providing examples from the text.

✳ Yes. Some of the information can be proven true. The life span of most spiders and female trap-door spiders can be proven. It's an opinion that they're not pretty.

12   Daily Fundamentals • EMC 3244 • © Evan-Moor Corp.

Page 13

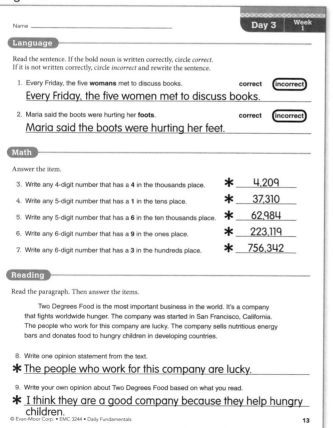

Name _____

Day 3 | Week 1

Language

Read the sentence. If the bold noun is written correctly, circle *correct*.
If it is not written correctly, circle *incorrect* and rewrite the sentence.

1. Every Friday, the five **womans** met to discuss books.   correct (incorrect)

Every Friday, the five women met to discuss books.

2. Maria said the boots were hurting her **foots**.   correct (incorrect)

Maria said the boots were hurting her feet.

Math

Answer the item.

3. Write any 4-digit number that has a **4** in the thousands place.   ✳ 4,209
4. Write any 5-digit number that has a **1** in the tens place.   ✳ 37,310
5. Write any 5-digit number that has a **6** in the ten thousands place. ✳ 62,984
6. Write any 6-digit number that has a **9** in the ones place.   ✳ 223,119
7. Write any 6-digit number that has a **3** in the hundreds place.   ✳ 756,342

Reading

Read the paragraph. Then answer the items.

Two Degrees Food is the most important business in the world. It's a company that fights worldwide hunger. The company was started in San Francisco, California. The people who work for this company are lucky. The company sells nutritious energy bars and donates food to hungry children in developing countries.

8. Write one opinion statement from the text.

✳ The people who work for this company are lucky.

9. Write your own opinion about Two Degrees Food based on what you read.

✳ I think they are a good company because they help hungry children.

© Evan-Moor Corp. • EMC 3244 • Daily Fundamentals   13

Page 14

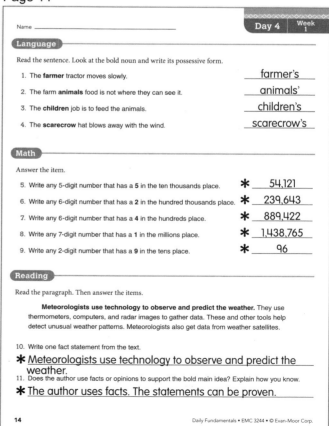

Name _____

Day 4 | Week 1

Language

Read the sentence. Look at the bold noun and write its possessive form.

1. The **farmer** tractor moves slowly.   farmer's
2. The farm **animals** food is not where they can see it.   animals'
3. The **children** job is to feed the animals.   children's
4. The **scarecrow** hat blows away with the wind.   scarecrow's

Math

Answer the item.

5. Write any 5-digit number that has a **5** in the ten thousands place.   ✳ 54,121
6. Write any 6-digit number that has a **2** in the hundred thousands place. ✳ 239,643
7. Write any 6-digit number that has a **4** in the hundreds place.   ✳ 889,422
8. Write any 7-digit number that has a **1** in the millions place.   ✳ 1,438,765
9. Write any 2-digit number that has a **9** in the tens place.   ✳ 96

Reading

Read the paragraph. Then answer the items.

Meteorologists use technology to observe and predict the weather. They use thermometers, computers, and radar images to gather data. These and other tools help detect unusual weather patterns. Meteorologists also get data from weather satellites.

10. Write one fact statement from the text.

✳ Meteorologists use technology to observe and predict the weather.

11. Does the author use facts or opinions to support the bold main idea? Explain how you know.

✳ The author uses facts. The statements can be proven.

14   Daily Fundamentals • EMC 3244 • © Evan-Moor Corp.

Page 15

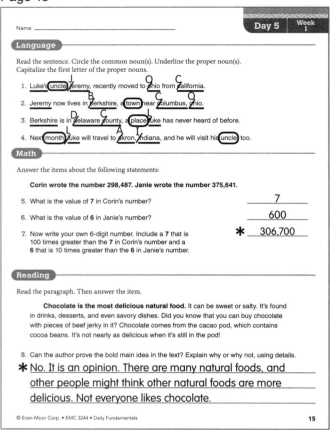

Name _____

Day 5 | Week 1

Language

Read the sentence. Circle the common noun(s). Underline the proper noun(s). Capitalize the first letter of the proper nouns.

1. Luke's (uncle) Jeremy, recently moved to Ohio from California.
2. Jeremy now lives in Berkshire, a (town) near Columbus, Ohio.
3. Berkshire is in Delaware (county), a (place) Luke has never heard of before.
4. Next (month) Luke will travel to Akron, Indiana, and he will visit his (uncle) too.

Math

Answer the items about the following statements:

Corin wrote the number 298,487. Janie wrote the number 375,641.

5. What is the value of **7** in Corin's number?   7
6. What is the value of **6** in Janie's number?   600
7. Now write your own 6-digit number. Include a **7** that is 100 times greater than the **7** in Corin's number and a **6** that is 10 times greater than the **6** in Janie's number.   ✳ 306,700

Reading

Read the paragraph. Then answer the item.

Chocolate is the most delicious natural food. It can be sweet or salty. It's found in drinks, desserts, and even savory dishes. Did you know that you can buy chocolate with pieces of beef jerky in it? Chocolate comes from the cacao pod, which contains cocoa beans. It's not nearly as delicious when it's still in the pod!

8. Can the author prove the bold main idea in the text? Explain why or why not, using details.

✳ No. It is an opinion. There are many natural foods, and other people might think other natural foods are more delicious. Not everyone likes chocolate.

© Evan-Moor Corp. • EMC 3244 • Daily Fundamentals   15

Page 16

Name _____

Day 1 | Week 2

Language

Read the sentence. Write an adjective to complete the sentence.

✳ 1. Pam enjoys spending time with her friendly neighbors.
✳ 2. The Hendersons have a cat and a shy dog.
✳ 3. Terry's family just got a huge trampoline.
✳ 4. The Jacksons live in the colorful house.

Math

Write the given number in expanded form.

5. standard form: 48,364

   expanded form: 40,000 + 8,000 + 300 + 60 + 4

6. standard form: 399,571

   expanded form: 300,000 + 90,000 + 9,000 + 500 + 70 + 1

Reading

Read the paragraph. Then answer the item.

Arachne could weave beautiful cloths. People gave her gifts because they liked her cloths so much. She usually didn't think the gifts were nice enough and refused them. When people complimented her, she would say, "Of course, I'm an excellent weaver."

7. Would you be friends with Arachne? Explain why or why not.

✳ I would not be friends with Arachne because she does not seem appreciative, and she does not consider other people's feelings.

16   Daily Fundamentals • EMC 3244 • © Evan-Moor Corp.

Page 17

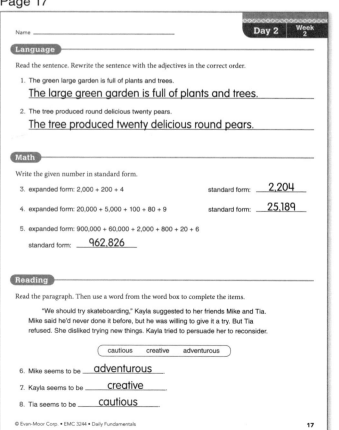

Name _____

Day 2 | Week 2

Language

Read the sentence. Rewrite the sentence with the adjectives in the correct order.

1. The green large garden is full of plants and trees.
   The large green garden is full of plants and trees.

2. The tree produced round delicious twenty pears.
   The tree produced twenty delicious round pears.

Math

Write the given number in standard form.

3. expanded form: 2,000 + 200 + 4   standard form: 2,204

4. expanded form: 20,000 + 5,000 + 100 + 80 + 9   standard form: 25,189

5. expanded form: 900,000 + 60,000 + 2,000 + 800 + 20 + 6

   standard form: 962,826

Reading

Read the paragraph. Then use a word from the word box to complete the items.

"We should try skateboarding," Kayla suggested to her friends Mike and Tia. Mike said he'd never done it before, but he was willing to give it a try. But Tia refused. She disliked trying new things. Kayla tried to persuade her to reconsider.

cautious   creative   adventurous

6. Mike seems to be adventurous
7. Kayla seems to be creative
8. Tia seems to be cautious

© Evan-Moor Corp. • EMC 3244 • Daily Fundamentals   17

Page 18

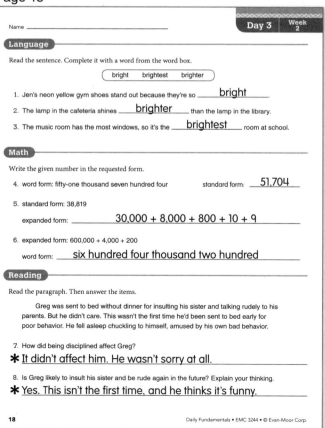

Name _____

Day 3 | Week 2

Language

Read the sentence. Complete it with a word from the word box.

bright   brightest   brighter

1. Jen's neon yellow gym shoes stand out because they're so bright
2. The lamp in the cafeteria shines brighter than the lamp in the library.
3. The music room has the most windows, so it's the brightest room at school.

Math

Write the given number in the requested form.

4. word form: fifty-one thousand seven hundred four   standard form: 51,704

5. standard form: 38,819

   expanded form: 30,000 + 8,000 + 800 + 10 + 9

6. expanded form: 600,000 + 4,000 + 200

   word form: six hundred four thousand two hundred

Reading

Read the paragraph. Then answer the items.

Greg was sent to bed without dinner for insulting his sister and talking rudely to his parents. But he didn't care. This wasn't the first time he'd been sent to bed early for poor behavior. He fell asleep chuckling to himself, amused by his own bad behavior.

7. How did being disciplined affect Greg?

✳ It didn't affect him. He wasn't sorry at all.

8. Is Greg likely to insult his sister and be rude again in the future? Explain your thinking.

✳ Yes. This isn't the first time, and he thinks it's funny.

18   Daily Fundamentals • EMC 3244 • © Evan-Moor Corp.

Page 19

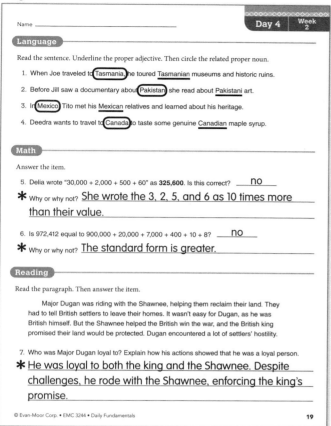

Name _____

Language

Read the sentence. Underline the proper adjective. Then circle the related proper noun.

1. When Joe traveled to (Tasmania,) he toured Tasmanian museums and historic ruins.

2. Before Jill saw a documentary about (Pakistan,) she read about Pakistani art.

3. In (Mexico,) Tito met his Mexican relatives and learned about his heritage.

4. Deedra wants to travel to (Canada) to taste some genuine Canadian maple syrup.

Math

Answer the item.

5. Delia wrote "30,000 + 2,000 + 500 + 60" as **325,600**. Is this correct? __no__

✱ Why or why not? __She wrote the 3, 2, 5, and 6 as 10 times more than their value.__

6. Is 972,412 equal to 900,000 + 20,000 + 7,000 + 400 + 10 + 8? __no__

✱ Why or why not? __The standard form is greater.__

Reading

Read the paragraph. Then answer the item.

Major Dugan was riding with the Shawnee, helping them reclaim their land. They had to tell British settlers to leave their homes. It wasn't easy for Dugan, as he was British himself. But the Shawnee helped the British win the war, and the British king promised their land would be protected. Dugan encountered a lot of settlers' hostility.

7. Who was Major Dugan loyal to? Explain how his actions showed that he was a loyal person.

✱ __He was loyal to both the king and the Shawnee. Despite challenges, he rode with the Shawnee, enforcing the king's promise.__

© Evan-Moor Corp. • EMC 3244 • Daily Fundamentals   19

Page 20

Name _____

Language

Write a possessive adjective from the word box to complete the sentence.

| my | your | his | her | its | our | their |

1. Denise and Carter have a trampoline. They jump on __their__ trampoline.

2. Danny and I rode bikes to the library. Then we left __our__ bikes outside.

3. Dad finally built a treehouse. Inside, __its__ floor is painted red.

Math

Answer the item.

4. Write a number in expanded form that is less than 19,799.

✱ __9,000 + 700 + 90 + 4__

5. Write a number in expanded form that is greater than 243,411.

✱ __700,000 + 30,000 + 800 + 60__

Reading

Read the paragraph. Then answer the items.

Sara and her friend Tasha were at the mall. Sara saw shoes she liked. "Oh, those aren't cute," said Tasha. Sara quickly agreed and decided not to buy them. For lunch, Sara really wanted a pretzel. But she got a taco because that's what Tasha wanted.

6. Write two adjectives that describe Sara.

✱ __agreeable, meek__

7. Explain how details in the text support the descriptive adjectives you wrote.

✱ __The text shows that Sara agrees with Tasha even though she does not feel that way inside.__

20   Daily Fundamentals • EMC 3244 • © Evan-Moor Corp.

Page 21

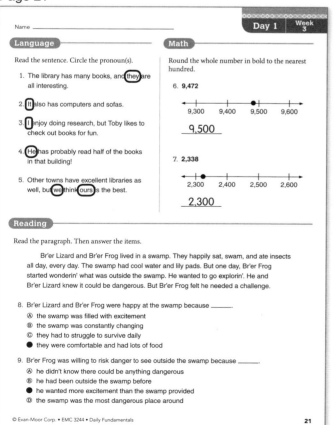

Name _____

Language

Read the sentence. Circle the pronoun(s).

1. The library has many books, and (they) are all interesting.

2. (It) also has computers and sofas.

3. (I) enjoy doing research, but Toby likes to check out books for fun.

4. (He) has probably read half of the books in that building!

5. Other towns have excellent libraries as well, but (we) think (ours) is the best.

Math

Round the whole number in bold to the nearest hundred.

6. **9,472**

9,300   9,400   9,500   9,600

__9,500__

7. **2,338**

2,300   2,400   2,500   2,600

__2,300__

Reading

Read the paragraph. Then answer the items.

Br'er Lizard and Br'er Frog lived in a swamp. They happily sat, swam, and ate insects all day, every day. The swamp had cool water and lily pads. But one day, Br'er Frog started wonderin' what was outside the swamp. He wanted to go explorin'. He and Br'er Lizard knew it could be dangerous. But Br'er Frog felt he needed a challenge.

8. Br'er Lizard and Br'er Frog were happy at the swamp because _____.
   Ⓐ the swamp was filled with excitement
   Ⓑ the swamp was constantly changing
   Ⓒ they had to struggle to survive daily
   ● they were comfortable and had lots of food

9. Br'er Frog was willing to risk danger to see outside the swamp because _____.
   Ⓐ he didn't know there could be anything dangerous
   Ⓑ he had been outside the swamp before
   ● he wanted more excitement than the swamp provided
   Ⓓ the swamp was the most dangerous place around

© Evan-Moor Corp. • EMC 3244 • Daily Fundamentals   21

Page 22

Name _____

Language

Read the sentence. Write a pronoun in place of the underlined word or words.

1. Cody called his dad.
   Cody called __him__.

2. Alicia and I play chess.
   __We__ play chess.

3. Shelly is out of town.
   __She__ is out of town.

4. Ben saw Sue and Alex.
   Ben saw __them__.

Math

Round the whole number to the nearest ten thousand.

5. 38,942   __40,000__
6. 67,800   __70,000__
7. 709,689   __710,000__
8. 813,222   __810,000__
9. 541,200   __540,000__
10. 931,620   __930,000__
11. 262,123   __260,000__
12. 478,321   __480,000__

Reading

Read the poem stanza. Then answer the items.

"Will you walk into my parlor?" said the Spider to the Fly.
"'Tis the prettiest little parlor that ever you did spy;
The way into my parlor is up a winding stair,
And I've many curious things to show you when you are there."

13. What is the spider's "parlor"? What is the "winding stair"? Explain how you know, using the picture and details from the poem.

✱ __The parlor is the center of the web. The "winding stair" is the web. The web kind of looks like a winding staircase.__

14. Do you think the fly should accept the spider's invitation? Why or why not?

✱ __No, the fly should not accept the invitation because spiders eat flies.__

22   Daily Fundamentals • EMC 3244 • © Evan-Moor Corp.

✱ These answers will vary. Examples are given.

Page 23

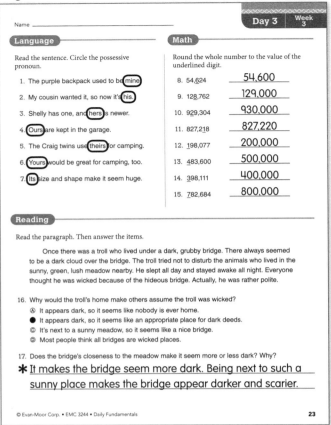

Day 3 — Week 3

Language

Read the sentence. Circle the possessive pronoun.

1. The purple backpack used to be (mine).
2. My cousin wanted it, so now it's (his).
3. Shelly has one, and (hers) is newer.
4. (Ours) are kept in the garage.
5. The Craig twins use (theirs) for camping.
6. (Yours) would be great for camping, too.
7. (Its) size and shape make it seem huge.

Math

Round the whole number to the value of the underlined digit.

8. 54,6̲24 — 54,600
9. 12̲8,762 — 129,000
10. 9̲29,304 — 930,000
11. 827,2̲18 — 827,220
12. 1̲98,077 — 200,000
13. 4̲83,600 — 500,000
14. 3̲98,111 — 400,000
15. 7̲82,684 — 800,000

Reading

Read the paragraph. Then answer the items.

Once there was a troll who lived under a dark, grubby bridge. There always seemed to be a dark cloud over the bridge. The troll tried not to disturb the animals who lived in the sunny, green, lush meadow nearby. He slept all day and stayed awake all night. Everyone thought he was wicked because of the hideous bridge. Actually, he was rather polite.

16. Why would the troll's home make others assume the troll was wicked?
   Ⓐ It appears dark, so it seems like nobody is ever home.
   ● It appears dark, so it seems like an appropriate place for dark deeds.
   Ⓒ It's next to a sunny meadow, so it seems like a nice bridge.
   Ⓓ Most people think all bridges are wicked places.

17. Does the bridge's closeness to the meadow make it seem more or less dark? Why?

✱ It makes the bridge seem more dark. Being next to such a sunny place makes the bridge appear darker and scarier.

Page 24

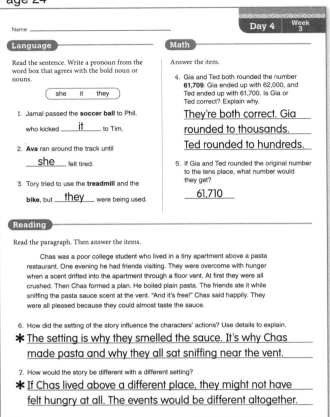

Day 4 — Week 3

Language

Read the sentence. Write a pronoun from the word box that agrees with the bold noun or nouns.

| she | it | they |

1. Jamal passed the **soccer ball** to Phil, who kicked ___it___ to Tim.
2. **Ava** ran around the track until ___she___ felt tired.
3. Tory tried to use the **treadmill** and the **bike**, but ___they___ were being used.

Math

Answer the item.

4. Gia and Ted both rounded the number **61,709**. Gia ended up with 62,000, and Ted ended up with 61,700. Is Gia or Ted correct? Explain why.

   They're both correct. Gia rounded to thousands. Ted rounded to hundreds.

5. If Gia and Ted rounded the original number to the tens place, what number would they get?

   61,710

Reading

Read the paragraph. Then answer the items.

Chas was a poor college student who lived in a tiny apartment above a pasta restaurant. One evening he had friends visiting. They were overcome with hunger when a scent drifted into the apartment through a floor vent. At first they were all crushed. Then Chas formed a plan. He boiled plain pasta. The friends ate it while sniffing the pasta sauce scent at the vent. "And it's free!" Chas said happily. They were all pleased because they could almost taste the sauce.

6. How did the setting of the story influence the characters' actions? Use details to explain.

✱ The setting is why they smelled the sauce. It's why Chas made pasta and why they all sat sniffing near the vent.

7. How would the story be different with a different setting?

✱ If Chas lived above a different place, they might not have felt hungry at all. The events would be different altogether.

Page 25

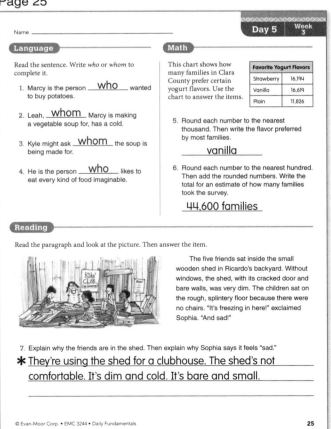

Day 5 — Week 3

Language

Read the sentence. Write *who* or *whom* to complete it.

1. Marcy is the person ___who___ wanted to buy potatoes.
2. Leah, ___whom___ Marcy is making a vegetable soup for, has a cold.
3. Kyle might ask ___whom___ the soup is being made for.
4. He is the person ___who___ likes to eat every kind of food imaginable.

Math

This chart shows how many families in Clara County prefer certain yogurt flavors. Use the chart to answer the items.

Favorite Yogurt Flavors	
Strawberry	16,194
Vanilla	16,619
Plain	11,826

5. Round each number to the nearest thousand. Then write the flavor preferred by most families.

   vanilla

6. Round each number to the nearest hundred. Then add the rounded numbers. Write the total for an estimate of how many families took the survey.

   44,600 families

Reading

Read the paragraph and look at the picture. Then answer the item.

The five friends sat inside the small wooden shed in Ricardo's backyard. Without windows, the shed, with its cracked door and bare walls, was very dim. The children sat on the rough, splintery floor because there were no chairs. "It's freezing in here!" exclaimed Sophia. "And sad!"

7. Explain why the friends are in the shed. Then explain why Sophia says it feels "sad."

✱ They're using the shed for a clubhouse. The shed's not comfortable. It's dim and cold. It's bare and small.

Page 26

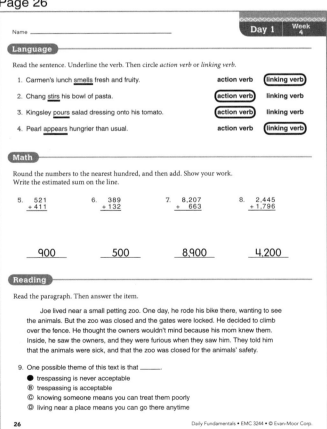

Day 1 — Week 4

Language

Read the sentence. Underline the verb. Then circle *action verb* or *linking verb*.

1. Carmen's lunch <u>smells</u> fresh and fruity.   action verb   (linking verb)
2. Chang <u>stirs</u> his bowl of pasta.   (action verb)   linking verb
3. Kingsley <u>pours</u> salad dressing onto his tomato.   (action verb)   linking verb
4. Pearl <u>appears</u> hungrier than usual.   action verb   (linking verb)

Math

Round the numbers to the nearest hundred, and then add. Show your work. Write the estimated sum on the line.

5. 521
   + 411
   ___900___

6. 389
   + 132
   ___500___

7. 8,207
   + 663
   ___8,900___

8. 2,445
   + 1,796
   ___4,200___

Reading

Read the paragraph. Then answer the item.

Joe lived near a small petting zoo. One day, he rode his bike there, wanting to see the animals. But the zoo was closed and the gates were locked. He decided to climb over the fence. He thought the owners wouldn't mind because his mom knew them. Inside, he saw the owners, and they were furious when they saw him. They told him that the animals were sick, and that the zoo was closed for the animals' safety.

9. One possible theme of this text is that _____.
   ● trespassing is never acceptable
   Ⓑ trespassing is acceptable
   Ⓒ knowing someone means you can treat them poorly
   Ⓓ living near a place means you can go there anytime

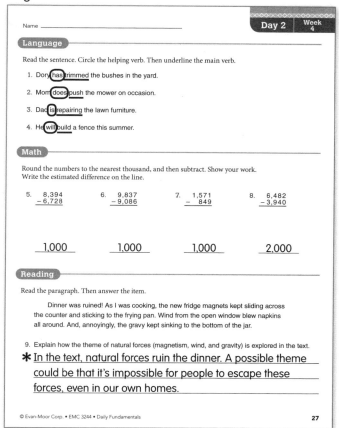

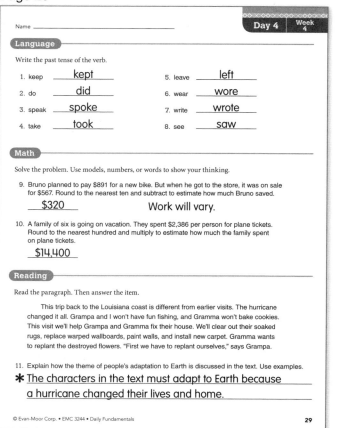

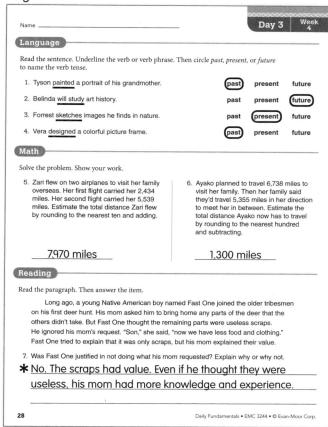

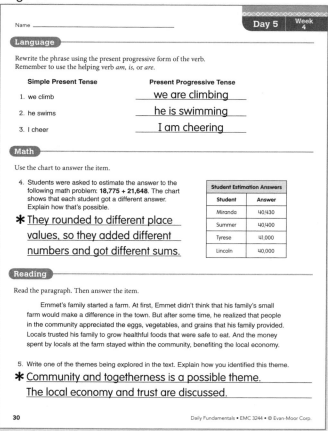

✳ These answers will vary. Examples are given.

Page 27

Name _____

Day 2 | Week 4

Language

Read the sentence. Circle the helping verb. Then underline the main verb.

1. Dory (has) trimmed the bushes in the yard.
2. Mom (does) push the mower on occasion.
3. Dad (is) repairing the lawn furniture.
4. He (will) build a fence this summer.

Math

Round the numbers to the nearest thousand, and then subtract. Show your work. Write the estimated difference on the line.

5. 8,394 − 6,728 = __1,000__
6. 9,837 − 9,086 = __1,000__
7. 1,571 − 849 = __1,000__
8. 6,482 − 3,940 = __2,000__

Reading

Read the paragraph. Then answer the item.

Dinner was ruined! As I was cooking, the new fridge magnets kept sliding across the counter and sticking to the frying pan. Wind from the open window blew napkins all around. And, annoyingly, the gravy kept sinking to the bottom of the jar.

9. Explain how the theme of natural forces (magnetism, wind, and gravity) is explored in the text.

✳ In the text, natural forces ruin the dinner. A possible theme could be that it's impossible for people to escape these forces, even in our own homes.

Page 28

Name _____

Day 3 | Week 4

Language

Read the sentence. Underline the verb or verb phrase. Then circle *past*, *present*, or *future* to name the verb tense.

1. Tyson painted a portrait of his grandmother. — (past) present future
2. Belinda will study art history. — past present (future)
3. Forrest sketches images he finds in nature. — past (present) future
4. Vera designed a colorful picture frame. — (past) present future

Math

Solve the problem. Show your work.

5. Zari flew on two airplanes to visit her family overseas. Her first flight carried her 2,434 miles. Her second flight carried her 5,539 miles. Estimate the total distance Zari flew by rounding to the nearest ten and adding.

__7,970 miles__

6. Ayako planned to travel 6,738 miles to visit her family. Then her family said they'd travel 5,355 miles in her direction to meet her in between. Estimate the total distance Ayako now has to travel by rounding to the nearest hundred and subtracting.

__1,300 miles__

Reading

Read the paragraph. Then answer the item.

Long ago, a young Native American boy named Fast One joined the older tribesmen on his first deer hunt. His mom asked him to bring home any parts of the deer that the others didn't want. But Fast One thought the remaining parts were useless scraps. He ignored his mom's request. "Son," she said, "now we have less food and clothing." Fast One tried to explain that it was only scraps, but his mom explained their value.

7. Was Fast One justified in not doing what his mom requested? Explain why or why not.

✳ No. The scraps had value. Even if he thought they were useless, his mom had more knowledge and experience.

Page 29

Name _____

Day 4 | Week 4

Language

Write the past tense of the verb.

1. keep — __kept__
2. do — __did__
3. speak — __spoke__
4. take — __took__
5. leave — __left__
6. wear — __wore__
7. write — __wrote__
8. see — __saw__

Math

Solve the problem. Use models, numbers, or words to show your thinking.

9. Bruno planned to pay $891 for a new bike. But when he got to the store, it was on sale for $567. Round to the nearest ten and subtract to estimate how much Bruno saved.

__$320__   Work will vary.

10. A family of six is going on vacation. They spent $2,386 per person for plane tickets. Round to the nearest hundred and multiply to estimate how much the family spent on plane tickets.

__$14,400__

Reading

Read the paragraph. Then answer the item.

This trip back to the Louisiana coast is different from earlier visits. The hurricane changed it all. Grampa and I won't have fun fishing, and Gramma won't bake cookies. This visit we'll help Grampa and Gramma fix their house. We'll clear out their soaked rugs, replace warped wallboards, paint walls, and install new carpet. Gramma wants to replant the destroyed flowers. "First we have to replant ourselves," says Grampa.

11. Explain how the theme of people's adaptation to Earth is discussed in the text. Use examples.

✳ The characters in the text must adapt to Earth because a hurricane changed their lives and home.

Page 30

Name _____

Day 5 | Week 4

Language

Rewrite the phrase using the present progressive form of the verb. Remember to use the helping verb *am, is,* or *are.*

Simple Present Tense	Present Progressive Tense
1. we climb	we are climbing
2. he swims	he is swimming
3. I cheer	I am cheering

Math

Use the chart to answer the item.

4. Students were asked to estimate the answer to the following math problem: **18,775 + 21,648.** The chart shows that each student got a different answer. Explain how that's possible.

✳ They rounded to different place values, so they added different numbers and got different sums.

Student Estimation Answers	
Student	**Answer**
Miranda	40,430
Summer	40,400
Tyrese	41,000
Lincoln	40,000

Reading

Read the paragraph. Then answer the item.

Emmet's family started a farm. At first, Emmet didn't think that his family's small farm would make a difference in the town. But after some time, he realized that people in the community appreciated the eggs, vegetables, and grains that his family provided. Locals trusted his family to grow healthful foods that were safe to eat. And the money spent by locals at the farm stayed within the community, benefiting the local economy.

5. Write one of the themes being explored in the text. Explain how you identified this theme.

✳ Community and togetherness is a possible theme. The local economy and trust are discussed.

Page 31

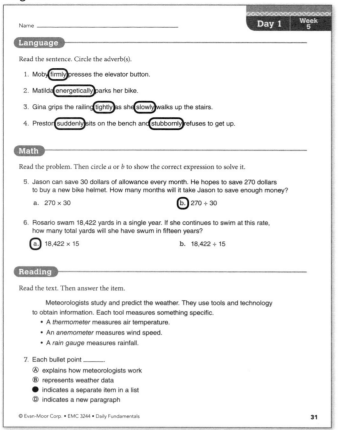

Name _____

Day 1 | Week 5

Language

Read the sentence. Circle the adverb(s).

1. Moby (firmly) presses the elevator button.
2. Matilda (energetically) parks her bike.
3. Gina grips the railing (tightly) as she (slowly) walks up the stairs.
4. Preston (suddenly) sits on the bench and (stubbornly) refuses to get up.

Math

Read the problem. Then circle *a* or *b* to show the correct expression to solve it.

5. Jason can save 30 dollars of allowance every month. He hopes to save 270 dollars to buy a new bike helmet. How many months will it take Jason to save enough money?

   a. 270 × 30   (b.) 270 ÷ 30

6. Rosario swam 18,422 yards in a single year. If she continues to swim at this rate, how many total yards will she have swum in fifteen years?

   (a.) 18,422 × 15   b. 18,422 ÷ 15

Reading

Read the text. Then answer the item.

Meteorologists study and predict the weather. They use tools and technology to obtain information. Each tool measures something specific.
- A *thermometer* measures air temperature.
- An *anemometer* measures wind speed.
- A *rain gauge* measures rainfall.

7. Each bullet point _____.
   Ⓐ explains how meteorologists work
   Ⓑ represents weather data
   ● indicates a separate item in a list
   Ⓓ indicates a new paragraph

© Evan-Moor Corp. • EMC 3244 • Daily Fundamentals   31

Page 32

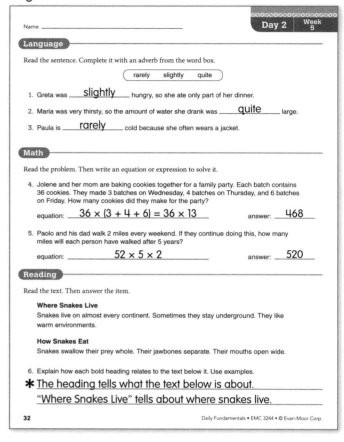

Name _____

Day 2 | Week 5

Language

Read the sentence. Complete it with an adverb from the word box.

    rarely   slightly   quite

1. Greta was ___slightly___ hungry, so she ate only part of her dinner.
2. Maria was very thirsty, so the amount of water she drank was ___quite___ large.
3. Paula is ___rarely___ cold because she often wears a jacket.

Math

Read the problem. Then write an equation or expression to solve it.

4. Jolene and her mom are baking cookies together for a family party. Each batch contains 36 cookies. They made 3 batches on Wednesday, 4 batches on Thursday, and 6 batches on Friday. How many cookies did they make for the party?

   equation: __$36 \times (3 + 4 + 6) = 36 \times 13$__   answer: __468__

5. Paolo and his dad walk 2 miles every weekend. If they continue doing this, how many miles will each person have walked after 5 years?

   equation: __$52 \times 5 \times 2$__   answer: __520__

Reading

Read the text. Then answer the item.

Where Snakes Live
Snakes live on almost every continent. Sometimes they stay underground. They like warm environments.

How Snakes Eat
Snakes swallow their prey whole. Their jawbones separate. Their mouths open wide.

6. Explain how each bold heading relates to the text below it. Use examples.

✳ The heading tells what the text below is about. "Where Snakes Live" tells about where snakes live.

32   Daily Fundamentals • EMC 3244 • © Evan-Moor Corp.

Page 33

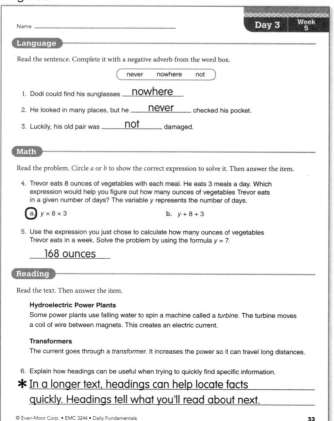

Name _____

Day 3 | Week 5

Language

Read the sentence. Complete it with a negative adverb from the word box.

    never   nowhere   not

1. Dodi could find his sunglasses ___nowhere___.
2. He looked in many places, but he ___never___ checked his pocket.
3. Luckily, his old pair was ___not___ damaged.

Math

Read the problem. Circle *a* or *b* to show the correct expression to solve it. Then answer the item.

4. Trevor eats 8 ounces of vegetables with each meal. He eats 3 meals a day. Which expression would help you figure out how many ounces of vegetables Trevor eats in a given number of days? The variable *y* represents the number of days.

   (a.) $y \times 8 \times 3$ b. $y + 8 + 3$

5. Use the expression you just chose to calculate how many ounces of vegetables Trevor eats in a week. Solve the problem by using the formula *y* = 7.

   __168 ounces__

Reading

Read the text. Then answer the item.

Hydroelectric Power Plants
Some power plants use falling water to spin a machine called a *turbine*. The turbine moves a coil of wire between magnets. This creates an electric current.

Transformers
The current goes through a *transformer*. It increases the power so it can travel long distances.

6. Explain how headings can be useful when trying to quickly find specific information.

✳ In a longer text, headings can help locate facts quickly. Headings tell what you'll read about next.

© Evan-Moor Corp. • EMC 3244 • Daily Fundamentals   33

Page 34

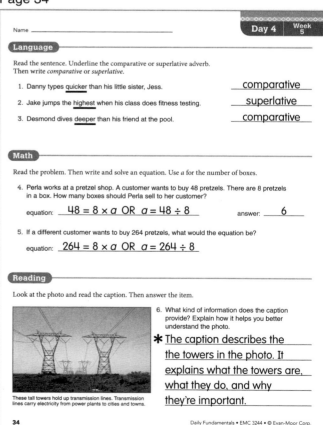

Name _____

Day 4 | Week 5

Language

Read the sentence. Underline the comparative or superlative adverb. Then write *comparative* or *superlative*.

1. Danny types quicker than his little sister, Jess.   comparative
2. Jake jumps the highest when his class does fitness testing.   superlative
3. Desmond dives deeper than his friend at the pool.   comparative

Math

Read the problem. Then write and solve an equation. Use *a* for the number of boxes.

4. Perla works at a pretzel shop. A customer wants to buy 48 pretzels. There are 8 pretzels in a box. How many boxes should Perla sell to her customer?

   equation: __$48 = 8 \times a$ OR $a = 48 \div 8$__   answer: __6__

5. If a different customer wants to buy 264 pretzels, what would the equation be?

   equation: __$264 = 8 \times a$ OR $a = 264 \div 8$__

Reading

Look at the photo and read the caption. Then answer the item.

These tall towers hold up transmission lines. Transmission lines carry electricity from power plants to cities and towns.

6. What kind of information does the caption provide? Explain how it helps you better understand the photo.

✳ The caption describes the the towers in the photo. It explains what the towers are, what they do, and why they're important.

34   Daily Fundamentals • EMC 3244 • © Evan-Moor Corp.

These answers will vary. Examples are given.

Page 35

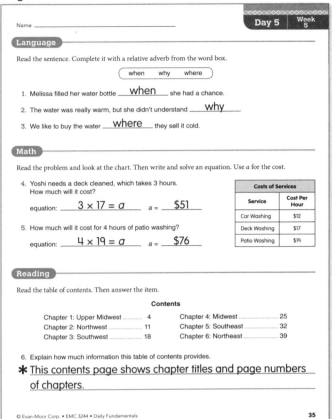

Name _____

Day 5 | Week 5

Language

Read the sentence. Complete it with a relative adverb from the word box.

> when   why   where

1. Melissa filled her water bottle __when__ she had a chance.

2. The water was really warm, but she didn't understand __why__.

3. We like to buy the water __where__ they sell it cold.

Math

Read the problem and look at the chart. Then write and solve an equation. Use *a* for the cost.

4. Yoshi needs a deck cleaned, which takes 3 hours. How much will it cost?

equation: __3 × 17 = a__   a = __$51__

5. How much will it cost for 4 hours of patio washing?

equation: __4 × 19 = a__   a = __$76__

Costs of Services	
Service	Cost Per Hour
Car Washing	$12
Deck Washing	$17
Patio Washing	$19

Reading

Read the table of contents. Then answer the item.

Contents

Chapter 1: Upper Midwest 4
Chapter 2: Northwest 11
Chapter 3: Southwest 18
Chapter 4: Midwest 25
Chapter 5: Southeast 32
Chapter 6: Northeast 39

6. Explain how much information this table of contents provides.

✳ __This contents page shows chapter titles and page numbers__ __of chapters.__

Page 36

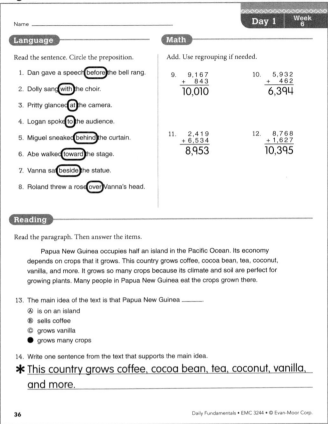

Name _____

Day 1 | Week 6

Language

Read the sentence. Circle the preposition.

1. Dan gave a speech (before) the bell rang.

2. Dolly sang (with) the choir.

3. Pritty glanced (at) the camera.

4. Logan spoke (to) the audience.

5. Miguel sneaked (behind) the curtain.

6. Abe walked (toward) the stage.

7. Vanna sat (beside) the statue.

8. Roland threw a rose (over) Vanna's head.

Math

Add. Use regrouping if needed.

9. $\begin{array}{r} 9,167 \\ +843 \\ \hline 10,010 \end{array}$ 10. $\begin{array}{r} 5,932 \\ +462 \\ \hline 6,394 \end{array}$

11. $\begin{array}{r} 2,419 \\ +6,534 \\ \hline 8,953 \end{array}$ 12. $\begin{array}{r} 8,768 \\ +1,627 \\ \hline 10,395 \end{array}$

Reading

Read the paragraph. Then answer the items.

Papua New Guinea occupies half an island in the Pacific Ocean. Its economy depends on crops that it grows. This country grows coffee, cocoa bean, tea, coconut, vanilla, and more. It grows so many crops because its climate and soil are perfect for growing plants. Many people in Papua New Guinea eat the crops grown there.

13. The main idea of the text is that Papua New Guinea _____.
Ⓐ is on an island
Ⓑ sells coffee
Ⓒ grows vanilla
● grows many crops

14. Write one sentence from the text that supports the main idea.

✳ __This country grows coffee, cocoa bean, tea, coconut, vanilla,__ __and more.__

Page 37

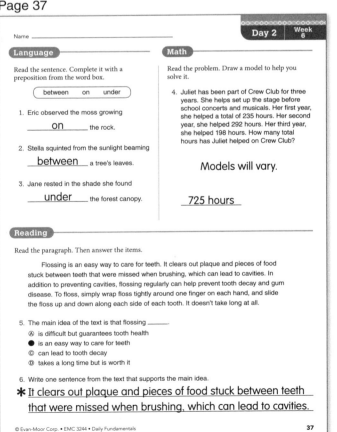

Name _____

Day 2 | Week 6

Language

Read the sentence. Complete it with a preposition from the word box.

> between   on   under

1. Eric observed the moss growing __on__ the rock.

2. Stella squinted from the sunlight beaming __between__ a tree's leaves.

3. Jane rested in the shade she found __under__ the forest canopy.

Math

Read the problem. Draw a model to help you solve it.

4. Juliet has been part of Crew Club for three years. She helps set up the stage before school concerts and musicals. Her first year, she helped a total of 235 hours. Her second year, she helped 292 hours. Her third year, she helped 198 hours. How many total hours has Juliet helped on Crew Club?

Models will vary.

__725 hours__

Reading

Read the paragraph. Then answer the items.

Flossing is an easy way to care for teeth. It clears out plaque and pieces of food stuck between teeth that were missed when brushing, which can lead to cavities. In addition to preventing cavities, flossing regularly can help prevent tooth decay and gum disease. To floss, simply wrap floss tightly around one finger on each hand, and slide the floss up and down along each side of each tooth. It doesn't take long at all.

5. The main idea of the text is that flossing _____.
Ⓐ is difficult but guarantees tooth health
● is an easy way to care for teeth
Ⓒ can lead to tooth decay
Ⓓ takes a long time but is worth it

6. Write one sentence from the text that supports the main idea.

✳ __It clears out plaque and pieces of food stuck between teeth__ __that were missed when brushing, which can lead to cavities.__

Page 38

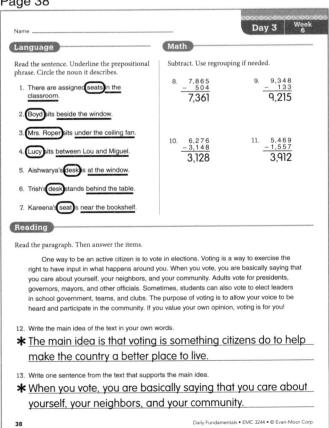

Name _____

Day 3 | Week 6

Language

Read the sentence. Underline the prepositional phrase. Circle the noun it describes.

1. There are assigned (seats) in the classroom.

2. (Boyd) sits beside the window.

3. (Mrs. Roper) sits under the ceiling fan.

4. (Lucy) sits between Lou and Miguel.

5. Aishwarya's (desk) is at the window.

6. Trish's (desk) stands behind the table.

7. Kareena's (seat) is near the bookshelf.

Math

Subtract. Use regrouping if needed.

8. $\begin{array}{r} 7,865 \\ -504 \\ \hline 7,361 \end{array}$ 9. $\begin{array}{r} 9,348 \\ -133 \\ \hline 9,215 \end{array}$

10. $\begin{array}{r} 6,276 \\ -3,148 \\ \hline 3,128 \end{array}$ 11. $\begin{array}{r} 5,469 \\ -1,557 \\ \hline 3,912 \end{array}$

Reading

Read the paragraph. Then answer the items.

One way to be an active citizen is to vote in elections. Voting is a way to exercise the right to have input in what happens around you. When you vote, you are basically saying that you care about yourself, your neighbors, and your community. Adults vote for presidents, governors, mayors, and other officials. Sometimes, students can also vote to elect leaders in school government, teams, and clubs. The purpose of voting is to allow your voice to be heard and participate in the community. If you value your own opinion, voting is for you!

12. Write the main idea of the text in your own words.

✳ __The main idea is that voting is something citizens do to help__ __make the country a better place to live.__

13. Write one sentence from the text that supports the main idea.

✳ __When you vote, you are basically saying that you care about__ __yourself, your neighbors, and your community.__

Page 39

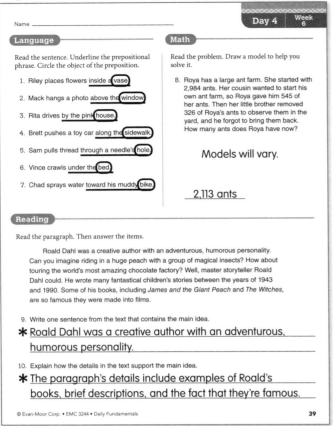

Name _____

Day 4 | Week 6

Language

Read the sentence. Underline the prepositional phrase. Circle the object of the preposition.

1. Riley places flowers inside a (vase).
2. Mack hangs a photo above the (window).
3. Rita drives by the pink (house).
4. Brett pushes a toy car along the (sidewalk).
5. Sam pulls thread through a needle's (hole).
6. Vince crawls under the (bed).
7. Chad sprays water toward his muddy (bike).

Math

Read the problem. Draw a model to help you solve it.

8. Roya has a large ant farm. She started with 2,984 ants. Her cousin wanted to start his own ant farm, so Roya gave him 545 of her ants. Then her little brother removed 326 of Roya's ants to observe them in the yard, and he forgot to bring them back. How many ants does Roya have now?

Models will vary.

__2,113 ants__

Reading

Read the paragraph. Then answer the items.

Roald Dahl was a creative author with an adventurous, humorous personality. Can you imagine riding in a huge peach with a group of magical insects? How about touring the world's most amazing chocolate factory? Well, master storyteller Roald Dahl could. He wrote many fantastical children's stories between the years of 1943 and 1990. Some of his books, including *James and the Giant Peach* and *The Witches*, are so famous they were made into films.

9. Write one sentence from the text that contains the main idea.

✳ Roald Dahl was a creative author with an adventurous, humorous personality.

10. Explain how the details in the text support the main idea.

✳ The paragraph's details include examples of Roald's books, brief descriptions, and the fact that they're famous.

© Evan-Moor Corp. • EMC 3244 • Daily Fundamentals   **39**

Page 40

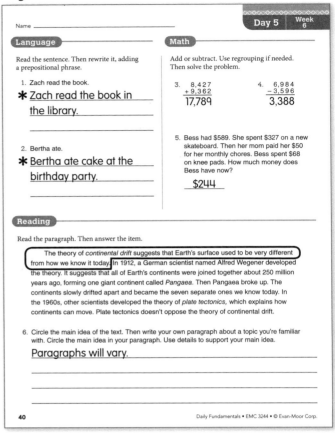

Name _____

Day 5 | Week 6

Language

Read the sentence. Then rewrite it, adding a prepositional phrase.

1. Zach read the book.

✳ Zach read the book in the library.

2. Bertha ate.

✳ Bertha ate cake at the birthday party.

Math

Add or subtract. Use regrouping if needed. Then solve the problem.

3. $\begin{array}{r} 8,427 \\ +9,362 \\ \hline 17,789 \end{array}$

4. $\begin{array}{r} 6,984 \\ -3,596 \\ \hline 3,388 \end{array}$

5. Bess had $589. She spent $327 on a new skateboard. Then her mom paid her $50 for her monthly chores. Bess spent $68 on knee pads. How much money does Bess have now?

__$244__

Reading

Read the paragraph. Then answer the item.

The theory of *continental drift* suggests that Earth's surface used to be very different from how we know it today. In 1912, a German scientist named Alfred Wegener developed the theory. It suggests that all of Earth's continents were joined together about 250 million years ago, forming one giant continent called *Pangaea*. Then Pangaea broke up. The continents slowly drifted apart and became the seven separate ones we know today. In the 1960s, other scientists developed the theory of *plate tectonics*, which explains how continents can move. Plate tectonics doesn't oppose the theory of continental drift.

6. Circle the main idea of the text. Then write your own paragraph about a topic you're familiar with. Circle the main idea in your paragraph. Use details to support your main idea.

Paragraphs will vary.

40   Daily Fundamentals • EMC 3244 • © Evan-Moor Corp.

Page 41

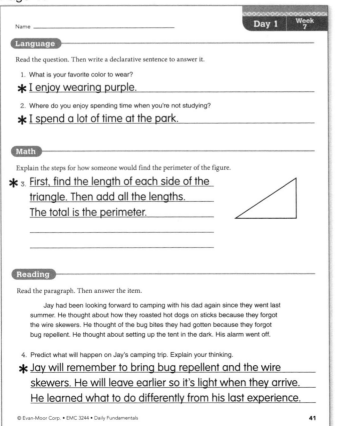

Name _____

Day 1 | Week 7

Language

Read the question. Then write a declarative sentence to answer it.

1. What is your favorite color to wear?

✳ I enjoy wearing purple.

2. Where do you enjoy spending time when you're not studying?

✳ I spend a lot of time at the park.

Math

Explain the steps for how someone would find the perimeter of the figure.

✳ 3. First, find the length of each side of the triangle. Then add all the lengths. The total is the perimeter.

Reading

Read the paragraph. Then answer the item.

Jay had been looking forward to camping with his dad again since they went last summer. He thought about how they roasted hot dogs on sticks because they forgot the wire skewers. He thought of the bug bites they had gotten because they forgot bug repellent. He thought about setting up the tent in the dark. His alarm went off.

4. Predict what will happen on Jay's camping trip. Explain your thinking.

✳ Jay will remember to bring bug repellent and the wire skewers. He will leave earlier so it's light when they arrive. He learned what to do differently from his last experience.

© Evan-Moor Corp. • EMC 3244 • Daily Fundamentals   **41**

Page 42

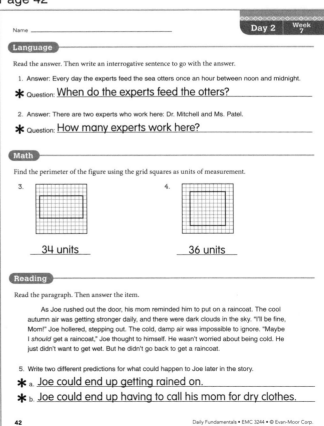

Name _____

Day 2 | Week 7

Language

Read the answer. Then write an interrogative sentence to go with the answer.

1. Answer: Every day the experts feed the sea otters once an hour between noon and midnight.

✳ Question: When do the experts feed the otters?

2. Answer: There are two experts who work here: Dr. Mitchell and Ms. Patel.

✳ Question: How many experts work here?

Math

Find the perimeter of the figure using the grid squares as units of measurement.

3.

__34 units__

4.

__36 units__

Reading

Read the paragraph. Then answer the item.

As Joe rushed out the door, his mom reminded him to put on a raincoat. The cool autumn air was getting stronger daily, and there were dark clouds in the sky. "I'll be fine, Mom!" Joe hollered, stepping out. The cold, damp air was impossible to ignore. "Maybe I *should* get a raincoat," Joe thought to himself. He wasn't worried about being cold. He just didn't want to get wet. But he didn't go back to get a raincoat.

5. Write two different predictions for what could happen to Joe later in the story.

✳ a. Joe could end up getting rained on.

✳ b. Joe could end up having to call his mom for dry clothes.

42   Daily Fundamentals • EMC 3244 • © Evan-Moor Corp.

Page 43

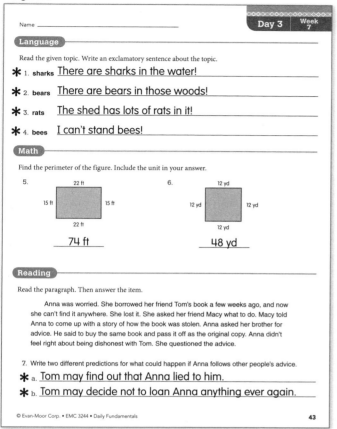

Name _____

Day 3 | Week 7

Language

Read the given topic. Write an exclamatory sentence about the topic.

* 1. sharks — There are sharks in the water!

* 2. bears — There are bears in those woods!

* 3. rats — The shed has lots of rats in it!

* 4. bees — I can't stand bees!

Math

Find the perimeter of the figure. Include the unit in your answer.

5. [rectangle: 22 ft, 15 ft, 15 ft, 22 ft] — 74 ft

6. [square: 12 yd on each side] — 48 yd

Reading

Read the paragraph. Then answer the item.

Anna was worried. She borrowed her friend Tom's book a few weeks ago, and now she can't find it anywhere. She lost it. She asked her friend Macy what to do. Macy told Anna to come up with a story of how the book was stolen. Anna asked her brother for advice. He said to buy the same book and pass it off as the original copy. Anna didn't feel right about being dishonest with Tom. She questioned the advice.

7. Write two different predictions for what could happen if Anna follows other people's advice.

* a. Tom may find out that Anna lied to him.

* b. Tom may decide not to loan Anna anything ever again.

Page 44

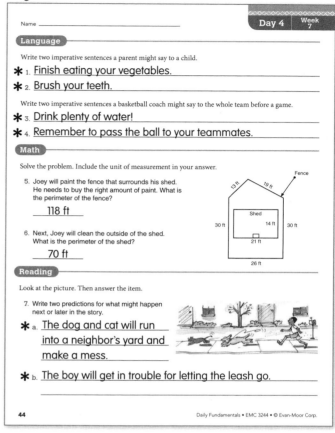

Name _____

Day 4 | Week 7

Language

Write two imperative sentences a parent might say to a child.

* 1. Finish eating your vegetables.

* 2. Brush your teeth.

Write two imperative sentences a basketball coach might say to the whole team before a game.

* 3. Drink plenty of water!

* 4. Remember to pass the ball to your teammates.

Math

Solve the problem. Include the unit of measurement in your answer.

5. Joey will paint the fence that surrounds his shed. He needs to buy the right amount of paint. What is the perimeter of the fence?

___118 ft___

6. Next, Joey will clean the outside of the shed. What is the perimeter of the shed?

___70 ft___

[diagram: Fence with house shape; 13 ft, 19 ft on roof slopes; 30 ft on left side, 30 ft on right side; Shed inside with 14 ft, 21 ft; 26 ft on bottom]

Reading

Look at the picture. Then answer the item.

7. Write two predictions for what might happen next or later in the story.

* a. The dog and cat will run into a neighbor's yard and make a mess.

* b. The boy will get in trouble for letting the leash go.

Page 45

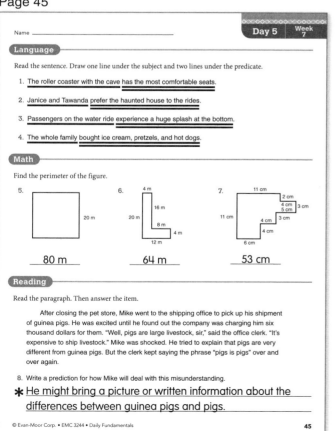

Name _____

Day 5 | Week 7

Language

Read the sentence. Draw one line under the subject and two lines under the predicate.

1. The roller coaster with the cave has the most comfortable seats.

2. Janice and Tawanda prefer the haunted house to the rides.

3. Passengers on the water ride experience a huge splash at the bottom.

4. The whole family bought ice cream, pretzels, and hot dogs.

Math

Find the perimeter of the figure.

5. [square: 20 m] — 80 m

6. [L-shaped figure: 4 m, 16 m, 20 m, 8 m, 4 m, 12 m] — 64 m

7. [figure: 11 cm, 2 cm, 4 cm, 5 cm, 3 cm, 11 cm, 4 cm, 3 cm, 4 cm, 6 cm] — 53 cm

Reading

Read the paragraph. Then answer the item.

After closing the pet store, Mike went to the shipping office to pick up his shipment of guinea pigs. He was excited until he found out the company was charging him six thousand dollars for them. "Well, pigs are large livestock, sir," said the office clerk. "It's expensive to ship livestock." Mike was shocked. He tried to explain that pigs are very different from guinea pigs. But the clerk kept saying the phrase "pigs is pigs" over and over again.

8. Write a prediction for how Mike will deal with this misunderstanding.

* He might bring a picture or written information about the differences between guinea pigs and pigs.

Page 46

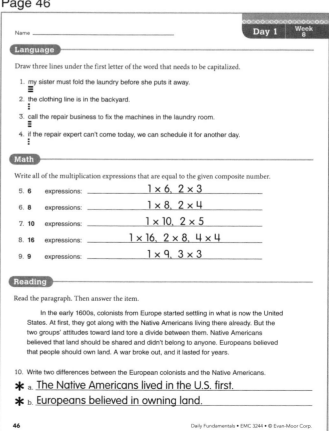

Name _____

Day 1 | Week 8

Language

Draw three lines under the first letter of the word that needs to be capitalized.

1. my sister must fold the laundry before she puts it away.

2. the clothing line is in the backyard.

3. call the repair business to fix the machines in the laundry room.

4. if the repair expert can't come today, we can schedule it for another day.

Math

Write all of the multiplication expressions that are equal to the given composite number.

5. 6 — expressions: 1×6, 2×3

6. 8 — expressions: 1×8, 2×4

7. 10 — expressions: 1×10, 2×5

8. 16 — expressions: 1×16, 2×8, 4×4

9. 9 — expressions: 1×9, 3×3

Reading

Read the paragraph. Then answer the item.

In the early 1600s, colonists from Europe started settling in what is now the United States. At first, they got along with the Native Americans living there already. But the two groups' attitudes toward land tore a divide between them. Native Americans believed that land should be shared and didn't belong to anyone. Europeans believed that people should own land. A war broke out, and it lasted for years.

10. Write two differences between the European colonists and the Native Americans.

* a. The Native Americans lived in the U.S. first.

* b. Europeans believed in owning land.

These answers will vary. Examples are given.

Page 47

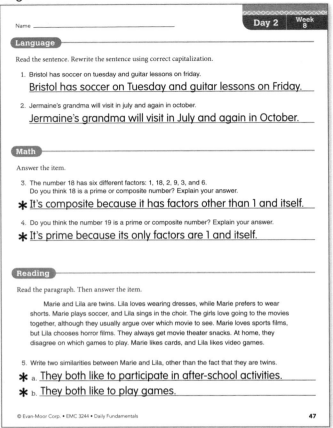

Name _____

Day 2 | **Week 8**

Language

Read the sentence. Rewrite the sentence using correct capitalization.

1. Bristol has soccer on tuesday and guitar lessons on friday.

   Bristol has soccer on Tuesday and guitar lessons on Friday.

2. Jermaine's grandma will visit in july and again in october.

   Jermaine's grandma will visit in July and again in October.

Math

Answer the item.

3. The number 18 has six different factors: 1, 18, 2, 9, 3, and 6.
   Do you think 18 is a prime or composite number? Explain your answer.

   * It's composite because it has factors other than 1 and itself.

4. Do you think the number 19 is a prime or composite number? Explain your answer.

   * It's prime because its only factors are 1 and itself.

Reading

Read the paragraph. Then answer the item.

Marie and Lila are twins. Lila loves wearing dresses, while Marie prefers to wear shorts. Marie plays soccer, and Lila sings in the choir. The girls love going to the movies together, although they usually argue over which movie to see. Marie loves sports films, but Lila chooses horror films. They always get movie theater snacks. At home, they disagree on which games to play. Marie likes cards, and Lila likes video games.

5. Write two similarities between Marie and Lila, other than the fact that they are twins.

   * a. They both like to participate in after-school activities.

   * b. They both like to play games.

© Evan-Moor Corp. • EMC 3244 • Daily Fundamentals

47

Page 48

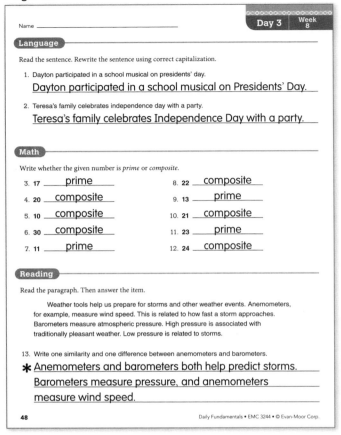

Name _____

Day 3 | **Week 8**

Language

Read the sentence. Rewrite the sentence using correct capitalization.

1. Dayton participated in a school musical on presidents' day.

   Dayton participated in a school musical on Presidents' Day.

2. Teresa's family celebrates independence day with a party.

   Teresa's family celebrates Independence Day with a party.

Math

Write whether the given number is *prime* or *composite*.

3. 17 ___prime___
4. 20 ___composite___
5. 10 ___composite___
6. 30 ___composite___
7. 11 ___prime___
8. 22 ___composite___
9. 13 ___prime___
10. 21 ___composite___
11. 23 ___prime___
12. 24 ___composite___

Reading

Read the paragraph. Then answer the item.

Weather tools help us prepare for storms and other weather events. Anemometers, for example, measure wind speed. This is related to how fast a storm approaches. Barometers measure atmospheric pressure. High pressure is associated with traditionally pleasant weather. Low pressure is related to storms.

13. Write one similarity and one difference between anemometers and barometers.

   * Anemometers and barometers both help predict storms. Barometers measure pressure, and anemometers measure wind speed.

48

Daily Fundamentals • EMC 3244 • © Evan-Moor Corp.

Page 49

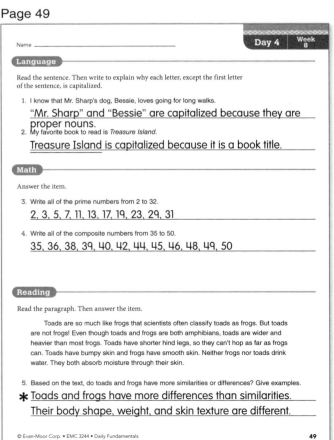

Name _____

Day 4 | **Week 8**

Language

Read the sentence. Then write to explain why each letter, except the first letter of the sentence, is capitalized.

1. I know that Mr. Sharp's dog, Bessie, loves going for long walks.

   "Mr. Sharp" and "Bessie" are capitalized because they are proper nouns.

2. My favorite book to read is *Treasure Island*.

   Treasure Island is capitalized because it is a book title.

Math

Answer the item.

3. Write all of the prime numbers from 2 to 32.

   2, 3, 5, 7, 11, 13, 17, 19, 23, 29, 31

4. Write all of the composite numbers from 35 to 50.

   35, 36, 38, 39, 40, 42, 44, 45, 46, 48, 49, 50

Reading

Read the paragraph. Then answer the item.

Toads are so much like frogs that scientists often classify toads as frogs. But toads are not frogs! Even though toads and frogs are both amphibians, toads are wider and heavier than most frogs. Toads have shorter hind legs, so they can't hop as far as frogs can. Toads have bumpy skin and frogs have smooth skin. Neither frogs nor toads drink water. They both absorb moisture through their skin.

5. Based on the text, do toads and frogs have more similarities or differences? Give examples.

   * Toads and frogs have more differences than similarities. Their body shape, weight, and skin texture are different.

© Evan-Moor Corp. • EMC 3244 • Daily Fundamentals

49

Page 50

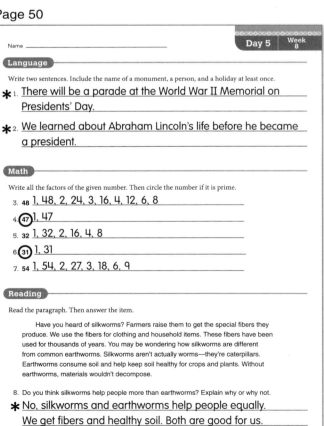

Name _____

Day 5 | **Week 8**

Language

Write two sentences. Include the name of a monument, a person, and a holiday at least once.

* 1. There will be a parade at the World War II Memorial on Presidents' Day.

* 2. We learned about Abraham Lincoln's life before he became a president.

Math

Write all the factors of the given number. Then circle the number if it is prime.

3. 48 — 1, 48, 2, 24, 3, 16, 4, 12, 6, 8
4. (47) — 1, 47
5. 32 — 1, 32, 2, 16, 4, 8
6. (31) — 1, 31
7. 54 — 1, 54, 2, 27, 3, 18, 6, 9

Reading

Read the paragraph. Then answer the item.

Have you heard of silkworms? Farmers raise them to get the special fibers they produce. We use the fibers for clothing and household items. These fibers have been used for thousands of years. You may be wondering how silkworms are different from common earthworms. Silkworms aren't actually worms—they're caterpillars. Earthworms consume soil and help keep soil healthy for crops and plants. Without earthworms, materials wouldn't decompose.

8. Do you think silkworms help people more than earthworms? Explain why or why not.

   * No, silkworms and earthworms help people equally. We get fibers and healthy soil. Both are good for us.

50

Daily Fundamentals • EMC 3244 • © Evan-Moor Corp.

Page 51

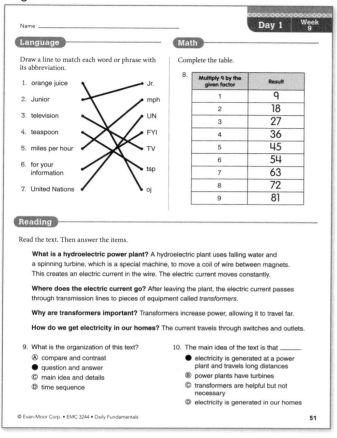

Day 1 Week 9

Language

Draw a line to match each word or phrase with its abbreviation.

1. orange juice
2. Junior
3. television
4. teaspoon
5. miles per hour
6. for your information
7. United Nations

Jr.
mph
UN
FYI
TV
tsp
oj

Math

Complete the table.

8.

Multiply 9 by the given factor	Result
1	9
2	18
3	27
4	36
5	45
6	54
7	63
8	72
9	81

Reading

Read the text. Then answer the items.

What is a hydroelectric power plant? A hydroelectric plant uses falling water and a spinning turbine, which is a special machine, to move a coil of wire between magnets. This creates an electric current in the wire. The electric current moves constantly.

Where does the electric current go? After leaving the plant, the electric current passes through transmission lines to pieces of equipment called *transformers*.

Why are transformers important? Transformers increase power, allowing it to travel far.

How do we get electricity in our homes? The current travels through switches and outlets.

9. What is the organization of this text?
   Ⓐ compare and contrast
   ● question and answer
   Ⓒ main idea and details
   Ⓓ time sequence

10. The main idea of the text is that _____.
   ● electricity is generated at a power plant and travels long distances
   Ⓑ power plants have turbines
   Ⓒ transformers are helpful but not necessary
   Ⓓ electricity is generated in our homes

© Evan-Moor Corp. • EMC 3244 • Daily Fundamentals — 51

Page 52

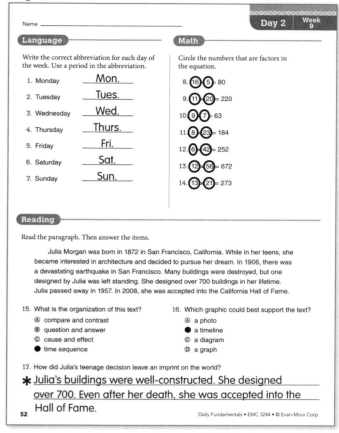

Day 2 Week 9

Language

Write the correct abbreviation for each day of the week. Use a period in the abbreviation.

1. Monday — Mon.
2. Tuesday — Tues.
3. Wednesday — Wed.
4. Thursday — Thurs.
5. Friday — Fri.
6. Saturday — Sat.
7. Sunday — Sun.

Math

Circle the numbers that are factors in the equation.

8. (16) (5) = 80
9. (11) (20) = 220
10. (9) (7) = 63
11. (8) (23) = 184
12. (6) (42) = 252
13. (12) (56) = 672
14. (13) (21) = 273

Reading

Read the paragraph. Then answer the items.

Julia Morgan was born in 1872 in San Francisco, California. While in her teens, she became interested in architecture and decided to pursue her dream. In 1906, there was a devastating earthquake in San Francisco. Many buildings were destroyed, but one designed by Julia was left standing. She designed over 700 buildings in her lifetime. Julia passed away in 1957. In 2008, she was accepted into the California Hall of Fame.

15. What is the organization of this text?
   Ⓐ compare and contrast
   Ⓑ question and answer
   Ⓒ cause and effect
   ● time sequence

16. Which graphic could best support the text?
   Ⓐ a photo
   ● a timeline
   Ⓒ a diagram
   Ⓓ a graph

17. How did Julia's teenage decision leave an imprint on the world?

✱ Julia's buildings were well-constructed. She designed over 700. Even after her death, she was accepted into the Hall of Fame.

52 — Daily Fundamentals • EMC 3244 • © Evan-Moor Corp.

Page 53

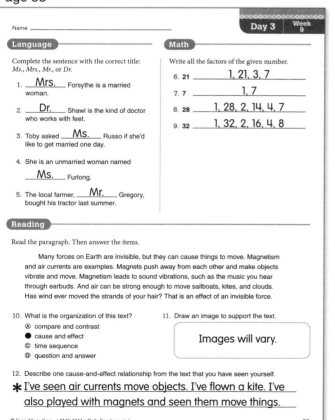

Day 3 Week 9

Language

Complete the sentence with the correct title: *Ms., Mrs., Mr.,* or *Dr.*

1. **Mrs.** Forsythe is a married woman.
2. **Dr.** Shawl is the kind of doctor who works with feet.
3. Toby asked **Ms.** Russo if she'd like to get married one day.
4. She is an unmarried woman named **Ms.** Furlong.
5. The local farmer, **Mr.** Gregory, bought his tractor last summer.

Math

Write all the factors of the given number.

6. **21** — 1, 21, 3, 7
7. **7** — 1, 7
8. **28** — 1, 28, 2, 14, 4, 7
9. **32** — 1, 32, 2, 16, 4, 8

Reading

Read the paragraph. Then answer the items.

Many forces on Earth are invisible, but they can cause things to move. Magnetism and air currents are examples. Magnets push away from each other and make objects vibrate and move. Magnetism leads to sound vibrations, such as the music you hear through earbuds. And air can be strong enough to move sailboats, kites, and clouds. Has wind ever moved the strands of your hair? That is an effect of an invisible force.

10. What is the organization of this text?
   Ⓐ compare and contrast
   ● cause and effect
   Ⓒ time sequence
   Ⓓ question and answer

11. Draw an image to support the text.

   Images will vary.

12. Describe one cause-and-effect relationship from the text that you have seen yourself.

✱ I've seen air currents move objects. I've flown a kite. I've also played with magnets and seen them move things.

© Evan-Moor Corp. • EMC 3244 • Daily Fundamentals — 53

Page 54

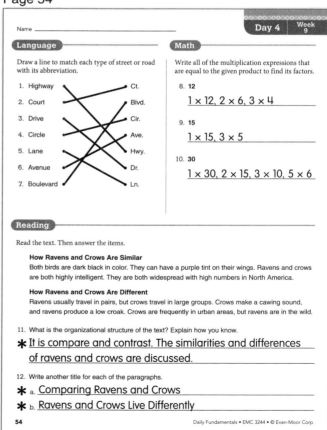

Day 4 Week 9

Language

Draw a line to match each type of street or road with its abbreviation.

1. Highway
2. Court
3. Drive
4. Circle
5. Lane
6. Avenue
7. Boulevard

Ct.
Blvd.
Cir.
Ave.
Hwy.
Dr.
Ln.

Math

Write all of the multiplication expressions that are equal to the given product to find its factors.

8. **12**
   1 × 12, 2 × 6, 3 × 4
9. **15**
   1 × 15, 3 × 5
10. **30**
   1 × 30, 2 × 15, 3 × 10, 5 × 6

Reading

Read the text. Then answer the items.

How Ravens and Crows Are Similar
Both birds are dark black in color. They can have a purple tint on their wings. Ravens and crows are both highly intelligent. They are both widespread with high numbers in North America.

How Ravens and Crows Are Different
Ravens usually travel in pairs, but crows travel in large groups. Crows make a cawing sound, and ravens produce a low croak. Crows are frequently in urban areas, but ravens are in the wild.

11. What is the organizational structure of the text? Explain how you know.

✱ It is compare and contrast. The similarities and differences of ravens and crows are discussed.

12. Write another title for each of the paragraphs.

✱ a. Comparing Ravens and Crows

✱ b. Ravens and Crows Live Differently

54 — Daily Fundamentals • EMC 3244 • © Evan-Moor Corp.

Page 55

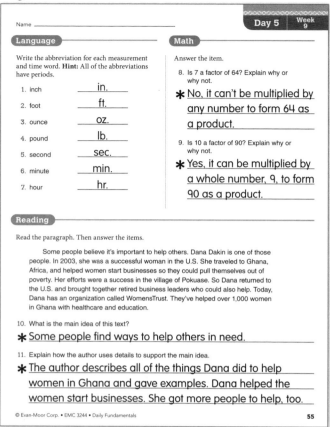

Name _____

Day 5 | **Week 9**

Language

Write the abbreviation for each measurement and time word. **Hint:** All of the abbreviations have periods.

1. inch — in.
2. foot — ft.
3. ounce — oz.
4. pound — lb.
5. second — sec.
6. minute — min.
7. hour — hr.

Math

Answer the item.

8. Is 7 a factor of 64? Explain why or why not.

✳ No, it can't be multiplied by any number to form 64 as a product.

9. Is 10 a factor of 90? Explain why or why not.

✳ Yes, it can be multiplied by a whole number, 9, to form 90 as a product.

Reading

Read the paragraph. Then answer the items.

Some people believe it's important to help others. Dana Dakin is one of those people. In 2003, she was a successful woman in the U.S. She traveled to Ghana, Africa, and helped women start businesses so they could pull themselves out of poverty. Her efforts were a success in the village of Pokuase. So Dana returned to the U.S. and brought together retired business leaders who could also help. Today, Dana has an organization called WomensTrust. They've helped over 1,000 women in Ghana with healthcare and education.

10. What is the main idea of this text?

✳ Some people find ways to help others in need.

11. Explain how the author uses details to support the main idea.

✳ The author describes all of the things Dana did to help women in Ghana and gave examples. Dana helped the women start businesses. She got more people to help, too.

© Evan-Moor Corp. • EMC 3244 • Daily Fundamentals   55

Page 56

Name _____

Day 1 | **Week 10**

Language

Read the pair of sentences. Write the correct end punctuation for each sentence.

✳ 1. Cory plays the violin . Did Cory play the saxophone in the past ?

✳ 2. Aretha, you did such a great job ! Did you feel nervous when you were onstage ?

✳ 3. Quickly grab your drumsticks ! Antonio and Yosef want to have a jam session .

✳ 4. I need to buy a new clarinet reed . Run to the car as fast as you can !

Math

Complete the table. Then answer the item.

5.

Factor	Factor	Product
6	5	30
6	10	60
6	11	66
6	20	120

6. The products are all multiples of ___6___ .

Reading

Read the paragraph. Then answer the item.

It was just a regular morning, and Corbin was making himself a snack at home. As he unpeeled his banana, out burst a purple cloud. It floated above his head and grew bigger. Then it spoke! "Corbin, I'll grant you three wishes," the cloud said. "Use your wishes wisely." Corbin was overjoyed. His first wish was to become human and stop being a monkey. He was tired of living in a tree! He wanted to live in a house and go to school.

7. Explain why this text would **not** be considered realistic fiction.

✳ The main character is a monkey who thinks and understands a purple cloud that talks. Neither could actually happen.

56   Daily Fundamentals • EMC 3244 • © Evan-Moor Corp.

Page 57

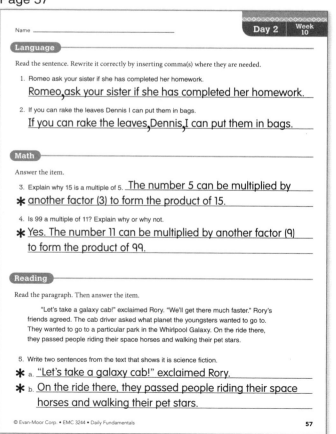

Name _____

Day 2 | **Week 10**

Language

Read the sentence. Rewrite it correctly by inserting comma(s) where they are needed.

1. Romeo ask your sister if she has completed her homework.
   Romeo, ask your sister if she has completed her homework.

2. If you can rake the leaves Dennis I can put them in bags.
   If you can rake the leaves, Dennis, I can put them in bags.

Math

Answer the item.

3. Explain why 15 is a multiple of 5. The number 5 can be multiplied by
✳ another factor (3) to form the product of 15.

4. Is 99 a multiple of 11? Explain why or why not.
✳ Yes. The number 11 can be multiplied by another factor (9) to form the product of 99.

Reading

Read the paragraph. Then answer the item.

"Let's take a galaxy cab!" exclaimed Rory. "We'll get there much faster." Rory's friends agreed. The cab driver asked what planet the youngsters wanted to go to. They wanted to go to a particular park in the Whirlpool Galaxy. On the ride there, they passed people riding their space horses and walking their pet stars.

5. Write two sentences from the text that shows it is science fiction.

✳ a. "Let's take a galaxy cab!" exclaimed Rory.

✳ b. On the ride there, they passed people riding their space horses and walking their pet stars.

© Evan-Moor Corp. • EMC 3244 • Daily Fundamentals   57

Page 58

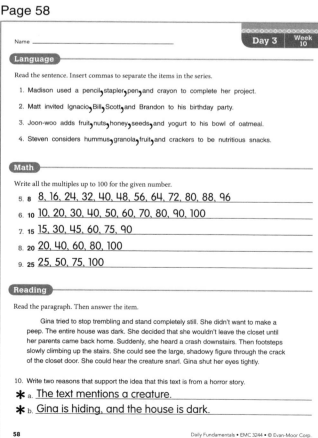

Name _____

Day 3 | **Week 10**

Language

Read the sentence. Insert commas to separate the items in the series.

1. Madison used a pencil, stapler, pen, and crayon to complete her project.

2. Matt invited Ignacio, Bill, Scott, and Brandon to his birthday party.

3. Joon-woo adds fruit, nuts, honey, seeds, and yogurt to his bowl of oatmeal.

4. Steven considers hummus, granola, fruit, and crackers to be nutritious snacks.

Math

Write all the multiples up to 100 for the given number.

5. 8   8, 16, 24, 32, 40, 48, 56, 64, 72, 80, 88, 96
6. 10   10, 20, 30, 40, 50, 60, 70, 80, 90, 100
7. 15   15, 30, 45, 60, 75, 90
8. 20   20, 40, 60, 80, 100
9. 25   25, 50, 75, 100

Reading

Read the paragraph. Then answer the item.

Gina tried to stop trembling and stand completely still. She didn't want to make a peep. The entire house was dark. She decided that she wouldn't leave the closet until her parents came back home. Suddenly, she heard a crash downstairs. Then footsteps slowly climbing up the stairs. She could see the large, shadowy figure through the crack of the closet door. She could hear the creature snarl. Gina shut her eyes tightly.

10. Write two reasons that support the idea that this text is from a horror story.

✳ a. The text mentions a creature.

✳ b. Gina is hiding, and the house is dark.

58   Daily Fundamentals • EMC 3244 • © Evan-Moor Corp.

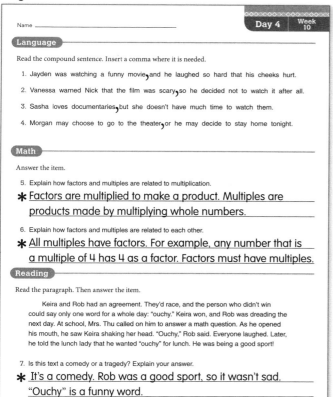

✱ These answers will vary. Examples are given.

Page 59

Name _____

Day 4 | **Week 10**

Language

Read the compound sentence. Insert a comma where it is needed.

1. Jayden was watching a funny movie**,** and he laughed so hard that his cheeks hurt.

2. Vanessa warned Nick that the film was scary**,** so he decided not to watch it after all.

3. Sasha loves documentaries**,** but she doesn't have much time to watch them.

4. Morgan may choose to go to the theater**,** or he may decide to stay home tonight.

Math

Answer the item.

5. Explain how factors and multiples are related to multiplication.

✱ Factors are multiplied to make a product. Multiples are products made by multiplying whole numbers.

6. Explain how factors and multiples are related to each other.

✱ All multiples have factors. For example, any number that is a multiple of 4 has 4 as a factor. Factors must have multiples.

Reading

Read the paragraph. Then answer the item.

Keira and Rob had an agreement. They'd race, and the person who didn't win could say only one word for a whole day: "ouchy." Keira won, and Rob was dreading the next day. At school, Mrs. Thu called on him to answer a math question. As he opened his mouth, he saw Keira shaking her head. "Ouchy," Rob said. Everyone laughed. Later, he told the lunch lady that he wanted "ouchy" for lunch. He was being a good sport!

7. Is this text a comedy or a tragedy? Explain your answer.

✱ It's a comedy. Rob was a good sport, so it wasn't sad. "Ouchy" is a funny word.

© Evan-Moor Corp. • EMC 3244 • Daily Fundamentals — 59

Page 60

Name _____

Day 5 | **Week 10**

Language

Read the complex sentence. Insert a comma if one is needed.

1. While he listened to the radio**,** Eddie was able to get his chores done.

2. Terrence will arrive at the stadium before the players run onto the field.

3. Unless he has an umbrella**,** Bob's clothes will get soaked in the rain.

4. Joel remembers his first day of school whenever he hears classical music.

Math

Answer the item.

5. Write the first seven multiples of 4. 4, 8, 12, 16, 20, 24, 28

6. Write the first ten multiples of 11. 11, 22, 33, 44, 55, 66, 77, 88, 99, 110

7. Write the first eight multiples of 7. 7, 14, 21, 28, 35, 42, 49, 56

8. Write the first six multiples of 12. 12, 24, 36, 48, 60, 72

9. Write the first nine multiples of 10. 10, 20, 30, 40, 50, 60, 70, 80, 90

Reading

Read the paragraph. Then answer the item.

"Son, jump out of the wagon and help me set up the family's camp for tonight," hollered Pa. "We'll eat the rest of that buffalo meat and potatoes for supper." Jeffrey helped his dad. The family of eight were headed west to California. They had a covered wagon, two horses, and two oxen. Some of them were walking on foot. They had months of travel ahead of them. The biggest threats were cholera and exhaustion.

10. Is this fictional text set in the present, past, or future? Explain why.

✱ The past. There's a covered wagon, and it's taking months to travel to California. Some people are walking.

60 — Daily Fundamentals • EMC 3244 • © Evan-Moor Corp.

Page 61

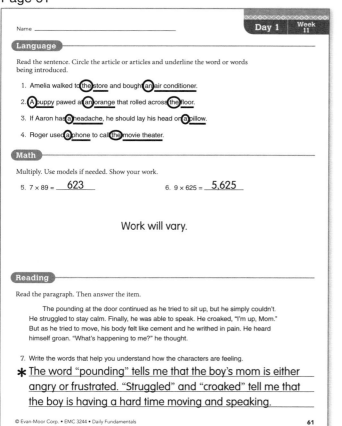

Name _____

Day 1 | **Week 11**

Language

Read the sentence. Circle the article or articles and underline the word or words being introduced.

1. Amelia walked to (the) store and bought (an) air conditioner.

2. (A) puppy pawed at (an) orange that rolled across (the) floor.

3. If Aaron has (a) headache, he should lay his head on (a) pillow.

4. Roger used (a) phone to call (the) movie theater.

Math

Multiply. Use models if needed. Show your work.

5. 7 × 89 = ___623___   6. 9 × 625 = ___5,625___

Work will vary.

Reading

Read the paragraph. Then answer the item.

The pounding at the door continued as he tried to sit up, but he simply couldn't. He struggled to stay calm. Finally, he was able to speak. He croaked, "I'm up, Mom." But as he tried to move, his body felt like cement and he writhed in pain. He heard himself groan. "What's happening to me?" he thought.

7. Write the words that help you understand how the characters are feeling.

✱ The word "pounding" tells me that the boy's mom is either angry or frustrated. "Struggled" and "croaked" tell me that the boy is having a hard time moving and speaking.

© Evan-Moor Corp. • EMC 3244 • Daily Fundamentals — 61

Page 62

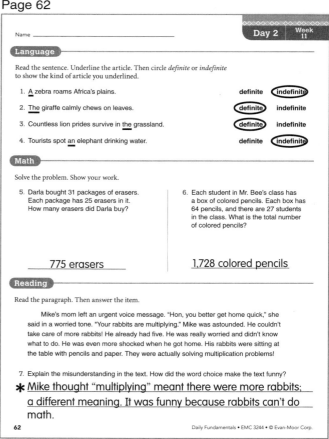

Name _____

Day 2 | **Week 11**

Language

Read the sentence. Underline the article. Then circle *definite* or *indefinite* to show the kind of article you underlined.

1. A zebra roams Africa's plains.   definite   (indefinite)

2. The giraffe calmly chews on leaves.   (definite)   indefinite

3. Countless lion prides survive in the grassland. (definite)   indefinite

4. Tourists spot an elephant drinking water.   definite   (indefinite)

Math

Solve the problem. Show your work.

5. Darla bought 31 packages of erasers. Each package has 25 erasers in it. How many erasers did Darla buy?

___775 erasers___

6. Each student in Mr. Bee's class has a box of colored pencils. Each box has 64 pencils, and there are 27 students in the class. What is the total number of colored pencils?

___1,728 colored pencils___

Reading

Read the paragraph. Then answer the item.

Mike's mom left an urgent voice message. "Hon, you better get home quick," she said in a worried tone. "Your rabbits are multiplying." Mike was astounded. He couldn't take care of more rabbits! He already had five. He was really worried and didn't know what to do. He was even more shocked when he got home. His rabbits were sitting at the table with pencils and paper. They were actually solving multiplication problems!

7. Explain the misunderstanding in the text. How did the word choice make the text funny?

✱ Mike thought "multiplying" meant there were more rabbits; a different meaning. It was funny because rabbits can't do math.

62 — Daily Fundamentals • EMC 3244 • © Evan-Moor Corp.

© Evan-Moor Corp. • EMC 3244 • *Daily Fundamentals*   **173**

Page 63

Name _____

Day 3 | Week 11

Language

Read the sentence. Complete it with the correct word from the word box.

> they're   there   their

1. Hal will leave here at noon and arrive ___there___ at midnight.

2. James and Ernie made ___their___ dog a birthday cake.

3. If the party is this Saturday, ___they're___ not going to be able to make it.

Math

Divide. Show your work.

4. 964 ÷ 4 = ___241___   5. 768 ÷ 8 = ___96___

Work will vary.

Reading

Read the paragraph. Then answer the items.

You've seen Br'er Lizard. He's been runnin' 'round and standin' on all fours in the yard. But I'm a-guessin' you've never seen him sittin'. He used to sit on a lily pad, jus' like his pal, ol' Br'er Frog. They did some swimmin' and pushin' and squeezin' through fences. Then everything changed. Poor ol' Br'er Lizard got himself a-flattened.

6. Explain how the text uses nontraditional spelling.

✱ Apostrophes replace letters and affect how words sound.

7. How would the text be different using more traditional spelling of the words?

✱ The story wouldn't sound as special, fun, or unique.

Page 64

Name _____

Day 4 | Week 11

Language

Read the sentence. Write *good* or *well* to complete the sentence.

1. Bertha knows the scenes of this movie ___well___.

2. Carl thought the book was ___good___, even though he disliked the ending.

3. Although Peggy normally cooks ___well___, the dinner she made tonight was odd.

4. Rob is a ___good___ friend because he is always there when I need him.

Math

Solve the problem. Show your work.

5. Maria has downloaded 856 songs. She has them evenly categorized in 8 different playlists. How many songs does Maria have in each playlist?

___107 songs___

6. Mom bought a big basket that contained 435 strawberries. She divided them equally among 5 relatives. How many strawberries did each relative get?

___87 strawberries___

Reading

Read the paragraph. Then answer the items.

Dina, Amy, and Yoko were hanging out in Amy's room. Amy left the room briefly. As she was returning, she overheard Dina saying, "Amy's nice but also extreme and forceful." This hurt Amy's feelings a little. She always thought of herself as energetic and lively. Amy knew Dina was a good friend. She'd ask her about it later.

7. How did Amy react to Dina's word choice?

✱ Amy didn't think of herself that way, so the words hurt her.

8. Write two words that have a similar meaning to *extreme* and *forceful*.

✱ excessive, assertive

Page 65

Name _____

Day 5 | Week 11

Language

Read the sentence. Write *bad* or *badly* to complete the sentence.

1. The park ranger saw litter on the trail, which was a ___bad___ sign.

2. Dave's room is still messy because he cleaned it ___badly___.

3. Paul got sprayed by a skunk, so now he smells ___bad___.

4. Louisa washes dishes ___badly___ because she doesn't use enough soap.

Math

Multiply or divide. Show your work.

5. 65 × 17 = ___1,105___   7. 38 ÷ 2 = ___19___

Work will vary.

6. 93 × 52 = ___4,836___   8. 388 ÷ 4 = ___97___

Reading

Read the paragraph. Then answer the items.

Forests can give us a <u>continuous</u> supply of <u>raw materials</u>. In order to stay healthy and <u>productive</u>, forests must be <u>managed carefully</u>. This means making sure that trees are not cut down faster than they can be replanted. Some companies cut down <u>numerous</u> trees in order to sell more tree products and make <u>higher profits</u>. All around the world, the <u>demand</u> for goods from trees is high.

9. Is the vocabulary in the text serious and formal, or fun and informal? Explain why.

✱ It's more serious/formal. The words are big and not simple.

✱ 10. Underline the words in the text that support your answer for number 9.

Page 66

Name _____

Day 1 | Week 12

Language

Draw a line to match the base word to the same word with an affix.

1. luck
2. appear
3. build
4. heat
5. write
6. do
7. hope

hopeful
rewrite
undo
lucky
buildable
preheat
disappear

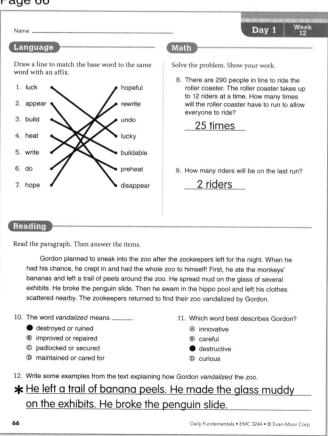

Math

Solve the problem. Show your work.

8. There are 290 people in line to ride the roller coaster. The roller coaster takes up to 12 riders at a time. How many times will the roller coaster have to run to allow everyone to ride?

___25 times___

9. How many riders will be on the last run?

___2 riders___

Reading

Read the paragraph. Then answer the items.

Gordon planned to sneak into the zoo after the zookeepers left for the night. When he had his chance, he crept in and had the whole zoo to himself! First, he ate the monkeys' bananas and left a trail of peels around the zoo. He spread mud on the glass of several exhibits. He broke the penguin slide. Then he swam in the hippo pool and left his clothes scattered nearby. The zookeepers returned to find their zoo vandalized by Gordon.

10. The word *vandalized* means _____.
- ● destroyed or ruined
- Ⓑ improved or repaired
- Ⓒ padlocked or secured
- Ⓓ maintained or cared for

11. Which word best describes Gordon?
- Ⓐ innovative
- Ⓑ careful
- ● destructive
- Ⓓ curious

12. Write some examples from the text explaining how Gordon *vandalized* the zoo.

✱ He left a trail of banana peels. He made the glass muddy on the exhibits. He broke the penguin slide.

Page 67

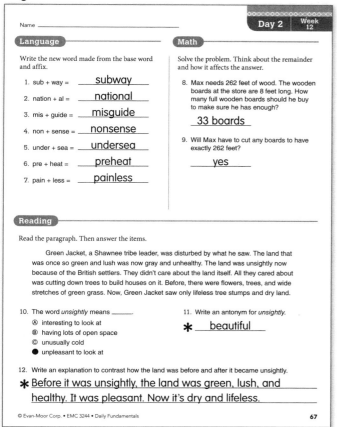

Name _____

Day 2 | Week 12

Language

Write the new word made from the base word and affix.

1. sub + way = __subway__
2. nation + al = __national__
3. mis + guide = __misguide__
4. non + sense = __nonsense__
5. under + sea = __undersea__
6. pre + heat = __preheat__
7. pain + less = __painless__

Math

Solve the problem. Think about the remainder and how it affects the answer.

8. Max needs 262 feet of wood. The wooden boards at the store are 8 feet long. How many full wooden boards should he buy to make sure he has enough?

__33 boards__

9. Will Max have to cut any boards to have exactly 262 feet?

__yes__

Reading

Read the paragraph. Then answer the items.

Green Jacket, a Shawnee tribe leader, was disturbed by what he saw. The land that was once so green and lush was now gray and unhealthy. The land was unsightly now because of the British settlers. They didn't care about the land itself. All they cared about was cutting down trees to build houses on it. Before, there were flowers, trees, and wide stretches of green grass. Now, Green Jacket saw only lifeless tree stumps and dry land.

10. The word *unsightly* means _____.
Ⓐ interesting to look at
Ⓑ having lots of open space
Ⓒ unusually cold
● unpleasant to look at

11. Write an antonym for *unsightly*.
※ __beautiful__

12. Write an explanation to contrast how the land was before and after it became unsightly.
※ __Before it was unsightly, the land was green, lush, and healthy. It was pleasant. Now it's dry and lifeless.__

Page 68

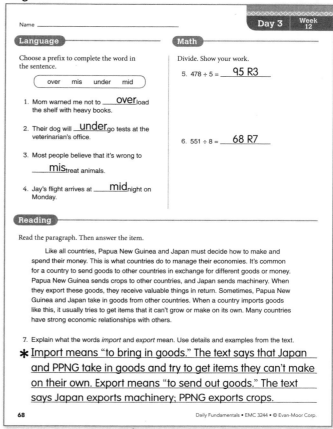

Name _____

Day 3 | Week 12

Language

Choose a prefix to complete the word in the sentence.

over   mis   under   mid

1. Mom warned me not to __over__load the shelf with heavy books.
2. Their dog will __under__go tests at the veterinarian's office.
3. Most people believe that it's wrong to __mis__treat animals.
4. Jay's flight arrives at __mid__night on Monday.

Math

Divide. Show your work.

5. 478 ÷ 5 = __95 R3__

6. 551 ÷ 8 = __68 R7__

Reading

Read the paragraph. Then answer the item.

Like all countries, Papua New Guinea and Japan must decide how to make and spend their money. This is what countries do to manage their economies. It's common for a country to send goods to other countries in exchange for different goods or money. Papua New Guinea sends crops to other countries, and Japan sends machinery. When they export these goods, they receive valuable things in return. Sometimes, Papua New Guinea and Japan take in goods from other countries. When a country imports goods like this, it usually tries to get items that it can't grow or make on its own. Many countries have strong economic relationships with others.

7. Explain what the words *import* and *export* mean. Use details and examples from the text.
※ __Import means "to bring in goods." The text says that Japan and PPNG take in goods and try to get items they can't make on their own. Export means "to send out goods." The text says Japan exports machinery; PPNG exports crops.__

Page 69

Name _____

Day 4 | Week 12

Language

Choose a suffix to complete the word in the sentence.

less   ful   ation   ment

1. Sara needs some relax__ation__ after her long school day.
2. Barb is looking forward to the quiz because she is hope__ful__ she'll do well.
3. Tim is naturally good at sports and finds baseball effort__less__.
4. There is a lot of excite__ment__ when De visits her cousins.

Math

Solve the problem.

5. Margo has 93 lemons. She'll give each of her 9 friends 10 lemons. How many lemons will she have left?

__3 lemons__

6. Tran ate 365 bowls of cereal last year. Each box of cereal contained enough cereal for 9 bowls. How many full boxes of cereal did Tran eat last year?

__40 boxes__

Reading

Read the paragraph. Then answer the items.

In the early 1600s, European colonists began settling what is now the United States. A Native American chief named Massasoit maintained peaceful relations with the colonists for decades. But tensions grew after Massasoit's death. His son believed the colonists wanted to rid the land of his people entirely. He formed an alliance with other Native American tribes. As a result of the alliance, different groups of Native Americans combined their efforts for the common goal of wiping out the colonists. They wanted to prevent the colonists from driving away all of the Native Americans from their homes. The tribes started a war in 1675.

7. Explain what an *alliance* is.
※ __An alliance is a joining of people with a common goal.__

8. How did the alliance mentioned in the text affect history?
※ __It led to war in 1675. It caused different groups of Native Americans to join together and fight against colonists.__

Page 70

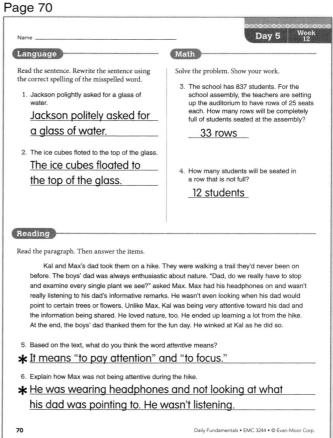

Name _____

Day 5 | Week 12

Language

Read the sentence. Rewrite the sentence using the correct spelling of the misspelled word.

1. Jackson polightly asked for a glass of water.
__Jackson politely asked for a glass of water.__

2. The ice cubes floted to the top of the glass.
__The ice cubes floated to the top of the glass.__

Math

Solve the problem. Show your work.

3. The school has 837 students. For the school assembly, the teachers are setting up the auditorium to have rows of 25 seats each. How many rows will be completely full of students seated at the assembly?

__33 rows__

4. How many students will be seated in a row that is not full?

__12 students__

Reading

Read the paragraph. Then answer the items.

Kal and Max's dad took them on a hike. They were walking a trail they'd never been on before. The boys' dad was always enthusiastic about nature. "Dad, do we really have to stop and examine every single plant we see?" asked Max. Max had his headphones on and wasn't really listening to his dad's informative remarks. He wasn't even looking when his dad would point to certain trees or flowers. Unlike Max, Kal was being very attentive toward his dad and the information being shared. He loved nature, too. He ended up learning a lot from the hike. At the end, the boys' dad thanked them for the fun day. He winked at Kal as he did so.

5. Based on the text, what do you think the word *attentive* means?
※ __It means "to pay attention" and "to focus."__

6. Explain how Max was not being attentive during the hike.
※ __He was wearing headphones and not looking at what his dad was pointing to. He wasn't listening.__

Page 71

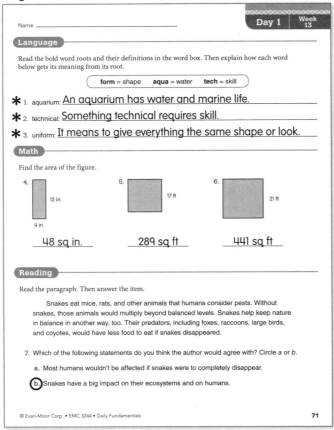

Name _____

Day 1 | **Week 13**

Language

Read the bold word roots and their definitions in the word box. Then explain how each word below gets its meaning from its root.

form = shape   **aqua** = water   **tech** = skill

* 1. aquarium: An aquarium has water and marine life.
* 2. technical: Something technical requires skill.
* 3. uniform: It means to give everything the same shape or look.

Math

Find the area of the figure.

4. 12 in. / 4 in.   48 sq in.

5. 17 ft   289 sq ft

6. 21 ft   441 sq ft

Reading

Read the paragraph. Then answer the item.

Snakes eat mice, rats, and other animals that humans consider pests. Without snakes, those animals would multiply beyond balanced levels. Snakes help keep nature in balance in another way, too. Their predators, including foxes, raccoons, large birds, and coyotes, would have less food to eat if snakes disappeared.

7. Which of the following statements do you think the author would agree with? Circle *a* or *b*.

a. Most humans wouldn't be affected if snakes were to completely disappear.

(b.) Snakes have a big impact on their ecosystems and on humans.

© Evan-Moor Corp. • EMC 3244 • Daily Fundamentals   71

Page 72

Name _____

Day 2 | **Week 13**

Language

Match the prefix to a base word to create a new word. Write the new word on the same line as the prefix it has.

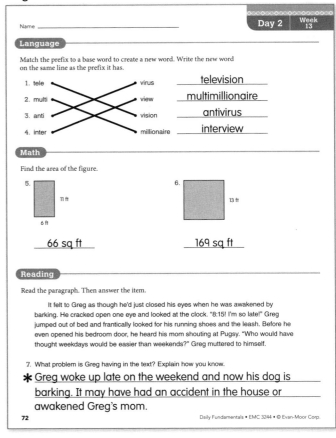

1. tele — vision   television
2. multi — millionaire   multimillionaire
3. anti — virus   antivirus
4. inter — view   interview

Math

Find the area of the figure.

5. 11 ft / 6 ft   66 sq ft

6. 13 ft   169 sq ft

Reading

Read the paragraph. Then answer the item.

It felt to Greg as though he'd just closed his eyes when he was awakened by barking. He cracked open one eye and looked at the clock. "8:15! I'm so late!" Greg jumped out of bed and frantically looked for his running shoes and the leash. Before he even opened his bedroom door, he heard his mom shouting at Pugsy. "Who would have thought weekdays would be easier than weekends?" Greg muttered to himself.

7. What problem is Greg having in the text? Explain how you know.

* Greg woke up late on the weekend and now his dog is barking. It may have had an accident in the house or awakened Greg's mom.

72   Daily Fundamentals • EMC 3244 • © Evan-Moor Corp.

Page 73

Name _____

Day 3 | **Week 13**

Language

Match the base word to a suffix to create a new word. Write the new word on the same line as the suffix it has.

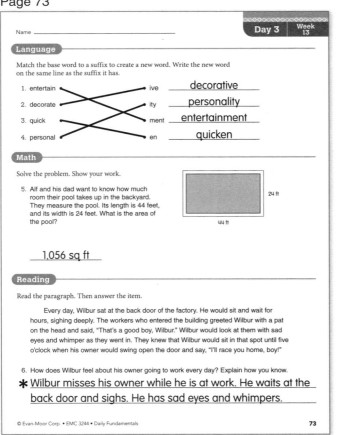

1. entertain — ive   decorative
2. decorate — ity   personality
3. quick — ment   entertainment
4. personal — en   quicken

Math

Solve the problem. Show your work.

5. Alf and his dad want to know how much room their pool takes up in the backyard. They measure the pool. Its length is 44 feet, and its width is 24 feet. What is the area of the pool?

24 ft / 44 ft

1,056 sq ft

Reading

Read the paragraph. Then answer the item.

Every day, Wilbur sat at the back door of the factory. He would sit and wait for hours, sighing deeply. The workers who entered the building greeted Wilbur with a pat on the head and said, "That's a good boy, Wilbur." Wilbur would look at them with sad eyes and whimper as they went in. They knew that Wilbur would sit in that spot until five o'clock when his owner would swing open the door and say, "I'll race you home, boy!"

6. How does Wilbur feel about his owner going to work every day? Explain how you know.

* Wilbur misses his owner while he is at work. He waits at the back door and sighs. He has sad eyes and whimpers.

© Evan-Moor Corp. • EMC 3244 • Daily Fundamentals   73

Page 74

Name _____

Day 4 | **Week 13**

Language

Underline the affix in the word. Then write the base word.

1. strengthen   strength
2. interstate   state
3. multipurpose   purpose
4. attachment   attach
5. telephone   phone
6. antifreeze   freeze
7. expressive   express
8. electricity   electric

Math

Solve the problem. Show your work.

9. Charity's mom is ordering a new dresser online. She wants to figure out how much floor space up to clear to make room for it, so she needs to calculate the dresser's area. The website states that the dresser is 4 ft long and 2 ft wide. What is the area of the floor space that Charity's mom should clear?

8 sq ft

10. Patsy has a toy chest that is 72 in. long and 42 in. wide. What is its area?

3,024 sq in.

Reading

Read the paragraph. Then answer the item.

After the sun sets in Tasmania, the Tasmanian devils wake up. These scavengers are one of nature's important garbage collectors. They feed on dead animals. In fact, their favorite food is rotten meat. Their sharp teeth can crush the toughest foods. They even swallow bones. And the poisons and germs they eat don't seem to harm them. Their eating habits actually stop bacteria and disease from spreading to other animals.

11. What relationship does the Tasmanian devil have with other animals?

* It has a good relationship because it eats dead animals and prevents live animals from getting bacteria and disease.

74   Daily Fundamentals • EMC 3244 • © Evan-Moor Corp.

Page 75

Name _____

Day 5 | Week **13**

Language

Explain how the affix changes the meaning of the base word.

* 1. recalculate <u>The prefix "re" makes it "calculate again."</u>

* 2. politely <u>The suffix "ly" turns "polite" into an adverb.</u>

* 3. sensitivity <u>It turned into a noun form of "sensitive."</u>

* 4. interact <u>The prefix makes it "do with another."</u>

Math

Solve the problem. Show your work.

5. Edwin is planting a big cabbage garden. The garden will have 16 rows of 13 heads of cabbage. Each head of cabbage has its own square-shaped growth area that is 14 in. wide. What will be the total area of Edwin's cabbage garden?

<u>40,768 sq in.</u>

Reading

Read the paragraph. Then answer the item.

Emmet changed into comfortable clothes so he could do his chores. He was in charge of the chickens, which meant he had to feed them, collect and wash their eggs, and keep the chickens and their pens clean. His dad fertilized the crops with compost from the pile that Mom tended. Everyone helped harvest the crops as they ripened, and all spare time was spent pulling weeds and eliminating pests.

6. Where does Emmet live? Explain your thinking.

* <u>Emmet lives on a farm. He has chores related to chickens</u>
  <u>and harvesting crops.</u>

Page 76

Name _____

Day 1 | Week **14**

Language

Read the sentence. Underline the adjective. Then circle the noun the adjective is describing.

1. Craig is a fan of snacks, especially <u>stinky</u> (cheese)

2. His favorite thing about it is the <u>salty</u> (flavor)

3. He once received an <u>exotic</u> (collection) of cheeses from overseas.

4. Sometimes he uses cheese to create a <u>delicious</u> (meal)

Math

Answer the item.

5. This circle has been divided into equal parts. What is the measure of each angle formed? Explain how you know.

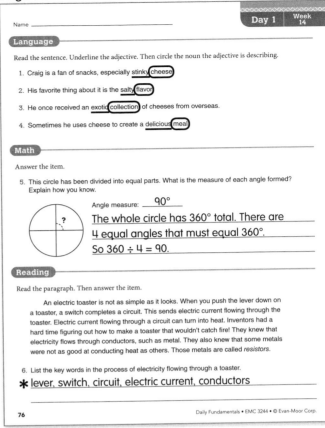

Angle measure: <u>90°</u>

<u>The whole circle has 360° total. There are</u>
<u>4 equal angles that must equal 360°.</u>
<u>So 360 ÷ 4 = 90.</u>

Reading

Read the paragraph. Then answer the item.

An electric toaster is not as simple as it looks. When you push the lever down on a toaster, a switch completes a circuit. This sends electric current flowing through the toaster. Electric current flowing through a circuit can turn into heat. Inventors had a hard time figuring out how to make a toaster that wouldn't catch fire! They knew that electricity flows through conductors, such as metal. They also knew that some metals were not as good at conducting heat as others. Those metals are called *resistors*.

6. List the key words in the process of electricity flowing through a toaster.

* <u>lever, switch, circuit, electric current, conductors</u>

Page 77

Name _____

Day 2 | Week **14**

Language

Read the sentence. Complete it with an adjective from the word box. Then underline the noun that the adjective is describing.

| calm   talented   strong |

1. Ryan is a <u>talented</u> kayaker.

2. He uses <u>strong</u> <u>paddles</u> to move the kayak in the water.

3. Ryan especially loves kayaking on days when the <u>water</u> is <u>calm</u>.

Math

Shade part of the circle to match the given angle measurement.

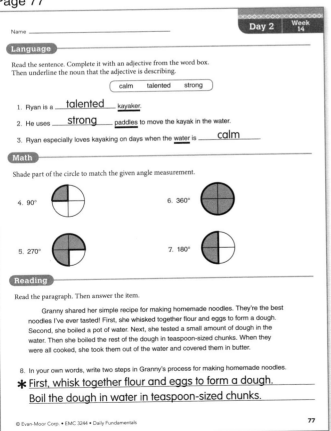

4. 90°

6. 360°

5. 270°

7. 180°

Reading

Read the paragraph. Then answer the item.

Granny shared her simple recipe for making homemade noodles. They're the best noodles I've ever tasted! First, she whisked together flour and eggs to form a dough. Second, she boiled a pot of water. Next, she tested a small amount of dough in the water. Then she boiled the rest of the dough in teaspoon-sized chunks. When they were all cooked, she took them out of the water and covered them in butter.

8. In your own words, write two steps in Granny's process for making homemade noodles.

* <u>First, whisk together flour and eggs to form a dough.</u>
  <u>Boil the dough in water in teaspoon-sized chunks.</u>

Page 78

Name _____

Day 3 | Week **14**

Language

Read the paragraph. Write your own adjectives to complete it.

* 1. Joe used a <u>tall</u> ladder to reach the <u>dented</u> bowl on the top shelf. He wanted to use it to mix <u>sour</u> berries with <u>sweet</u> granola. This day was going to be <u>tiresome</u>, so Joe wanted to have a <u>special</u> breakfast. He felt extra <u>anxious</u> this morning.

Math

Write the measurement of the angle that is marked. Then explain how you found it.

2. <u>90°</u>

3. <u>45°</u>

* <u>It's a perpendicular angle</u>
  <u>or a right triangle.</u>

* <u>It's a split right angle,</u>
  <u>or half a 90° angle.</u>

Reading

Read the text. Then answer the item.

Follow these steps each day while I am out of town:
1) Pour fresh filtered water into Sparkle's red bowl.
2) Fill Sparkle's yellow bowl with 2 cups of dry dog food.
3) Go outside with Sparkle, on leash, for a 20-minute walk.
4) Throw the ball for Sparkle for 10 minutes.

4. What kind of process does the list describe? Who is the author of this text?

* <u>It describes the process to care for the author's dog,</u>
  <u>Sparkle. The author is Sparkle's owner.</u>

✱ **These answers will vary. Examples are given.**

Page 79

Name _____

Day 4 | Week 14

Language

Write three sentences using the adjectives from the word box.

stylish   confusing   brave

✱ 1. Grandma is wearing a stylish new coat.

✱ 2. Coco's handwriting is confusing.

✱ 3. That is a brave little dog!

Math

Find the unknown angle measure without measuring.

4. 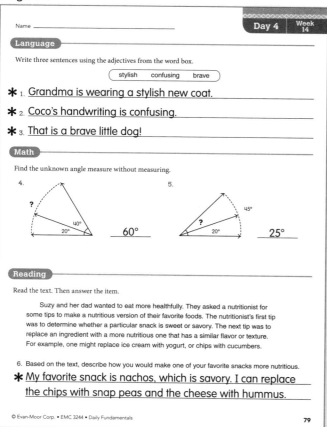 60°

5. 25°

Reading

Read the text. Then answer the item.

Suzy and her dad wanted to eat more healthfully. They asked a nutritionist for some tips to make a nutritious version of their favorite foods. The nutritionist's first tip was to determine whether a particular snack is sweet or savory. The next tip was to replace an ingredient with a more nutritious one that has a similar flavor or texture. For example, one might replace ice cream with yogurt, or chips with cucumbers.

6. Based on the text, describe how you would make one of your favorite snacks more nutritious.

✱ My favorite snack is nachos, which is savory. I can replace the chips with snap peas and the cheese with hummus.

© Evan-Moor Corp. • EMC 3244 • Daily Fundamentals   79

Page 80

Name _____

Day 5 | Week 14

Language

Answer the item.

1. Explain why adjectives are important when describing nouns.

✱ Adjectives give qualities to nouns and help create imagery. Nouns would be less special without adjectives.

2. List four adjectives that you enjoy using in your writing.

✱ fascinating, pretty, intelligent, odd

Math

Draw a figure that has the given angle or angles. Then circle the angle or angles.

3. a triangle with a right angle   4. a parallelogram with two acute angles

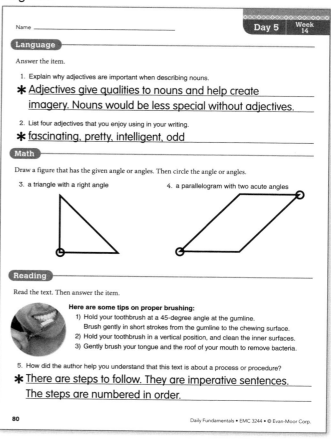

Reading

Read the text. Then answer the item.

Here are some tips on proper brushing:
1) Hold your toothbrush at a 45-degree angle at the gumline. Brush gently in short strokes from the gumline to the chewing surface.
2) Hold your toothbrush in a vertical position, and clean the inner surfaces.
3) Gently brush your tongue and the roof of your mouth to remove bacteria.

5. How did the author help you understand that this text is about a process or procedure?

✱ There are steps to follow. They are imperative sentences. The steps are numbered in order.

80   Daily Fundamentals • EMC 3244 • © Evan-Moor Corp.

Page 81

Name _____

Day 1 | Week 15

Language

Write the subject pronoun that replaces the given word or words.

1. Sheila and Don — they
2. Carlos — he
3. a dog and cat — they
4. Gloria — she
5. you and Paul — you
6. Ari and I — we
7. the bike — it

Math

Write *perpendicular*, *intersecting*, or *parallel* to describe the pair of lines.

8. perpendicular
9. parallel
10. intersecting
11. intersecting

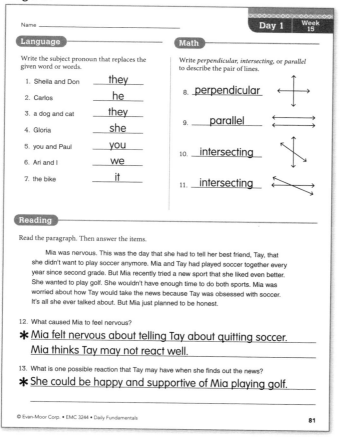

Reading

Read the paragraph. Then answer the items.

Mia was nervous. This was the day that she had to tell her best friend, Tay, that she didn't want to play soccer anymore. Mia and Tay had played soccer together every year since second grade. But Mia recently tried a new sport that she liked even better. She wanted to play golf. She wouldn't have enough time to do both sports. Mia was worried about how Tay would take the news because Tay was obsessed with soccer. It's all she ever talked about. But Mia just planned to be honest.

12. What caused Mia to feel nervous?

✱ Mia felt nervous about telling Tay about quitting soccer. Mia thinks Tay may not react well.

13. What is one possible reaction that Tay may have when she finds out the news?

✱ She could be happy and supportive of Mia playing golf.

© Evan-Moor Corp. • EMC 3244 • Daily Fundamentals   81

Page 82

Name _____

Day 2 | Week 15

Language

Write the object pronoun that replaces the given word or words.

1. Dory and Luis — them
2. Pablo — him
3. the pencil — it
4. Cory and me — us
5. you and Rita — you
6. Ramona — her
7. a leaf and a twig — them

Math

Write *obtuse*, *right*, *acute*, or *straight* to describe the angle.

8. straight
9. right
10. obtuse
11. acute

Reading

Look at the picture and read the caption. Then answer the items.

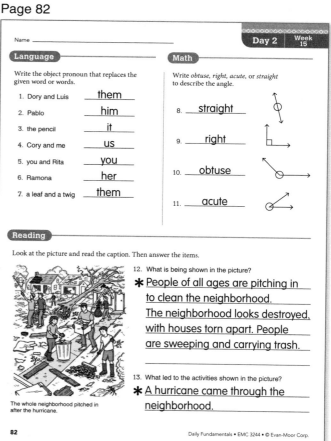

The whole neighborhood pitched in after the hurricane.

12. What is being shown in the picture?

✱ People of all ages are pitching in to clean the neighborhood. The neighborhood looks destroyed, with houses torn apart. People are sweeping and carrying trash.

13. What led to the activities shown in the picture?

✱ A hurricane came through the neighborhood.

82   Daily Fundamentals • EMC 3244 • © Evan-Moor Corp.

178   Daily Fundamentals • EMC 3244 • © Evan-Moor Corp.

These answers will vary. Examples are given.

Page 83

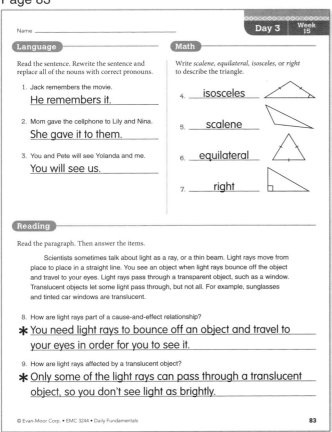

Name _____

Day 3 | Week 15

Language

Read the sentence. Rewrite the sentence and replace all of the nouns with correct pronouns.

1. Jack remembers the movie.
   He remembers it.

2. Mom gave the cellphone to Lily and Nina.
   She gave it to them.

3. You and Pete will see Yolanda and me.
   You will see us.

Math

Write *scalene, equilateral, isosceles,* or *right* to describe the triangle.

4. isosceles
5. scalene
6. equilateral
7. right

Reading

Read the paragraph. Then answer the items.

Scientists sometimes talk about light as a ray, or a thin beam. Light rays move from place to place in a straight line. You see an object when light rays bounce off the object and travel to your eyes. Light rays pass through a transparent object, such as a window. Translucent objects let some light pass through, but not all. For example, sunglasses and tinted car windows are translucent.

8. How are light rays part of a cause-and-effect relationship?
   * You need light rays to bounce off an object and travel to your eyes in order for you to see it.

9. How are light rays affected by a translucent object?
   * Only some of the light rays can pass through a translucent object, so you don't see light as brightly.

© Evan-Moor Corp. • EMC 3244 • Daily Fundamentals   83

Page 84

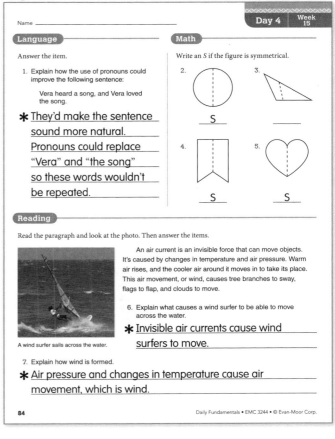

Name _____

Day 4 | Week 15

Language

Answer the item.

1. Explain how the use of pronouns could improve the following sentence:

   Vera heard a song, and Vera loved the song.

   * They'd make the sentence sound more natural. Pronouns could replace "Vera" and "the song" so these words wouldn't be repeated.

Math

Write an *S* if the figure is symmetrical.

2. S
3.
4.
5. S

S

Reading

Read the paragraph and look at the photo. Then answer the items.

An air current is an invisible force that can move objects. It's caused by changes in temperature and air pressure. Warm air rises, and the cooler air around it moves in to take its place. This air movement, or wind, causes tree branches to sway, flags to flap, and clouds to move.

A wind surfer sails across the water.

6. Explain what causes a wind surfer to be able to move across the water.
   * Invisible air currents cause wind surfers to move.

7. Explain how wind is formed.
   * Air pressure and changes in temperature cause air movement, which is wind.

84   Daily Fundamentals • EMC 3244 • © Evan-Moor Corp.

Page 85

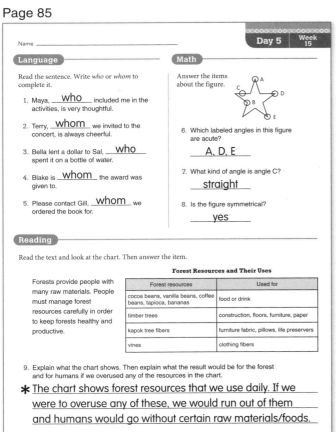

Name _____

Day 5 | Week 15

Language

Read the sentence. Write *who* or *whom* to complete it.

1. Maya, who included me in the activities, is very thoughtful.
2. Terry, whom we invited to the concert, is always cheerful.
3. Bella lent a dollar to Sal, who spent it on a bottle of water.
4. Blake is whom the award was given to.
5. Please contact Gill, whom we ordered the book for.

Math

Answer the items about the figure.

6. Which labeled angles in this figure are acute?
   A, D, E
7. What kind of angle is angle C?
   straight
8. Is the figure symmetrical?
   yes

Reading

Read the text and look at the chart. Then answer the item.

Forests provide people with many raw materials. People must manage forest resources carefully in order to keep forests healthy and productive.

Forest Resources and Their Uses

Forest resources	Used for
cocoa beans, vanilla beans, coffee beans, tapioca, bananas	food or drink
timber trees	construction, floors, furniture, paper
kapok tree fibers	furniture fabric, pillows, life preservers
vines	clothing fibers

9. Explain what the chart shows. Then explain what the result would be for the forest and for humans if we overused any of the resources in the chart.
   * The chart shows forest resources that we use daily. If we were to overuse any of these, we would run out of them and humans would go without certain raw materials/foods.

© Evan-Moor Corp. • EMC 3244 • Daily Fundamentals   85

Page 86

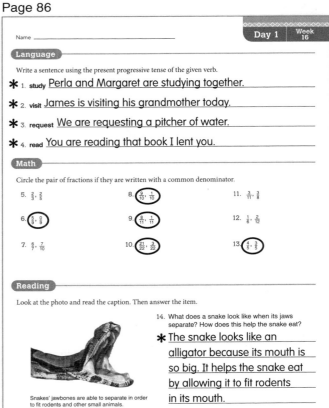

Name _____

Day 1 | Week 16

Language

Write a sentence using the present progressive tense of the given verb.

* 1. study Perla and Margaret are studying together.
* 2. visit James is visiting his grandmother today.
* 3. request We are requesting a pitcher of water.
* 4. read You are reading that book I lent you.

Math

Circle the pair of fractions if they are written with a common denominator.

5. $\frac{2}{3}, \frac{2}{5}$
6. $\frac{5}{9}, \frac{9}{9}$
7. $\frac{6}{7}, \frac{7}{10}$
8. $\frac{9}{10}, \frac{1}{10}$
9. $\frac{6}{11}, \frac{1}{11}$
10. $\frac{21}{22}, \frac{3}{22}$
11. $\frac{3}{11}, \frac{3}{8}$
12. $\frac{1}{6}, \frac{2}{12}$
13. $\frac{4}{5}, \frac{3}{5}$

Reading

Look at the photo and read the caption. Then answer the item.

14. What does a snake look like when its jaws separate? How does this help the snake eat?
    * The snake looks like an alligator because its mouth is so big. It helps the snake eat by allowing it to fit rodents in its mouth.

Snakes' jawbones are able to separate in order to fit rodents and other small animals.

86   Daily Fundamentals • EMC 3244 • © Evan-Moor Corp.

© Evan-Moor Corp. • EMC 3244 • Daily Fundamentals   **179**

Page 87

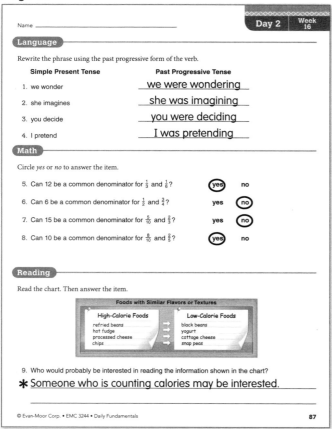

Name _____

Day 2 • Week 16

Language

Rewrite the phrase using the past progressive form of the verb.

Simple Present Tense	Past Progressive Tense
1. we wonder	we were wondering
2. she imagines	she was imagining
3. you decide	you were deciding
4. I pretend	I was pretending

Math

Circle *yes* or *no* to answer the item.

5. Can 12 be a common denominator for $\frac{1}{3}$ and $\frac{1}{8}$? (yes) no

6. Can 6 be a common denominator for $\frac{1}{2}$ and $\frac{3}{4}$? yes (no)

7. Can 15 be a common denominator for $\frac{5}{10}$ and $\frac{2}{3}$? yes (no)

8. Can 10 be a common denominator for $\frac{8}{10}$ and $\frac{2}{5}$? (yes) no

Reading

Read the chart. Then answer the item.

Foods with Similar Flavors or Textures

High-Calorie Foods	Low-Calorie Foods
refried beans	black beans
hot fudge	yogurt
processed cheese	cottage cheese
chips	snap peas

9. Who would probably be interested in reading the information shown in the chart?

 ✱ Someone who is counting calories may be interested.

© Evan-Moor Corp. • EMC 3244 • Daily Fundamentals   87

Page 88

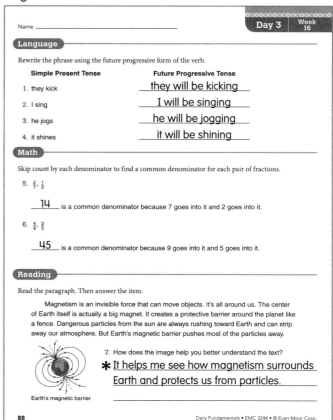

Name _____

Day 3 • Week 16

Language

Rewrite the phrase using the future progressive form of the verb.

Simple Present Tense	Future Progressive Tense
1. they kick	they will be kicking
2. I sing	I will be singing
3. he jogs	he will be jogging
4. it shines	it will be shining

Math

Skip count by each denominator to find a common denominator for each pair of fractions.

5. $\frac{2}{7}$, $\frac{1}{2}$

 __14__ is a common denominator because 7 goes into it and 2 goes into it.

6. $\frac{4}{9}$, $\frac{3}{5}$

 __45__ is a common denominator because 9 goes into it and 5 goes into it.

Reading

Read the paragraph. Then answer the item.

Magnetism is an invisible force that can move objects. It's all around us. The center of Earth itself is actually a big magnet. It creates a protective barrier around the planet like a fence. Dangerous particles from the sun are always rushing toward Earth and can strip away our atmosphere. But Earth's magnetic barrier pushes most of the particles away.

Earth's magnetic barrier

7. How does the image help you better understand the text?

 ✱ It helps me see how magnetism surrounds Earth and protects us from particles.

88   Daily Fundamentals • EMC 3244 • © Evan-Moor Corp.

Page 89

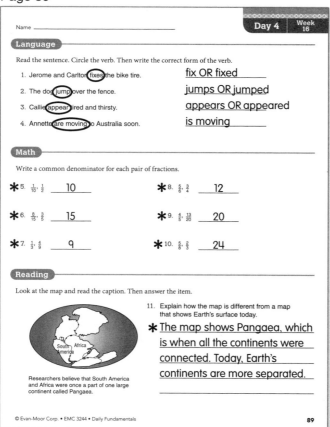

Name _____

Day 4 • Week 16

Language

Read the sentence. Circle the verb. Then write the correct form of the verb.

1. Jerome and Carlton (fixes) the bike tire. fix OR fixed

2. The dog (jump) over the fence. jumps OR jumped

3. Callie (appear) tired and thirsty. appears OR appeared

4. Annette (are moving) to Australia soon. is moving

Math

Write a common denominator for each pair of fractions.

✱ 5. $\frac{1}{10}$, $\frac{1}{2}$ 10

✱ 6. $\frac{8}{15}$, $\frac{1}{3}$ 15

✱ 7. $\frac{1}{3}$, $\frac{4}{9}$ 9

✱ 8. $\frac{5}{6}$, $\frac{3}{4}$ 12

✱ 9. $\frac{4}{5}$, $\frac{13}{20}$ 20

✱ 10. $\frac{5}{8}$, $\frac{2}{3}$ 24

Reading

Look at the map and read the caption. Then answer the item.

Researchers believe that South America and Africa were once a part of one large continent called Pangaea.

11. Explain how the map is different from a map that shows Earth's surface today.

 ✱ The map shows Pangaea, which is when all the continents were connected. Today, Earth's continents are more separated.

© Evan-Moor Corp. • EMC 3244 • Daily Fundamentals   89

Page 90

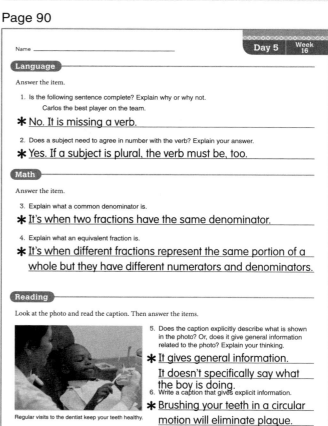

Name _____

Day 5 • Week 16

Language

Answer the item.

1. Is the following sentence complete? Explain why or why not.
Carlos the best player on the team.

 ✱ No. It is missing a verb.

2. Does a subject need to agree in number with the verb? Explain your answer.

 ✱ Yes. If a subject is plural, the verb must be, too.

Math

Answer the item.

3. Explain what a common denominator is.

 ✱ It's when two fractions have the same denominator.

4. Explain what an equivalent fraction is.

 ✱ It's when different fractions represent the same portion of a whole but they have different numerators and denominators.

Reading

Look at the photo and read the caption. Then answer the items.

Regular visits to the dentist keep your teeth healthy.

5. Does the caption explicitly describe what is shown in the photo? Or, does it give general information related to the photo? Explain your thinking.

 ✱ It gives general information. It doesn't specifically say what the boy is doing.

6. Write a caption that gives explicit information.

 ✱ Brushing your teeth in a circular motion will eliminate plaque.

90   Daily Fundamentals • EMC 3244 • © Evan-Moor Corp.

Page 91

Day 1 | Week 17

Language

Read the sentence. Circle the preposition. Then underline the noun that it is describing a location for.

1. A <u>fence</u> stands (around) the schoolyard.
2. The <u>bus</u> is parked (along) a sidewalk.
3. Their <u>house</u> faces (toward) the lake.
4. A <u>swing</u> hangs (from) the tree's branches.

Math

Write *equivalent* if the pair of shaded figures show equivalent fractions or *no* if not.

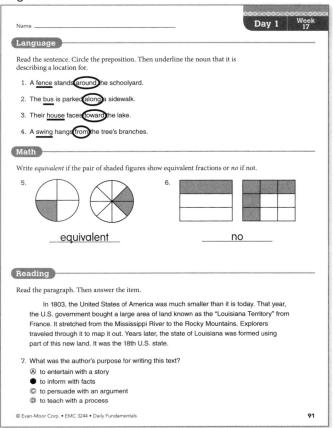

5. equivalent

6. no

Reading

Read the paragraph. Then answer the item.

In 1803, the United States of America was much smaller than it is today. That year, the U.S. government bought a large area of land known as the "Louisiana Territory" from France. It stretched from the Mississippi River to the Rocky Mountains. Explorers traveled through it to map it out. Years later, the state of Louisiana was formed using part of this new land. It was the 18th U.S. state.

7. What was the author's purpose for writing this text?
   Ⓐ to entertain with a story
   ● to inform with facts
   Ⓒ to persuade with an argument
   Ⓓ to teach with a process

Page 92

Day 2 | Week 17

Language

Read the sentence. Complete it with a prepositional phrase from the word box. Then circle the preposition.

toward a slide	through the air	at the park

1. Cole and I had so much fun (at) the park yesterday.
2. We felt as if we were flying (through) the air when we were on the swings.
3. After swinging, we made our way (toward) a slide.

Math

Shade the second picture in each pair to show equivalent fractions. Then write the name of each fraction.

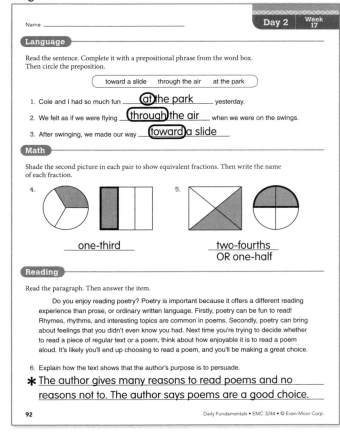

4. one-third

5. two-fourths OR one-half

Reading

Read the paragraph. Then answer the item.

Do you enjoy reading poetry? Poetry is important because it offers a different reading experience than prose, or ordinary written language. Firstly, poetry can be fun to read! Rhymes, rhythms, and interesting topics are common in poems. Secondly, poetry can bring about feelings that you didn't even know you had. Next time you're trying to decide whether to read a piece of regular text or a poem, think about how enjoyable it is to read a poem aloud. It's likely you'll end up choosing to read a poem, and you'll be making a great choice.

6. Explain how the text shows that the author's purpose is to persuade.

* The author gives many reasons to read poems and no reasons not to. The author says poems are a good choice.

Page 93

Day 3 | Week 17

Language

Read the sentence. Rewrite it, replacing the underlined prepositional phrase with a new one.

1. Judy left her glasses <u>beside her book</u>.

* Judy left her glasses on the dresser.

2. Rohan shook the saltshaker <u>over his food</u>.

* Rohan shook the saltshaker at the table.

Math

Find and label the fractions on the number lines. Then circle *yes* or *no* to answer the item.

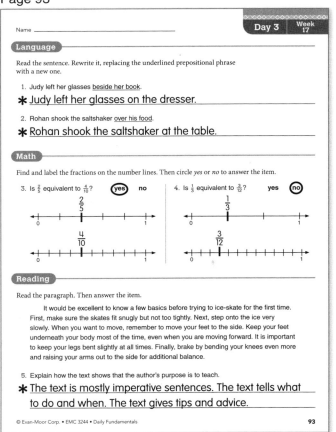

3. Is $\frac{2}{5}$ equivalent to $\frac{4}{10}$? (yes) no

$\frac{2}{5}$

$\frac{4}{10}$

4. Is $\frac{1}{3}$ equivalent to $\frac{3}{12}$? yes (no)

$\frac{1}{3}$

$\frac{3}{12}$

Reading

Read the paragraph. Then answer the item.

It would be excellent to know a few basics before trying to ice-skate for the first time. First, make sure the skates fit snugly but not too tightly. Next, step onto the ice very slowly. When you want to move, remember to move your feet to the side. Keep your feet underneath your body most of the time, even when you are moving forward. It is important to keep your legs bent slightly at all times. Finally, brake by bending your knees even more and raising your arms out to the side for additional balance.

5. Explain how the text shows that the author's purpose is to teach.

* The text is mostly imperative sentences. The text tells what to do and when. The text gives tips and advice.

Page 94

Day 4 | Week 17

Language

Read the sentence. Underline the prepositional phrase. Then circle the object of the preposition.

1. There are hundreds of geese <u>by the (pond)</u>.
2. We can see a huge flock <u>from the (bike trail)</u>.
3. We like to ride our bikes <u>through the (park)</u>.
4. We pass ducks when we cross <u>over the (bridge)</u>.

Math

Write an equivalent fraction.

* 5. $\frac{4}{5}$ $\frac{16}{20}$

* 6. $\frac{9}{12}$ $\frac{3}{4}$

* 7. $\frac{9}{10}$ $\frac{18}{20}$

* 8. $\frac{1}{6}$ $\frac{3}{18}$

* 9. $\frac{1}{2}$ $\frac{50}{100}$

* 10. $\frac{13}{26}$ $\frac{1}{2}$

Reading

Read the paragraph. Then answer the item.

Boom! Crash! Splat! "Oops!" exclaimed Jaya. "There goes another dozen eggs," she thought to herself. Jaya's visit to her aunt's egg ranch had been a disaster so far. In a short two hours, Jaya had managed to break two dozen eggs. Luckily, her aunt was so kind and patient. Aunt Dolma suggested that Jaya take a break from helping out. Jaya thought that was an excellent idea. She felt flustered. She got herself a glass of lemonade and went to sit down. But as soon as she sat, she heard a loud "crunch!" Oh well. There went another dozen!

11. Explain how the text shows that the author's purpose is to entertain.

* There are a lot of entertaining sound words, such as "boom" and "crash." There is humor in the text.

Page 95

Language

Answer the item.

1. What information do prepositions give about nouns in a sentence? Explain your answer.

* Prepositions tell where nouns are located or what position they are in. Prepositions relate nouns to each other.

2. Write a sentence that contains a prepositional phrase. Then circle it.

* Amanda prefers to hike (off the popular trail).

Math

Read the math story and answer the item.

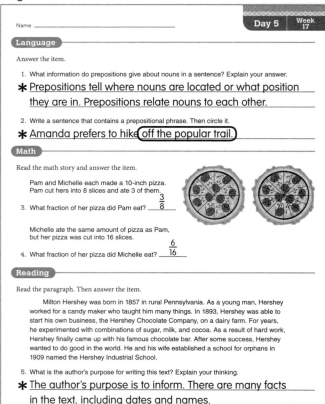

Pam and Michelle each made a 10-inch pizza. Pam cut hers into 8 slices and ate 3 of them.

3. What fraction of her pizza did Pam eat? $\frac{3}{8}$

Michelle ate the same amount of pizza as Pam, but her pizza was cut into 16 slices.

4. What fraction of her pizza did Michelle eat? $\frac{6}{16}$

Reading

Read the paragraph. Then answer the item.

Milton Hershey was born in 1857 in rural Pennsylvania. As a young man, Hershey worked for a candy maker who taught him many things. In 1893, Hershey was able to start his own business, the Hershey Chocolate Company, on a dairy farm. For years, he experimented with combinations of sugar, milk, and cocoa. As a result of hard work, Hershey finally came up with his famous chocolate bar. After some success, Hershey wanted to do good in the world. He and his wife established a school for orphans in 1909 named the Hershey Industrial School.

5. What is the author's purpose for writing this text? Explain your thinking.

* The author's purpose is to inform. There are many facts in the text, including dates and names.

Page 96

Language

Read the sentence. Circle the adverb. Then underline the verb it's describing.

1. Tom (quickly) makes a sandwich.

2. Jenny (selfishly) eats the last cookie.

3. Fa-Chen (quietly) reads her book.

4. Aleeya (rudely) replies to an email.

5. Shanice (cautiously) pours a cup of tea.

6. Shaquille (gently) waters the flowers.

7. Reagan (kindly) holds the door open for me.

Math

Write a mixed number to show what part is shaded.

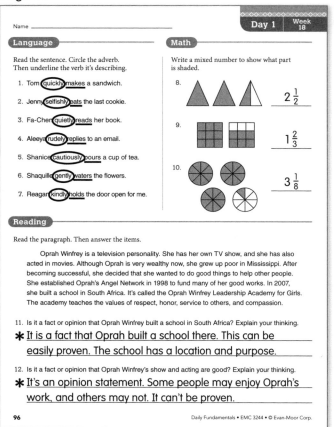

8. $2\frac{1}{2}$

9. $1\frac{2}{3}$

10. $3\frac{1}{8}$

Reading

Read the paragraph. Then answer the items.

Oprah Winfrey is a television personality. She has her own TV show, and she has also acted in movies. Although Oprah is very wealthy now, she grew up poor in Mississippi. After becoming successful, she decided that she wanted to do good things to help other people. She established Oprah's Angel Network in 1998 to fund many of her good works. In 2007, she built a school in South Africa. It's called the Oprah Winfrey Leadership Academy for Girls. The academy teaches the values of respect, honor, service to others, and compassion.

11. Is it a fact or opinion that Oprah Winfrey built a school in South Africa? Explain your thinking.

* It is a fact that Oprah built a school there. This can be easily proven. The school has a location and purpose.

12. Is it a fact or opinion that Oprah Winfrey's show and acting are good? Explain your thinking.

* It's an opinion statement. Some people may enjoy Oprah's work, and others may not. It can't be proven.

Page 97

Language

Read the sentence. Rewrite it, replacing the adverb with a new one.

1. The movie is unexpectedly funny.

* The movie is surprisingly funny.

2. Josh is cheerfully doing his chores.

* Josh is responsibly doing his chores.

Math

Write an improper fraction to show what part is shaded.

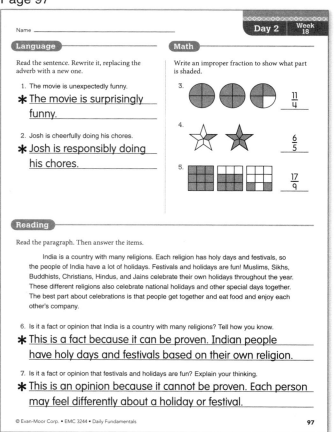

3. $\frac{11}{4}$

4. $\frac{6}{5}$

5. $\frac{17}{9}$

Reading

Read the paragraph. Then answer the items.

India is a country with many religions. Each religion has holy days and festivals, so the people of India have a lot of holidays. Festivals and holidays are fun! Muslims, Sikhs, Buddhists, Christians, Hindus, and Jains celebrate their own holidays throughout the year. These different religions also celebrate national holidays and other special days together. The best part about celebrations is that people get together and eat food and enjoy each other's company.

6. Is it a fact or opinion that India is a country with many religions? Tell how you know.

* This is a fact because it can be proven. Indian people have holy days and festivals based on their own religion.

7. Is it a fact or opinion that festivals and holidays are fun? Explain your thinking.

* This is an opinion because it cannot be proven. Each person may feel differently about a holiday or festival.

Page 98

Language

Write an adverb to describe the given verb.

* 1. sings ___loudly___

* 2. speaks ___honestly___

* 3. ___gracefully___ tiptoes

* 4. dances ___beautifully___

* 5. ___frantically___ searches

* 6. ___carefully___ examines

* 7. ___often___ forgets

* 8. ___angrily___ disagrees

Math

Convert the improper fraction to a mixed number.

9. $\frac{16}{5}$ $3\frac{1}{5}$ 10. $\frac{22}{5}$ $4\frac{2}{5}$

11. $\frac{17}{4}$ $4\frac{1}{4}$ 12. $\frac{19}{6}$ $3\frac{1}{6}$

13. $\frac{9}{2}$ $4\frac{1}{2}$ 14. $\frac{13}{3}$ $4\frac{1}{3}$

15. $\frac{11}{3}$ $3\frac{2}{3}$

Reading

Read the paragraph. Then answer the items.

Exercise benefits people of all ages. There are many different ways to exercise. Some exercises, such as those using weights, focus on strengthening muscles. Other exercises are cardiovascular, which means they focus on getting the heart pumping. Some cardiovascular exercises include jogging and doing jumping jacks. Some people prefer to exercise privately in their homes, while others enjoy taking fitness classes and going to the gym. There are also different exercise disciplines, such as yoga, Pilates, and martial arts.

16. Write your own opinion about the text.

* I think the text was interesting and helpful.

17. Write one additional fact that you know about exercise. Then list any additional types of exercise that you know about.

* Exercise can support healthy joints and bones. cycling, jumping rope, kickboxing, dancing

Page 99

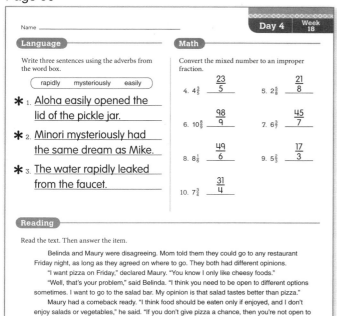

Day 4 | **Week 18**

Name _____

Language

Write three sentences using the adverbs from the word box.

rapidly   mysteriously   easily

✳ 1. Aloha easily opened the lid of the pickle jar.

✳ 2. Minori mysteriously had the same dream as Mike.

✳ 3. The water rapidly leaked from the faucet.

Math

Convert the mixed number to an improper fraction.

4. $4\frac{3}{5}$ — $\frac{23}{5}$

5. $2\frac{5}{8}$ — $\frac{21}{8}$

6. $10\frac{8}{9}$ — $\frac{98}{9}$

7. $6\frac{3}{7}$ — $\frac{45}{7}$

8. $8\frac{1}{6}$ — $\frac{49}{6}$

9. $5\frac{2}{3}$ — $\frac{17}{3}$

10. $7\frac{3}{4}$ — $\frac{31}{4}$

Reading

Read the text. Then answer the item.

Belinda and Maury were disagreeing. Mom told them they could go to any restaurant Friday night, as long as they agreed on where to go. They both had different opinions.

"I want pizza on Friday," declared Maury. "You know I only like cheesy foods."

"Well, that's your problem," said Belinda. "I think you need to be open to different options sometimes. I want to go to the salad bar. My opinion is that salad tastes better than pizza."

Maury had a comeback ready. "I think food should be eaten only if enjoyed, and I don't enjoy salads or vegetables," he said. "If you don't give pizza a chance, then you're not open to other options, either." Maury thought he'd made a good point, and Belinda would have to agree.

"Well, I usually don't give in to others," sighed Belinda, "but I will try it your way this time."

"Sweet," said Maury. "Next time, I'll try salad. Maybe my opinion about it will change."

11. Explain how opinions play a role in this text.

✳ Opinions caused conflict and led to a solution in the text. Maury and Belinda started out with different opinions. But they both admitted that opinions can sometimes change.

© Evan-Moor Corp. • EMC 3244 • Daily Fundamentals   99

Page 100

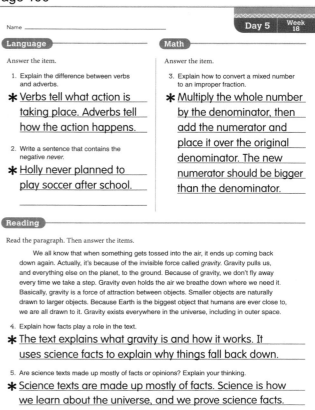

Day 5 | **Week 18**

Name _____

Language

Answer the item.

1. Explain the difference between verbs and adverbs.

✳ Verbs tell what action is taking place. Adverbs tell how the action happens.

2. Write a sentence that contains the negative *never*.

✳ Holly never planned to play soccer after school.

Math

Answer the item.

3. Explain how to convert a mixed number to an improper fraction.

✳ Multiply the whole number by the denominator, then add the numerator and place it over the original denominator. The new numerator should be bigger than the denominator.

Reading

Read the paragraph. Then answer the items.

We all know that when something gets tossed into the air, it ends up coming back down again. Actually, it's because of the invisible force called *gravity*. Gravity pulls us, and everything else on the planet, to the ground. Because of gravity, we don't fly away every time we take a step. Gravity even holds the air we breathe down where we need it. Basically, gravity is a force of attraction between objects. Smaller objects are naturally drawn to larger objects. Because Earth is the biggest object that humans are ever close to, we are all drawn to it. Gravity exists everywhere in the universe, including in outer space.

4. Explain how facts play a role in the text.

✳ The text explains what gravity is and how it works. It uses science facts to explain why things fall back down.

5. Are science texts made up mostly of facts or opinions? Explain your thinking.

✳ Science texts are made up mostly of facts. Science is how we learn about the universe, and we prove science facts.

100   Daily Fundamentals • EMC 3244 • © Evan-Moor Corp.

Page 101

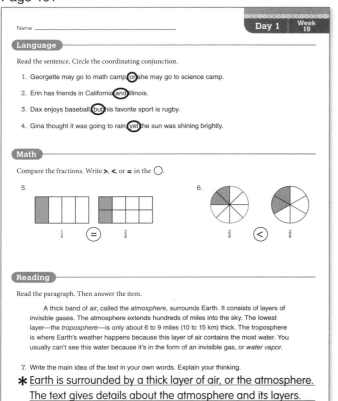

Day 1 | **Week 19**

Name _____

Language

Read the sentence. Circle the coordinating conjunction.

1. Georgette may go to math camp, (or) she may go to science camp.

2. Erin has friends in California (and) Illinois.

3. Dax enjoys baseball, (but) his favorite sport is rugby.

4. Gina thought it was going to rain, (yet) the sun was shining brightly.

Math

Compare the fractions. Write **>**, **<**, or **=** in the ◯.

5. $\frac{1}{4}$ ◯(=) $\frac{2}{8}$

6. $\frac{2}{8}$ ◯(<) $\frac{2}{6}$

Reading

Read the paragraph. Then answer the item.

A thick band of air, called the *atmosphere,* surrounds Earth. It consists of layers of invisible gases. The atmosphere extends hundreds of miles into the sky. The lowest layer—the *troposphere*—is only about 6 to 9 miles (10 to 15 km) thick. The troposphere is where Earth's weather happens because this layer of air contains the most water. You usually can't see this water because it's in the form of an invisible gas, or *water vapor*.

7. Write the main idea of the text in your own words. Explain your thinking.

✳ Earth is surrounded by a thick layer of air, or the atmosphere. The text gives details about the atmosphere and its layers.

© Evan-Moor Corp. • EMC 3244 • Daily Fundamentals   101

Page 102

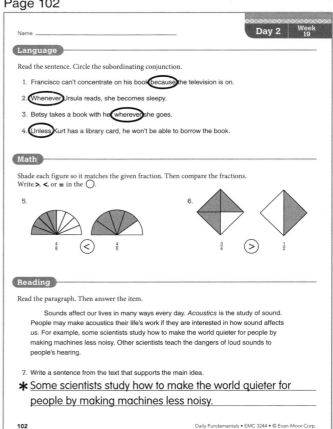

Day 2 | **Week 19**

Name _____

Language

Read the sentence. Circle the subordinating conjunction.

1. Francisco can't concentrate on his book (because) the television is on.

2. (Whenever) Ursula reads, she becomes sleepy.

3. Betsy takes a book with her (wherever) she goes.

4. (Unless) Kurt has a library card, he won't be able to borrow the book.

Math

Shade each figure so it matches the given fraction. Then compare the fractions. Write **>**, **<**, or **=** in the ◯.

5. $\frac{4}{8}$ ◯(<) $\frac{4}{6}$

6. $\frac{4}{10}$ ◯(>) $\frac{1}{2}$

Reading

Read the paragraph. Then answer the item.

Sounds affect our lives in many ways every day. *Acoustics* is the study of sound. People may make acoustics their life's work if they are interested in how sound affects us. For example, some scientists study how to make the world quieter for people by making machines less noisy. Other scientists teach the dangers of loud sounds to people's hearing.

7. Write a sentence from the text that supports the main idea.

✳ Some scientists study how to make the world quieter for people by making machines less noisy.

102   Daily Fundamentals • EMC 3244 • © Evan-Moor Corp.

Page 103

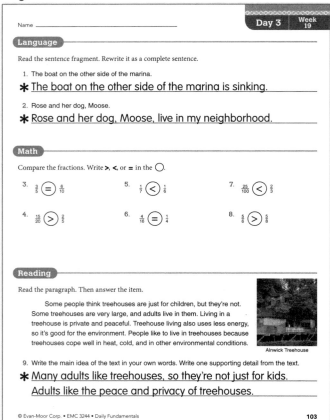

Name _____

Language

Read the sentence fragment. Rewrite it as a complete sentence.

1. The boat on the other side of the marina.

✱ The boat on the other side of the marina is sinking.

2. Rose and her dog, Moose.

✱ Rose and her dog, Moose, live in my neighborhood.

Math

Compare the fractions. Write >, <, or = in the ○.

3. $\frac{5}{5}$ = $\frac{8}{10}$ 5. $\frac{1}{7}$ < $\frac{1}{6}$ 7. $\frac{25}{100}$ < $\frac{2}{3}$

4. $\frac{15}{20}$ > $\frac{2}{5}$ 6. $\frac{4}{16}$ = $\frac{1}{4}$ 8. $\frac{5}{6}$ > $\frac{5}{8}$

Reading

Read the paragraph. Then answer the item.

Some people think treehouses are just for children, but they're not. Some treehouses are very large, and adults live in them. Living in a treehouse is private and peaceful. Treehouse living also uses less energy, so it's good for the environment. People like to live in treehouses because treehouses cope well in heat, cold, and in other environmental conditions.

Alnwick Treehouse

9. Write the main idea of the text in your own words. Write one supporting detail from the text.

✱ Many adults like treehouses, so they're not just for kids. Adults like the peace and privacy of treehouses.

Page 104

Name _____

Language

Read the run-on sentence. Correct it by dividing it into two simple sentences. Write the new sentences.

1. Drew is taking a kickboxing class he goes one day a week.

Drew is taking a kickboxing class. He goes one day a week.

2. Evan visits his grandma in Wyoming she is 92 years old.

Evan visits his grandma in Wyoming. She is 92 years old.

Math

Compare the fractions and write them in order from smallest to largest.

3. $\frac{4}{5}$ $\frac{1}{2}$ $\frac{25}{100}$ $\frac{7}{10}$

$\frac{25}{100}$ $\frac{1}{2}$ $\frac{7}{10}$ $\frac{4}{5}$

Reading

Read the paragraph. Then answer the item.

Two Degrees Food is a company that fights to end worldwide hunger while selling a healthy product. Lauren Walters and Will Hauser started the company in 2011. They wanted to create a healthy energy bar, not a candy bar. Their bar is made of fruit, nuts, and seeds. For every bar sold, Two Degrees Food donates a meal to a hungry child in a developing country in Asia or Africa.

4. Explain how the details in the text support the main idea.

✱ The text explains what Two Degrees Food does. It tells about their healthy energy bar and the meals they donate to children.

Page 105

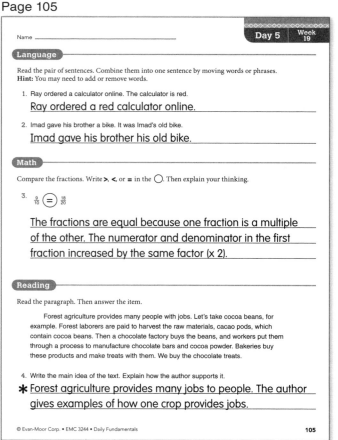

Name _____

Language

Read the pair of sentences. Combine them into one sentence by moving words or phrases. **Hint:** You may need to add or remove words.

1. Ray ordered a calculator online. The calculator is red.

Ray ordered a red calculator online.

2. Imad gave his brother a bike. It was Imad's old bike.

Imad gave his brother his old bike.

Math

Compare the fractions. Write >, <, or = in the ○. Then explain your thinking.

3. $\frac{9}{10}$ = $\frac{18}{20}$

The fractions are equal because one fraction is a multiple of the other. The numerator and denominator in the first fraction increased by the same factor (x 2).

Reading

Read the paragraph. Then answer the item.

Forest agriculture provides many people with jobs. Let's take cocoa beans, for example. Forest laborers are paid to harvest the raw materials, cacao pods, which contain cocoa beans. Then a chocolate factory buys the beans, and workers put them through a process to manufacture chocolate bars and cocoa powder. Bakeries buy these products and make treats with them. We buy the chocolate treats.

4. Write the main idea of the text. Explain how the author supports it.

✱ Forest agriculture provides many jobs to people. The author gives examples of how one crop provides jobs.

Page 106

Name _____

Language

Read the sentence. Rewrite it, making the underlined noun possessive.

1. The squirrel burrow went deep into the ground.

The squirrel's burrow went deep into the ground.

2. The student lunch was packed in a red bag.

The student's lunch was packed in a red bag.

Math

First, write each fraction as a sum of unit fractions. Then write the sum in a different way.

3. $\frac{5}{6}$ = $\frac{1}{6} + \frac{1}{6} + \frac{1}{6} + \frac{1}{6} + \frac{1}{6}$ ✱ $\frac{5}{6}$ = $\frac{3}{6} + \frac{2}{6}$

4. $\frac{3}{4}$ = $\frac{1}{4} + \frac{1}{4} + \frac{1}{4}$ ✱ $\frac{3}{4}$ = $\frac{1}{4} + \frac{2}{4}$

Reading

Read the paragraph. Then answer the item.

Claire sat in her backyard, enjoying the sunny afternoon. She often hung out there so she could be alone. She listened to the birds singing. She admired the colorful wildflowers. Suddenly, she heard her little brother, Jack, yelling in the distance. He was always so loud. Just then, gray clouds moved in front of the sun, covering the yard in a cold, dark shadow. Jack came around the corner, yelling, stick in hand.

5. How do the sun and clouds relate to what happened in the text? Explain your thinking.

✱ Claire was happy and the sun was out when she was alone. Then she heard Jack yelling, and dark clouds covered the sun.

Page 107

Name _____

Day 2 | Week 20

Language

Read the sentence. Insert a comma where it is needed.

1. The label on the sleeping bag reads, "Keep away from fire and heat."

2. Gia read the first sentence of the paragraph, which said, "Some days are truly memorable."

3. The sign by the pool cautioned, "Running or jogging near the pool is prohibited."

4. The food label reads, "This product contains milk and peanuts."

Math

Find two different ways to write the given number as a sum of fractions. Draw a model to help you.

Models will vary.

5. Write 1 as a sum of fifths.

$\frac{1}{5} + \frac{1}{5} + \frac{1}{5} + \frac{1}{5} + \frac{1}{5}$ ✱ $\frac{1}{5} + \frac{4}{5}$

6. Write 2 as a sum of thirds.

$\frac{1}{3} + \frac{1}{3} + \frac{1}{3} + \frac{1}{3} + \frac{1}{3} + \frac{1}{3}$ ✱ $\frac{2}{3} + \frac{4}{3}$

Reading

Read the paragraph. Then answer the item.

Ted whistled to himself as he carried the trash bags out to the garbage cans. He was so glad that he had trash duty instead of basement duty. That dark, dank basement gave him the creeps. He looked up at the blue sky, put on his bike helmet, and checked his pocket for his mom's grocery list. All of a sudden, he heard his dad calling his name from the web-covered basement. "Ted, there's a leak down here, can you help me?"

7. Did the text give a clue that Ted would end up going into the basement? Explain your answer.

✱ Yes, because it said that Ted did not like going into the basement and how glad he was that he did not have to.

Page 108

Name _____

Day 3 | Week 20

Language

Read the sentence. Rewrite it to correct the punctuation errors.

1. How "can I find the information I need"? Maya asked.

"How can I find the information I need?" Maya asked.

2. This game is complicated, Craig stated.

"This game is complicated," Craig stated.

Math

Find a common denominator for the pair of fractions. Then add the fractions. Show your work.

3. $\frac{2}{5} + \frac{8}{15} =$ $\frac{6}{15} + \frac{8}{15} = \frac{14}{15}$

4. $\frac{1}{3} + \frac{1}{2} =$ $\frac{2}{6} + \frac{3}{6} = \frac{5}{6}$

5. $\frac{5}{12} + \frac{2}{6} =$ $\frac{5}{12} + \frac{4}{12} = \frac{9}{12}$

Accept equivalent fractions.

6. $\frac{3}{4} + \frac{1}{20} =$ $\frac{15}{20} + \frac{1}{20} = \frac{16}{20}$

Reading

Read the paragraph. Then answer the item.

It was a dark, cloudy day. Tyler was nervous about his first day at the new school. "Why did we have to move?" he thought. He felt invisible as he entered the school. He walked alone through a stuffy, dim hallway, looking for his classroom. Then he saw a brightly lit, colorfully decorated room. He wondered if this was his class and walked faster. As he got closer, he saw a poster on the door that said, "Welcome, Tyler!"

7. How does lighting relate to what happened in the text? Explain your thinking.

✱ It was dark and cloudy, and the hall was dim when Tyler was unhappy. His mood changed when he saw the bright class.

Page 109

Name _____

Day 4 | Week 20

Language

Read the sentence. Rewrite it using quotation marks where they are needed.

1. Becca can play Buffalo Gals very well on the piano.

Becca can play "Buffalo Gals" very well on the piano.

2. Tory loves the rhymes in The Walrus and the Carpenter.

Tory loves the rhymes in "The Walrus and the Carpenter."

Math

Find a common denominator for the pair of fractions and then subtract. Show your work.

3. $\frac{3}{4} - \frac{5}{16} =$ $\frac{12}{16} - \frac{5}{16} = \frac{7}{16}$

4. $\frac{3}{5} - \frac{1}{2} =$ $\frac{6}{10} - \frac{5}{10} = \frac{1}{10}$

5. $\frac{8}{9} - \frac{2}{3} =$ $\frac{8}{9} - \frac{6}{9} = \frac{2}{9}$

Accept equivalent fractions.

6. $\frac{11}{14} - \frac{3}{7} =$ $\frac{11}{14} - \frac{6}{14} = \frac{5}{14}$

Reading

Read the paragraph. Then answer the item.

Walking to school, Tara thought she saw her grandma's dog, Sputnik, across the street. "No, can't be," she thought. "Sputnik lives with Grandma four hours away." Later, Tara thought she saw Sputnik outside her classroom window. She knew she was imagining things. On her walk home, a car stopped at a stop sign. Inside the car, she saw Sputnik. Tara raced home. To her surprise, Grandma and Sputnik were visiting!

7. Is there foreshadowing in the text? Explain your thinking.

✱ Yes. The foreshadowing was when Tara kept imagining Sputnik. Those were clues. She later saw the real Sputnik.

Page 110

Name _____

Day 5 | Week 20

Language

Read the paragraph. Underline the titles of books, movies, plays, television shows, newspapers, and magazines.

1. Jen and Tuck were going to the movie theater to see Woman of Mystery. It was based on a book called Lady Spy. The movie was getting great reviews in the New City Times. Jen had read an article in Entertainment Magazine that gave behind-the-scenes details about making the movie. It made her want to see the movie even more. Tuck was also willing to see the movie Fun Class.

Math

Add or subtract. Write the answer as a whole number or a mixed number.

2. $2\frac{2}{3}$
$+ 4\frac{1}{3}$
$\overline{7}$

3. $9\frac{5}{6}$
$- 3\frac{2}{7}$
$\overline{6\frac{3}{7}}$

4. $9\frac{6}{8}$
$+ 7\frac{1}{8}$
$\overline{16\frac{7}{8}}$

5. $10\frac{5}{6}$
$- 4\frac{5}{6}$
$\overline{6}$

6. $5\frac{3}{12}$
$+ 1\frac{5}{12}$
$\overline{6\frac{8}{12}}$

7. $11\frac{10}{11}$
$- 5\frac{8}{11}$
$\overline{6\frac{2}{11}}$

Reading

Read the paragraph. Then answer the item.

"We can't be late," Mom said for the hundredth time. Our whole family was in the van on our way to the airport. All five of us were flying to Oregon for vacation. The fog was thick and the traffic was bad. "We can't miss the flight," Mom said. Dad was driving, and he sighed deeply. The van was barely inching along. An hour later, we arrived at the airport. To our surprise, planes were sitting on the runway, delayed because of fog.

8. Did foreshadowing make the text more or less suspenseful? Explain your thinking.

✱ It made the text more suspenseful. The mom's focus on being late made me expect them to be late but hope not.

Page 111

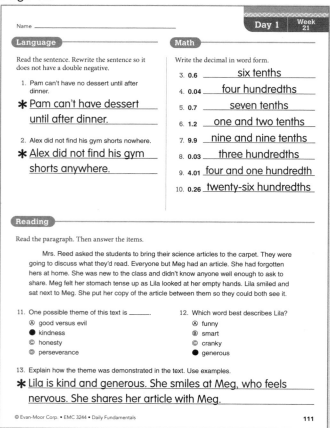

Name _____

Day 1 | Week 21

Language

Read the sentence. Rewrite the sentence so it does not have a double negative.

1. Pam can't have no dessert until after dinner.

✱ Pam can't have dessert until after dinner.

2. Alex did not find his gym shorts nowhere.

✱ Alex did not find his gym shorts anywhere.

Math

Write the decimal in word form.

3. 0.6 ___six tenths___

4. 0.04 ___four hundredths___

5. 0.7 ___seven tenths___

6. 1.2 ___one and two tenths___

7. 9.9 ___nine and nine tenths___

8. 0.03 ___three hundredths___

9. 4.01 ___four and one hundredth___

10. 0.26 ___twenty-six hundredths___

Reading

Read the paragraph. Then answer the items.

Mrs. Reed asked the students to bring their science articles to the carpet. They were going to discuss what they'd read. Everyone but Meg had an article. She had forgotten hers at home. She was new to the class and didn't know anyone well enough to ask to share. Meg felt her stomach tense up as Lila looked at her empty hands. Lila smiled and sat next to Meg. She put her copy of the article between them so they could both see it.

11. One possible theme of this text is _____.
   Ⓐ good versus evil
   ● kindness
   Ⓒ honesty
   Ⓓ perseverance

12. Which word best describes Lila?
   Ⓐ funny
   Ⓑ smart
   Ⓒ cranky
   ● generous

13. Explain how the theme was demonstrated in the text. Use examples.

✱ Lila is kind and generous. She smiles at Meg, who feels nervous. She shares her article with Meg.

© Evan-Moor Corp. • EMC 3244 • Daily Fundamentals   111

Page 112

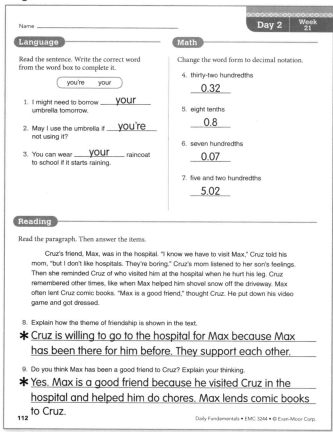

Name _____

Day 2 | Week 21

Language

Read the sentence. Write the correct word from the word box to complete it.

[you're   your]

1. I might need to borrow ___your___ umbrella tomorrow.

2. May I use the umbrella if ___you're___ not using it?

3. You can wear ___your___ raincoat to school if it starts raining.

Math

Change the word form to decimal notation.

4. thirty-two hundredths
   ___0.32___

5. eight tenths
   ___0.8___

6. seven hundredths
   ___0.07___

7. five and two hundredths
   ___5.02___

Reading

Read the paragraph. Then answer the items.

Cruz's friend, Max, was in the hospital. "I know we have to visit Max," Cruz told his mom, "but I don't like hospitals. They're boring." Cruz's mom listened to her son's feelings. Then she reminded Cruz of who visited him at the hospital when he hurt his leg. Cruz remembered other times, like when Max helped him shovel snow off the driveway. Max often lent Cruz comic books. "Max is a good friend," thought Cruz. He put down his video game and got dressed.

8. Explain how the theme of friendship is shown in the text.

✱ Cruz is willing to go to the hospital for Max because Max has been there for him before. They support each other.

9. Do you think Max has been a good friend to Cruz? Explain your thinking.

✱ Yes. Max is a good friend because he visited Cruz in the hospital and helped him do chores. Max lends comic books to Cruz.

112   Daily Fundamentals • EMC 3244 • © Evan-Moor Corp.

Page 113

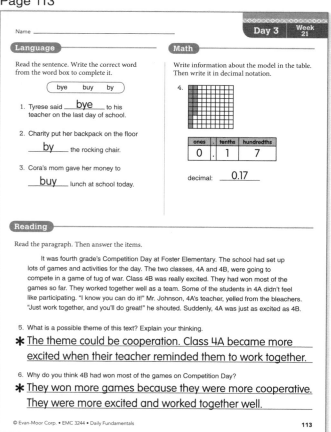

Name _____

Day 3 | Week 21

Language

Read the sentence. Write the correct word from the word box to complete it.

[bye   buy   by]

1. Tyrese said ___bye___ to his teacher on the last day of school.

2. Charity put her backpack on the floor ___by___ the rocking chair.

3. Cora's mom gave her money to ___buy___ lunch at school today.

Math

Write information about the model in the table. Then write it in decimal notation.

4.

ones	.	tenths	hundredths
0	.	1	7

decimal: ___0.17___

Reading

Read the paragraph. Then answer the items.

It was fourth grade's Competition Day at Foster Elementary. The school had set up lots of games and activities for the day. The two classes, 4A and 4B, were going to compete in a game of tug of war. Class 4B was really excited. They had won most of the games so far. They worked together well as a team. Some of the students in 4A didn't feel like participating. "I know you can do it!" Mr. Johnson, 4A's teacher, yelled from the bleachers. "Just work together, and you'll be great!" he shouted. Suddenly, 4A was just as excited as 4B.

5. What is a possible theme of this text? Explain your thinking.

✱ The theme could be cooperation. Class 4A became more excited when their teacher reminded them to work together.

6. Why do you think 4B had won most of the games on Competition Day?

✱ They won more games because they were more cooperative. They were more excited and worked together well.

© Evan-Moor Corp. • EMC 3244 • Daily Fundamentals   113

Page 114

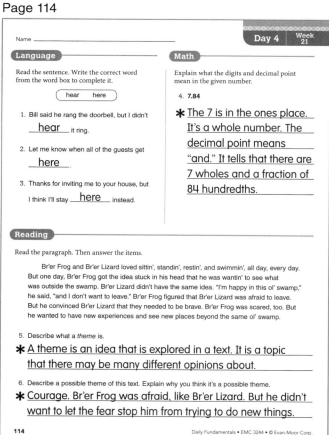

Name _____

Day 4 | Week 21

Language

Read the sentence. Write the correct word from the word box to complete it.

[hear   here]

1. Bill said he rang the doorbell, but I didn't ___hear___ it ring.

2. Let me know when all of the guests get ___here___.

3. Thanks for inviting me to your house, but I think I'll stay ___here___ instead.

Math

Explain what the digits and decimal point mean in the given number.

4. 7.84

✱ The 7 is in the ones place. It's a whole number. The decimal point means "and." It tells that there are 7 wholes and a fraction of 84 hundredths.

Reading

Read the paragraph. Then answer the items.

Br'er Frog and Br'er Lizard loved sittin', standin', restin', and swimmin', all day, every day. But one day, Br'er Frog got the idea stuck in his head that he was wantin' to see what was outside the swamp. Br'er Lizard didn't have the same idea. "I'm happy in this ol' swamp," he said, "and I don't want to leave." Br'er Frog figured that Br'er Lizard was afraid to leave. But he convinced Br'er Lizard that they needed to be brave. Br'er Frog was scared, too. But he wanted to have new experiences and see new places beyond the same ol' swamp.

5. Describe what a *theme* is.

✱ A theme is an idea that is explored in a text. It is a topic that there may be many different opinions about.

6. Describe a possible theme of this text. Explain why you think it's a possible theme.

✱ Courage. Br'er Frog was afraid, like Br'er Lizard. But he didn't want to let the fear stop him from trying to do new things.

114   Daily Fundamentals • EMC 3244 • © Evan-Moor Corp.

Page 115

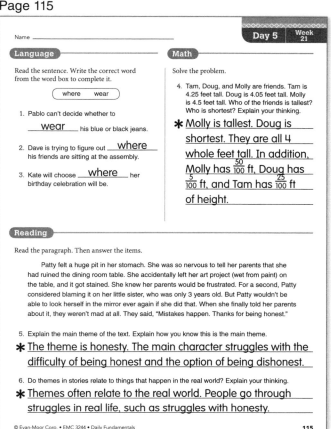

Name _____

Day 5 | **Week 21**

Language

Read the sentence. Write the correct word from the word box to complete it.

[where   wear]

1. Pablo can't decide whether to ___wear___ his blue or black jeans.

2. Dave is trying to figure out ___where___ his friends are sitting at the assembly.

3. Kate will choose ___where___ her birthday celebration will be.

Math

Solve the problem.

4. Tam, Doug, and Molly are friends. Tam is 4.25 feet tall. Doug is 4.05 feet tall. Molly is 4.5 feet tall. Who of the friends is tallest? Who is shortest? Explain your thinking.

* Molly is tallest. Doug is shortest. They are all 4 whole feet tall. In addition, Molly has $\frac{50}{100}$ ft, Doug has $\frac{5}{100}$ ft, and Tam has $\frac{25}{100}$ ft of height.

Reading

Read the paragraph. Then answer the items.

Patty felt a huge pit in her stomach. She was so nervous to tell her parents that she had ruined the dining room table. She accidentally left her art project (wet from paint) on the table, and it got stained. She knew her parents would be frustrated. For a second, Patty considered blaming it on her little sister, who was only 3 years old. But Patty wouldn't be able to look herself in the mirror ever again if she did that. When she finally told her parents about it, they weren't mad at all. They said, "Mistakes happen. Thanks for being honest."

5. Explain the main theme of the text. Explain how you know this is the main theme.

* The theme is honesty. The main character struggles with the difficulty of being honest and the option of being dishonest.

6. Do themes in stories relate to things that happen in the real world? Explain your thinking.

* Themes often relate to the real world. People go through struggles in real life, such as struggles with honesty.

Page 116

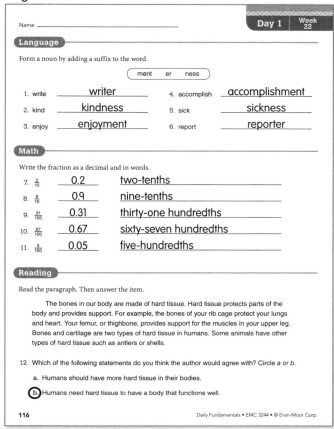

Name _____

Day 1 | **Week 22**

Language

Form a noun by adding a suffix to the word.

[ment   er   ness]

1. write ___writer___
2. kind ___kindness___
3. enjoy ___enjoyment___
4. accomplish ___accomplishment___
5. sick ___sickness___
6. report ___reporter___

Math

Write the fraction as a decimal and in words.

7. $\frac{2}{10}$ ___0.2___ two-tenths
8. $\frac{9}{10}$ ___0.9___ nine-tenths
9. $\frac{31}{100}$ ___0.31___ thirty-one hundredths
10. $\frac{67}{100}$ ___0.67___ sixty-seven hundredths
11. $\frac{5}{100}$ ___0.05___ five-hundredths

Reading

Read the paragraph. Then answer the item.

The bones in our body are made of hard tissue. Hard tissue protects parts of the body and provides support. For example, the bones of your rib cage protect your lungs and heart. Your femur, or thighbone, provides support for the muscles in your upper leg. Bones and cartilage are two types of hard tissue in humans. Some animals have other types of hard tissue such as antlers or shells.

12. Which of the following statements do you think the author would agree with? Circle *a* or *b*.

a. Humans should have more hard tissue in their bodies.

(b.) Humans need hard tissue to have a body that functions well.

Page 117

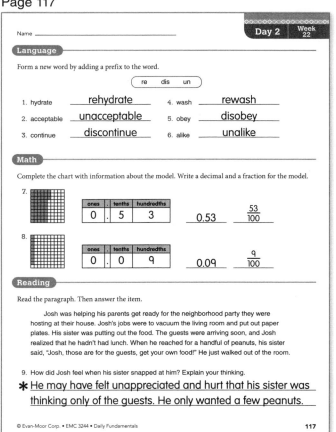

Name _____

Day 2 | **Week 22**

Language

Form a new word by adding a prefix to the word.

[re   dis   un]

1. hydrate ___rehydrate___
2. acceptable ___unacceptable___
3. continue ___discontinue___
4. wash ___rewash___
5. obey ___disobey___
6. alike ___unalike___

Math

Complete the chart with information about the model. Write a decimal and a fraction for the model.

7.

ones	.	tenths	hundredths
0	.	5	3

0.53 $\frac{53}{100}$

8.

ones	.	tenths	hundredths
0	.	0	9

0.09 $\frac{9}{100}$

Reading

Read the paragraph. Then answer the item.

Josh was helping his parents get ready for the neighborhood party they were hosting at their house. Josh's jobs were to vacuum the living room and put out paper plates. His sister was putting out the food. The guests were arriving soon, and Josh realized that he hadn't had lunch. When he reached for a handful of peanuts, his sister said, "Josh, those are for the guests, get your own food!" He just walked out of the room.

9. How did Josh feel when his sister snapped at him? Explain your thinking.

* He may have felt unappreciated and hurt that his sister was thinking only of the guests. He only wanted a few peanuts.

Page 118

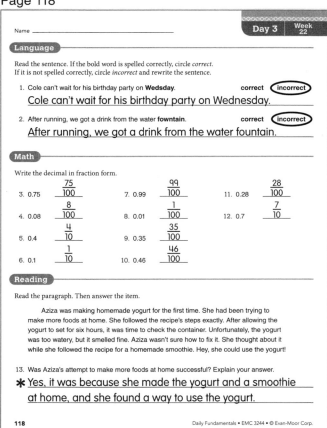

Name _____

Day 3 | **Week 22**

Language

Read the sentence. If the bold word is spelled correctly, circle *correct*. If it is not spelled correctly, circle *incorrect* and rewrite the sentence.

1. Cole can't wait for his birthday party on **Wedsday**.   correct   (incorrect)

Cole can't wait for his birthday party on Wednesday.

2. After running, we got a drink from the water **fowntain**.   correct   (incorrect)

After running, we got a drink from the water fountain.

Math

Write the decimal in fraction form.

3. 0.75 → $\frac{75}{100}$
4. 0.08 → $\frac{8}{100}$
5. 0.4 → $\frac{4}{10}$
6. 0.1 → $\frac{1}{10}$
7. 0.99 → $\frac{99}{100}$
8. 0.01 → $\frac{1}{100}$
9. 0.35 → $\frac{35}{100}$
10. 0.46 → $\frac{46}{100}$
11. 0.28 → $\frac{28}{100}$
12. 0.7 → $\frac{7}{10}$

Reading

Read the paragraph. Then answer the item.

Aziza was making homemade yogurt for the first time. She had been trying to make more foods at home. She followed the recipe's steps exactly. After allowing the yogurt to set for six hours, it was time to check the container. Unfortunately, the yogurt was too watery, but it smelled fine. Aziza wasn't sure how to fix it. She thought about it while she followed the recipe for a homemade smoothie. Hey, she could use the yogurt!

13. Was Aziza's attempt to make more foods at home successful? Explain your answer.

* Yes, it was because she made the yogurt and a smoothie at home, and she found a way to use the yogurt.

Page 119

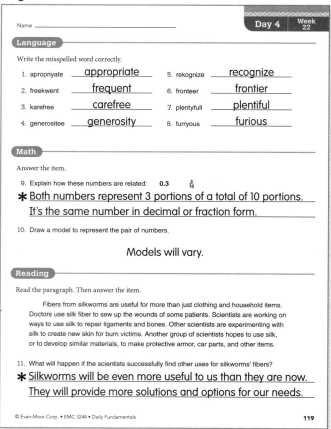

Name _____ Day 4 | Week 22

Language

Write the misspelled word correctly.

1. apropriyate — **appropriate**
2. freekwent — **frequent**
3. karefree — **carefree**
4. generositee — **generosity**
5. rekognize — **recognize**
6. fronteer — **frontier**
7. plentyfull — **plentiful**
8. furryous — **furious**

Math

Answer the item.

9. Explain how these numbers are related: 0.3 $\frac{3}{10}$

* **Both numbers represent 3 portions of a total of 10 portions. It's the same number in decimal or fraction form.**

10. Draw a model to represent the pair of numbers.

Models will vary.

Reading

Read the paragraph. Then answer the item.

Fibers from silkworms are useful for more than just clothing and household items. Doctors use silk fiber to sew up the wounds of some patients. Scientists are working on ways to use silk to repair ligaments and bones. Other scientists are experimenting with silk to create new skin for burn victims. Another group of scientists hopes to use silk, or to develop similar materials, to make protective armor, car parts, and other items.

11. What will happen if the scientists successfully find other uses for silkworms' fibers?

* **Silkworms will be even more useful to us than they are now. They will provide more solutions and options for our needs.**

© Evan-Moor Corp. • EMC 3244 • Daily Fundamentals   119

Page 120

Name _____ Day 5 | Week 22

Language

Read the paragraph. Cross out any word that is spelled incorrectly. Rewrite the word correctly above it.

1. Marie had a difficult day. First, she woke up late and almost missed the school bus. At school, she found math challenging. She just figured that she needed more practice with decimals. But the worst part of Marie's day was when she realized that she'd forgotten her lunch. She had to go to the school office to call her mom to bring lunch. Luckily, Marie's day got better after lunch.

(corrections: difficult, challenging, figured, practice, decimals, forgotten, office, Luckily)

Math

Solve the problem. Write the answer as a mixed number. Then convert it to decimal notation.

2. Mrs. Royple made lasagna for a dinner party. In addition to herself, her husband, her three kids, and her sister, Mrs. Royple invited the Hendersons, a family of five, and the Turlocks, a family of three. Each person ate $\frac{25}{100}$ of one tray of lasagna. How many trays of lasagna did they eat in all?

mixed number: **$3\frac{1}{2}$ trays**   decimal: **3.5 trays**

Reading

Read the paragraph. Then answer the item.

The Onondaga cave ecosystem in Missouri is home to many species. The bats there feed on insects. Salamanders and cavefish are predators that feed on tiny organisms. Cave spiders eat insects. Millipedes, centipedes, and crustaceans feed on tiny organisms and funguses. Cave beetles eat the eggs of cave crickets. The cave food web is also sometimes called a *cave food pyramid*. Decomposers are at the bottom.

3. How would the Onondaga cave ecosystem be different if all the tiny organisms disappeared?

* **The salamanders and cavefish would probably decrease or die because they depend on tiny organisms for food.**

120   Daily Fundamentals • EMC 3244 • © Evan-Moor Corp.

Page 121

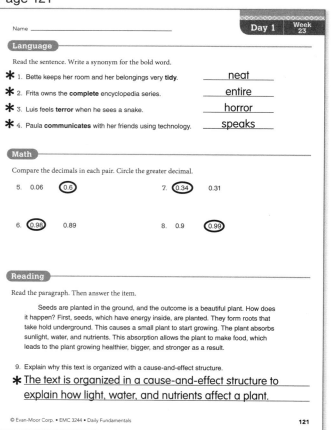

Name _____ Day 1 | Week 23

Language

Read the sentence. Write a synonym for the bold word.

* 1. Bette keeps her room and her belongings very **tidy**. — neat
* 2. Frita owns the **complete** encyclopedia series. — entire
* 3. Luis feels **terror** when he sees a snake. — horror
* 4. Paula **communicates** with her friends using technology. — speaks

Math

Compare the decimals in each pair. Circle the greater decimal.

5. 0.06 (0.6)   7. (0.34) 0.31
6. (0.98) 0.89   8. 0.9 (0.99)

Reading

Read the paragraph. Then answer the item.

Seeds are planted in the ground, and the outcome is a beautiful plant. How does it happen? First, seeds, which have energy inside, are planted. They form roots that take hold underground. This causes a small plant to start growing. The plant absorbs sunlight, water, and nutrients. This absorption allows the plant to make food, which leads to the plant growing healthier, bigger, and stronger as a result.

9. Explain why this text is organized with a cause-and-effect structure.

* **The text is organized in a cause-and-effect structure to explain how light, water, and nutrients affect a plant.**

© Evan-Moor Corp. • EMC 3244 • Daily Fundamentals   121

Page 122

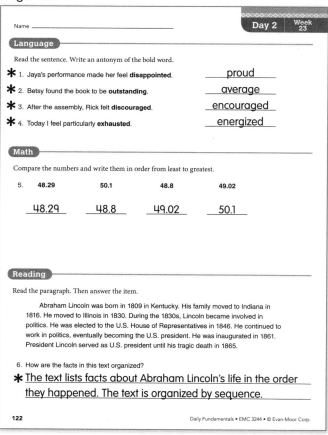

Name _____ Day 2 | Week 23

Language

Read the sentence. Write an antonym of the bold word.

* 1. Jaya's performance made her feel **disappointed**. — proud
* 2. Betsy found the book to be **outstanding**. — average
* 3. After the assembly, Rick felt **discouraged**. — encouraged
* 4. Today I feel particularly **exhausted**. — energized

Math

Compare the numbers and write them in order from least to greatest.

5. 48.29   50.1   48.8   49.02

48.29   48.8   49.02   50.1

Reading

Read the paragraph. Then answer the item.

Abraham Lincoln was born in 1809 in Kentucky. His family moved to Indiana in 1816. He moved to Illinois in 1830. During the 1830s, Lincoln became involved in politics. He was elected to the U.S. House of Representatives in 1846. He continued to work in politics, eventually becoming the U.S. president. He was inaugurated in 1861. President Lincoln served as U.S. president until his tragic death in 1865.

6. How are the facts in this text organized?

* **The text lists facts about Abraham Lincoln's life in the order they happened. The text is organized by sequence.**

122   Daily Fundamentals • EMC 3244 • © Evan-Moor Corp.

Page 123

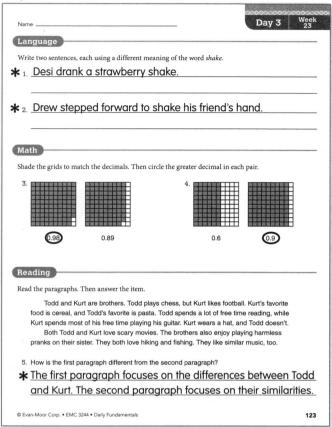

Name _____

Day 3 | Week 23

Language

Write two sentences, each using a different meaning of the word *shake*.

*1. Desi drank a strawberry shake.

*2. Drew stepped forward to shake his friend's hand.

Math

Shade the grids to match the decimals. Then circle the greater decimal in each pair.

3. (0.98)   0.89

4. 0.6   (0.9)

Reading

Read the paragraphs. Then answer the item.

Todd and Kurt are brothers. Todd plays chess, but Kurt likes football. Kurt's favorite food is cereal, and Todd's favorite is pasta. Todd spends a lot of free time reading, while Kurt spends most of his free time playing his guitar. Kurt wears a hat, and Todd doesn't. Both Todd and Kurt love scary movies. The brothers also enjoy playing harmless pranks on their sister. They both love hiking and fishing. They like similar music, too.

5. How is the first paragraph different from the second paragraph?

*The first paragraph focuses on the differences between Todd and Kurt. The second paragraph focuses on their similarities.

© Evan-Moor Corp. • EMC 3244 • Daily Fundamentals   **123**

Page 124

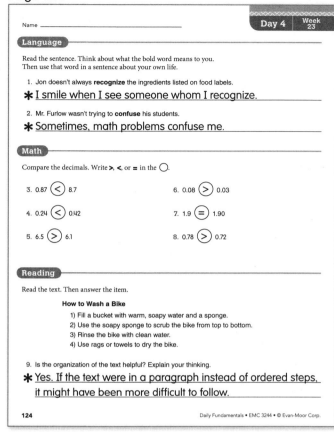

Name _____

Day 4 | Week 23

Language

Read the sentence. Think about what the bold word means to you. Then use that word in a sentence about your own life.

1. Jon doesn't always **recognize** the ingredients listed on food labels.

*I smile when I see someone whom I recognize.

2. Mr. Furlow wasn't trying to **confuse** his students.

*Sometimes, math problems confuse me.

Math

Compare the decimals. Write **>**, **<**, or **=** in the ◯.

3. 0.87 (<) 8.7

4. 0.24 (<) 0.42

5. 6.5 (>) 6.1

6. 0.08 (>) 0.03

7. 1.9 (=) 1.90

8. 0.78 (>) 0.72

Reading

Read the text. Then answer the item.

How to Wash a Bike
1) Fill a bucket with warm, soapy water and a sponge.
2) Use the soapy sponge to scrub the bike from top to bottom.
3) Rinse the bike with clean water.
4) Use rags or towels to dry the bike.

9. Is the organization of the text helpful? Explain your thinking.

*Yes. If the text were in a paragraph instead of ordered steps, it might have been more difficult to follow.

124   Daily Fundamentals • EMC 3244 • © Evan-Moor Corp.

Page 125

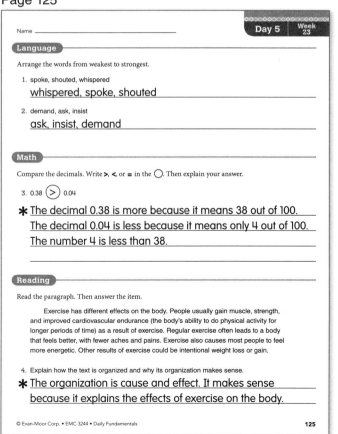

Name _____

Day 5 | Week 23

Language

Arrange the words from weakest to strongest.

1. spoke, shouted, whispered
whispered, spoke, shouted

2. demand, ask, insist
ask, insist, demand

Math

Compare the decimals. Write **>**, **<**, or **=** in the ◯. Then explain your answer.

3. 0.38 (>) 0.04

*The decimal 0.38 is more because it means 38 out of 100. The decimal 0.04 is less because it means only 4 out of 100. The number 4 is less than 38.

Reading

Read the paragraph. Then answer the item.

Exercise has different effects on the body. People usually gain muscle, strength, and improved cardiovascular endurance (the body's ability to do physical activity for longer periods of time) as a result of exercise. Regular exercise often leads to a body that feels better, with fewer aches and pains. Exercise also causes most people to feel more energetic. Other results of exercise could be intentional weight loss or gain.

4. Explain how the text is organized and why its organization makes sense.

*The organization is cause and effect. It makes sense because it explains the effects of exercise on the body.

© Evan-Moor Corp. • EMC 3244 • Daily Fundamentals   **125**

Page 126

Name _____

Day 1 | Week 24

Language

Read the sentence. Insert a comma where it is needed.

1. Ron plays golf, and he plays the flute.

2. Sean likes jogging, but he dislikes running laps.

3. Jada rides the bus every morning, and she walks home every afternoon.

4. Yoshi wants a new bike, yet the bike he has now works fine.

5. Maria is interested in trains, so she plans to visit the train museum soon.

Math

Add.

6. 2.46
  +0.23
   2.69

7. 0.89
  +0.45
   1.34

8. 0.74
  +0.94
   1.68

9. 3.25
  +4.61
   7.86

Reading

Read the paragraph. Then answer the items.

Kimani had always longed to live near the ocean. Unfortunately, she happened to grow up in a hot desert town. Because Kimani loved the ocean so much, she painted her bedroom walls, including the ceiling, blue. Her bedsheets and blankets were blue. She wore at least one piece of blue clothing every day. Almost everything she owned was blue, too.

10. What does the color blue symbolize to Kimani?
Ⓐ the desert
● the ocean
Ⓒ a town
Ⓓ her bedroom

11. What can you infer about Kimani?
● She is very certain of what she likes.
Ⓑ She does not have any interests.
Ⓒ Her goal is to be settled in the desert.
Ⓓ Comfort is her biggest concern.

12. Explain why Kimani surrounded herself with blue items, and how a color could be a symbol.

*By having blue around her, Kimani probably felt closer to the ocean. Blue represented something specific, so it's a symbol.

126   Daily Fundamentals • EMC 3244 • © Evan-Moor Corp.

✱ These answers will vary. Examples are given.

Page 127

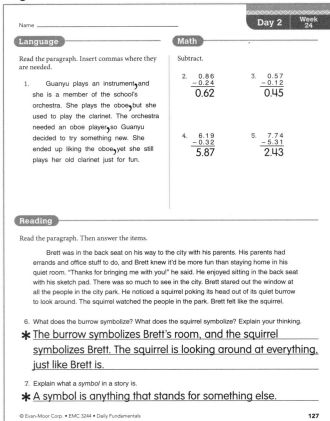

Name _____

Day 2 Week 24

Language

Read the paragraph. Insert commas where they are needed.

1. Guanyu plays an instrument, and she is a member of the school's orchestra. She plays the oboe, but she used to play the clarinet. The orchestra needed an oboe player, so Guanyu decided to try something new. She ended up liking the oboe, yet she still plays her old clarinet just for fun.

Math

Subtract.

2. $0.86 - 0.24 = 0.62$

3. $0.57 - 0.12 = 0.45$

4. $6.19 - 0.32 = 5.87$

5. $7.74 - 5.31 = 2.43$

Reading

Read the paragraph. Then answer the items.

Brett was in the back seat on his way to the city with his parents. His parents had errands and office stuff to do, and Brett knew it'd be more fun than staying home in his quiet room. "Thanks for bringing me with you!" he said. He enjoyed sitting in the back seat with his sketch pad. There was so much to see in the city. Brett stared out the window at all the people in the city park. He noticed a squirrel poking its head out of its quiet burrow to look around. The squirrel watched the people in the park. Brett felt like the squirrel.

6. What does the burrow symbolize? What does the squirrel symbolize? Explain your thinking.

✱ The burrow symbolizes Brett's room, and the squirrel symbolizes Brett. The squirrel is looking around at everything, just like Brett is.

7. Explain what a *symbol* in a story is.

✱ A symbol is anything that stands for something else.

© Evan-Moor Corp. • EMC 3244 • Daily Fundamentals 127

Page 128

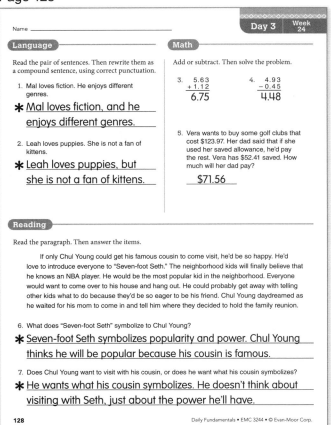

Name _____

Day 3 Week 24

Language

Read the pair of sentences. Then rewrite them as a compound sentence, using correct punctuation.

1. Mal loves fiction. He enjoys different genres.

✱ Mal loves fiction, and he enjoys different genres.

2. Leah loves puppies. She is not a fan of kittens.

✱ Leah loves puppies, but she is not a fan of kittens.

Math

Add or subtract. Then solve the problem.

3. $5.63 + 1.12 = 6.75$

4. $4.93 - 0.45 = 4.48$

5. Vera wants to buy some golf clubs that cost $123.97. Her dad said that if she used her saved allowance, he'd pay the rest. Vera has $52.41 saved. How much will her dad pay?

$71.56

Reading

Read the paragraph. Then answer the items.

If only Chul Young could get his famous cousin to come visit, he'd be so happy. He'd love to introduce everyone to "Seven-foot Seth." The neighborhood kids will finally believe that he knows an NBA player. He would be the most popular kid in the neighborhood. Everyone would want to come over to his house and hang out. He could probably get away with telling other kids what to do because they'd be so eager to be his friend. Chul Young daydreamed as he waited for his mom to come in and tell him where they decided to hold the family reunion.

6. What does "Seven-foot Seth" symbolize to Chul Young?

✱ Seven-foot Seth symbolizes popularity and power. Chul Young thinks he will be popular because his cousin is famous.

7. Does Chul Young want to visit with his cousin, or does he want what his cousin symbolizes?

✱ He wants what his cousin symbolizes. He doesn't think about visiting with Seth, just about the power he'll have.

128 Daily Fundamentals • EMC 3244 • © Evan-Moor Corp.

Page 129

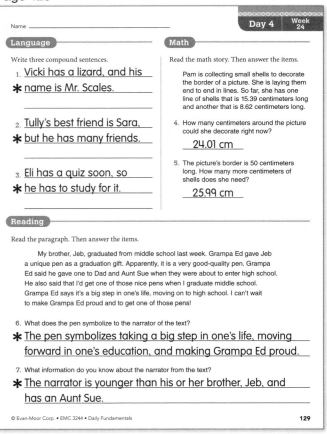

Name _____

Day 4 Week 24

Language

Write three compound sentences.

1. ✱ Vicki has a lizard, and his name is Mr. Scales.

2. ✱ Tully's best friend is Sara, but he has many friends.

3. ✱ Eli has a quiz soon, so he has to study for it.

Math

Read the math story. Then answer the items.

Pam is collecting small shells to decorate the border of a picture. She is laying them end to end in lines. So far, she has one line of shells that is 15.39 centimeters long and another that is 8.62 centimeters long.

4. How many centimeters around the picture could she decorate right now?

24.01 cm

5. The picture's border is 50 centimeters long. How many more centimeters of shells does she need?

25.99 cm

Reading

Read the paragraph. Then answer the items.

My brother, Jeb, graduated from middle school last week. Grampa Ed gave Jeb a unique pen as a graduation gift. Apparently, it is a very good-quality pen. Grampa Ed said he gave one to Dad and Aunt Sue when they were about to enter high school. He also said that I'd get one of those nice pens when I graduate middle school. Grampa Ed says it's a big step in one's life, moving on to high school. I can't wait to make Grampa Ed proud and to get one of those pens!

6. What does the pen symbolize to the narrator of the text?

✱ The pen symbolizes taking a big step in one's life, moving forward in one's education, and making Grampa Ed proud.

7. What information do you know about the narrator from the text?

✱ The narrator is younger than his or her brother, Jeb, and has an Aunt Sue.

© Evan-Moor Corp. • EMC 3244 • Daily Fundamentals 129

Page 130

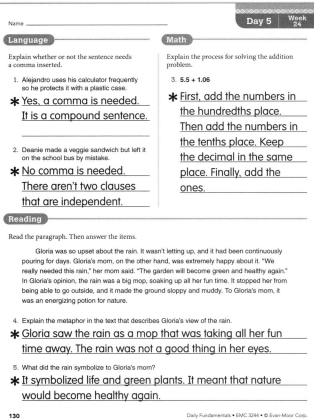

Name _____

Day 5 Week 24

Language

Explain whether or not the sentence needs a comma inserted.

1. Alejandro uses his calculator frequently so he protects it with a plastic case.

✱ Yes, a comma is needed. It is a compound sentence.

2. Deanie made a veggie sandwich but left it on the school bus by mistake.

✱ No comma is needed. There aren't two clauses that are independent.

Math

Explain the process for solving the addition problem.

3. **5.5 + 1.06**

✱ First, add the numbers in the hundredths place. Then add the numbers in the tenths place. Keep the decimal in the same place. Finally, add the ones.

Reading

Read the paragraph. Then answer the items.

Gloria was so upset about the rain. It wasn't letting up, and it had been continuously pouring for days. Gloria's mom, on the other hand, was extremely happy about it. "We really needed this rain," her mom said. "The garden will become green and healthy again." In Gloria's opinion, the rain was a big mop, soaking up all her fun time. It stopped her from being able to go outside, and it made the ground sloppy and muddy. To Gloria's mom, it was an energizing potion for nature.

4. Explain the metaphor in the text that describes Gloria's view of the rain.

✱ Gloria saw the rain as a mop that was taking all her fun time away. The rain was not a good thing in her eyes.

5. What did the rain symbolize to Gloria's mom?

✱ It symbolized life and green plants. It meant that nature would become healthy again.

130 Daily Fundamentals • EMC 3244 • © Evan-Moor Corp.

190 Daily Fundamentals • EMC 3244 • © Evan-Moor Corp.

These answers will vary. Examples are given.

Page 131

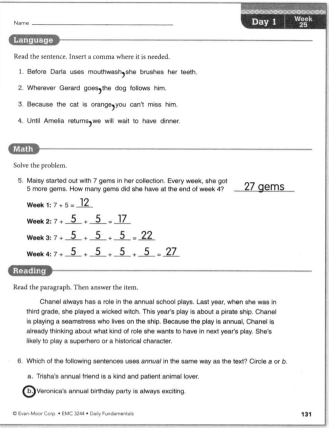

Name _____

Day 1 | **Week 25**

Language

Read the sentence. Insert a comma where it is needed.

1. Before Darla uses mouthwash, she brushes her teeth.

2. Wherever Gerard goes, the dog follows him.

3. Because the cat is orange, you can't miss him.

4. Until Amelia returns, we will wait to have dinner.

Math

Solve the problem.

5. Maisy started out with 7 gems in her collection. Every week, she got 5 more gems. How many gems did she have at the end of week 4?   **27 gems**

Week 1: 7 + 5 = __12__

Week 2: 7 + __5__ + __5__ = __17__

Week 3: 7 + __5__ + __5__ + __5__ = __22__

Week 4: 7 + __5__ + __5__ + __5__ + __5__ = __27__

Reading

Read the paragraph. Then answer the item.

Chanel always has a role in the annual school plays. Last year, when she was in third grade, she played a wicked witch. This year's play is about a pirate ship. Chanel is playing a seamstress who lives on the ship. Because the play is annual, Chanel is already thinking about what kind of role she wants to have in next year's play. She's likely to play a superhero or a historical character.

6. Which of the following sentences uses *annual* in the same way as the text? Circle *a* or *b*.

a. Trisha's annual friend is a kind and patient animal lover.

(b.) Veronica's annual birthday party is always exciting.

Page 132

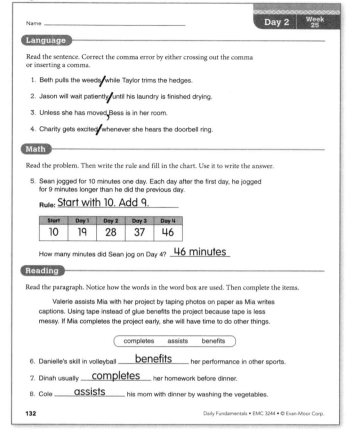

Name _____

Day 2 | **Week 25**

Language

Read the sentence. Correct the comma error by either crossing out the comma or inserting a comma.

1. Beth pulls the weeds / while Taylor trims the hedges.

2. Jason will wait patiently / until his laundry is finished drying.

3. Unless she has moved, Bess is in her room.

4. Charity gets excited / whenever she hears the doorbell ring.

Math

Read the problem. Then write the rule and fill in the chart. Use it to write the answer.

5. Sean jogged for 10 minutes one day. Each day after the first day, he jogged for 9 minutes longer than he did the previous day.

Rule: Start with 10. Add 9.

Start	Day 1	Day 2	Day 3	Day 4
10	19	28	37	46

How many minutes did Sean jog on Day 4?   **46 minutes**

Reading

Read the paragraph. Notice how the words in the word box are used. Then complete the items.

Valerie assists Mia with her project by taping photos on paper as Mia writes captions. Using tape instead of glue benefits the project because tape is less messy. If Mia completes the project early, she will have time to do other things.

completes   assists   benefits

6. Danielle's skill in volleyball __benefits__ her performance in other sports.

7. Dinah usually __completes__ her homework before dinner.

8. Cole __assists__ his mom with dinner by washing the vegetables.

Page 133

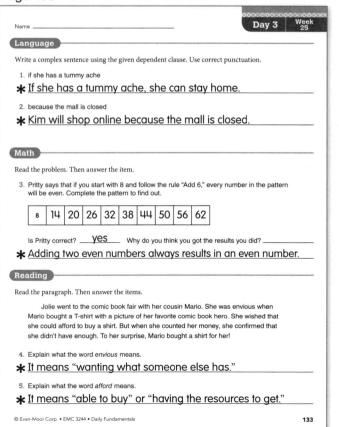

Name _____

Day 3 | **Week 25**

Language

Write a complex sentence using the given dependent clause. Use correct punctuation.

1. if she has a tummy ache

✳ If she has a tummy ache, she can stay home.

2. because the mall is closed

✳ Kim will shop online because the mall is closed.

Math

Read the problem. Then answer the item.

3. Pritty says that if you start with 8 and follow the rule "Add 6," every number in the pattern will be even. Complete the pattern to find out.

| 8 | 14 | 20 | 26 | 32 | 38 | 44 | 50 | 56 | 62 |

Is Pritty correct? __yes__   Why do you think you got the results you did? _____

✳ Adding two even numbers always results in an even number.

Reading

Read the paragraph. Then answer the items.

Jolie went to the comic book fair with her cousin Mario. She was envious when Mario bought a T-shirt with a picture of her favorite comic book hero. She wished that she could afford to buy a shirt. But when she counted her money, she confirmed that she didn't have enough. To her surprise, Mario bought a shirt for her!

4. Explain what the word *envious* means.

✳ It means "wanting what someone else has."

5. Explain what the word *afford* means.

✳ It means "able to buy" or "having the resources to get."

Page 134

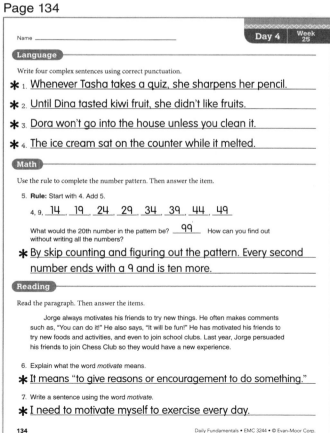

Name _____

Day 4 | **Week 25**

Language

Write four complex sentences using correct punctuation.

✳ 1. Whenever Tasha takes a quiz, she sharpens her pencil.

✳ 2. Until Dina tasted kiwi fruit, she didn't like fruits.

✳ 3. Dora won't go into the house unless you clean it.

✳ 4. The ice cream sat on the counter while it melted.

Math

Use the rule to complete the number pattern. Then answer the item.

5. **Rule:** Start with 4. Add 5.

4, 9, __14__, __19__, __24__, __29__, __34__, __39__, __44__, __49__

What would the 20th number in the pattern be? __99__   How can you find out without writing all the numbers?

✳ By skip counting and figuring out the pattern. Every second number ends with a 9 and is ten more.

Reading

Read the paragraph. Then answer the items.

Jorge always motivates his friends to try new things. He often makes comments such as, "You can do it!" He also says, "It will be fun!" He has motivated his friends to try new foods and activities, and even to join school clubs. Last year, Jorge persuaded his friends to join Chess Club so they would have a new experience.

6. Explain what the word *motivate* means.

✳ It means "to give reasons or encouragement to do something."

7. Write a sentence using the word *motivate*.

✳ I need to motivate myself to exercise every day.

These answers will vary. Examples are given.

Page 135

Language

Explain whether or not the sentence needs a comma inserted. If it does, correctly insert it.

1. After dinosaurs roamed the earth, the presence of humans increased.

* Yes, the dependent clause is at the start of the sentence.

2. Classes have been full since the school opened in August.

* No, the dependent clause is at the end of the sentence.

Math

Start with an odd number greater than 40 and follow the rule "Subtract 4."
Fill in the chart to show your results. Then answer the items.

* | 49 | 45 | 41 | 37 | 33 | 29 | 25 | 21 | 17 | 13 |

3. Did you get all even numbers, all odd numbers, or both? all odd numbers

4. Why do you think you got the results you did? When you add or subtract an

* even number from an odd one, the result is an odd number.

Reading

Read the paragraph. Then answer the item.

Amal's older brother, Rob, constantly claims that she can't do various things. But Amal protests, saying, "I am capable of doing that, Rob." Once, Rob claimed that Amal was not capable of bringing bricks from their dad's truck to the backyard when they were building a patio. Amal proved she was capable. She helped to carry many bricks.

5. Explain what *capable* means. Then explain how the text gives clues about its meaning.

* Capable means "able to do something." The text claims that
Amal is capable, then gives an example of how. Rob also
gives a clue about the opposite meaning of capable.

Page 136

Language

Read the sentence. Write the correct word from the word box to complete it.

worst   bad   worse

1. Joann made the worst sandwich because it was soggy.

2. Pearl's sandwich was worse than Ray's sandwich.

3. Ray made a bad sandwich because its bread was stale.

Math

Answer the item.

4. Continue this shape pattern until there are 10 shapes in all.

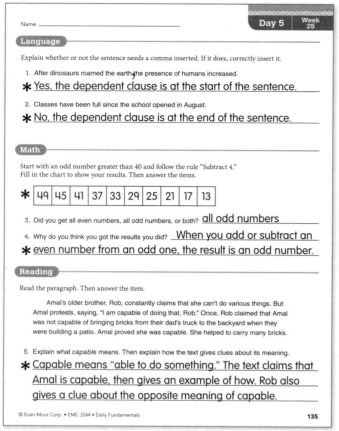

Describe the pattern. triangle triangle circle triangle triangle square

What will the 15th shape be? circle

Reading

Read the paragraph. Then answer the item.

In the American Civil War, the North and South fought against each other. Each side had different advantages. The North had more people, money, factories, and railroads. They had better supplies and weapons. The South had experienced military generals. Southern soldiers were more physically fit because of the demands of farm work. Most of the battles occurred on southern land, so the southern troops knew the land well.

5. Would you have preferred to have the advantages of the North or the South? Explain.

* I'd prefer the North's advantages because I think better
supplies and weapons are most important in war.

Page 137

Language

Read the sentence. Write the correct word from the word box to complete it.

better   best   good

1. Farida's song was good

2. Danica played her instrument better than her sister did.

3. Of everyone in the choir, Agatha sang best

Math

Answer the item.

4. Continue this shape pattern until there are 10 shapes in all.

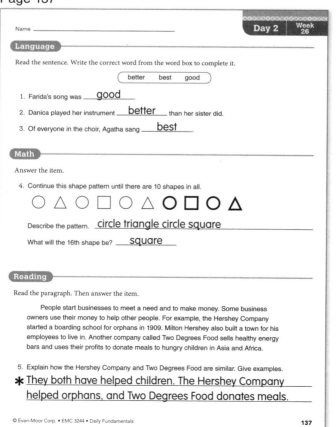

Describe the pattern. circle triangle circle square

What will the 16th shape be? square

Reading

Read the paragraph. Then answer the item.

People start businesses to meet a need and to make money. Some business owners use their money to help other people. For example, the Hershey Company started a boarding school for orphans in 1909. Milton Hershey also built a town for his employees to live in. Another company called Two Degrees Food sells healthy energy bars and uses their profits to donate meals to hungry children in Asia and Africa.

5. Explain how the Hershey Company and Two Degrees Food are similar. Give examples.

* They both have helped children. The Hershey Company
helped orphans, and Two Degrees Food donates meals.

Page 138

Language

Write two sentences using the words from the word box correctly.

than   then

* 1. The squirrel ran faster than the children.

* 2. If Mickey does his chores, then he can have fun.

Math

Answer the item.

3. Continue this shape pattern until there are 10 shapes in all.

Describe the pattern. square triangle triangle square circle circle

What will the 21st shape be? triangle

Reading

Read the paragraph. Then answer the item.

Birds and bats may seem similar. They both have wings and feet, and both fly. Birds eat insects, and some types of bats do, too. Both birds and bats may live in or on buildings or trees. However, in some ways, birds and bats are different. Birds are not mammals (birds hatch from eggs.) Bats sleep upside down. Birds have feathers, and bats have fur. Bats drink milk, and birds do not.

4. Explain why someone might mistake a bat for a bird.

* Birds and bats both have wings and fly. If a bat was seen
eating insects or in a building, someone might think it was
a bird.

Page 139

Name _____

Day 4 | Week 26

Language

Write two sentences using the words from the word box correctly.

(sit   set)

＊ 1. Grandma and Grampa sit on the bench together.

＊ 2. We set the tea sandwiches on the table.

Math

Look at the shape pattern. Continue the pattern three times by drawing in the boxes.

3.

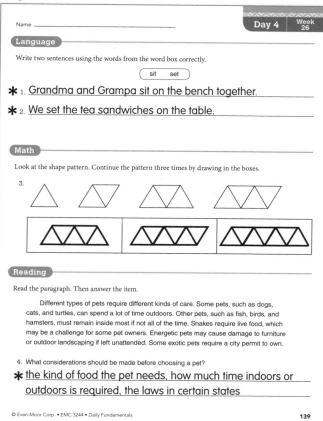

Reading

Read the paragraph. Then answer the item.

Different types of pets require different kinds of care. Some pets, such as dogs, cats, and turtles, can spend a lot of time outdoors. Other pets, such as fish, birds, and hamsters, must remain inside most if not all of the time. Snakes require live food, which may be a challenge for some pet owners. Energetic pets may cause damage to furniture or outdoor landscaping if left unattended. Some exotic pets require a city permit to own.

4. What considerations should be made before choosing a pet?

＊ the kind of food the pet needs, how much time indoors or outdoors is required, the laws in certain states

Page 140

Name _____

Day 5 | Week 26

Language

Write two sentences using the words from the word box correctly.

(raise   rise)

＊ 1. Try to raise the banner high in the air.

＊ 2. Please rise to greet Aunt Sandy when she arrives.

Math

Look at the shape pattern. Then answer the item.

3. Draw the fourth shape in the pattern.

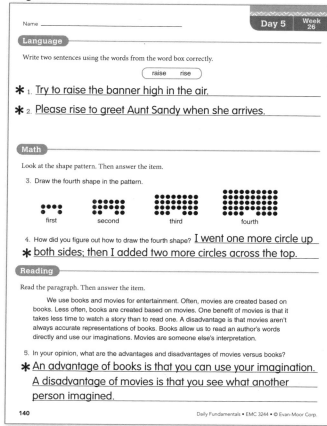

first   second   third   fourth

4. How did you figure out how to draw the fourth shape? I went one more circle up
＊ both sides; then I added two more circles across the top.

Reading

Read the paragraph. Then answer the item.

We use books and movies for entertainment. Often, movies are created based on books. Less often, books are created based on movies. One benefit of movies is that it takes less time to watch a story than to read one. A disadvantage is that movies aren't always accurate representations of books. Books allow us to read an author's words directly and use our imaginations. Movies are someone else's interpretation.

5. In your opinion, what are the advantages and disadvantages of movies versus books?

＊ An advantage of books is that you can use your imagination. A disadvantage of movies is that you see what another person imagined.

Page 141

Name _____

Day 1 | Week 27

Language

Write a sentence using the irregular past tense of the given verb.

1. **wear**

＊ My dad wore his dress shirt to do the gardening!

2. **know**

＊ Jess knew who gave her the lovely greeting card.

Math

Answer the item.

3. How many squares are in the figure?
Hint: Some squares may have other squares within them.

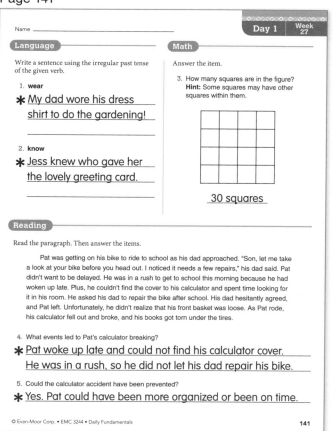

30 squares

Reading

Read the paragraph. Then answer the items.

Pat was getting on his bike to ride to school as his dad approached. "Son, let me take a look at your bike before you head out. I noticed it needs a few repairs," his dad said. Pat didn't want to be delayed. He was in a rush to get to school this morning because he had woken up late. Plus, he couldn't find the cover to his calculator and spent time looking for it in his room. He asked his dad to repair the bike after school. His dad hesitantly agreed, and Pat left. Unfortunately, he didn't realize that his front basket was loose. As Pat rode, his calculator fell out and broke, and his books got torn under the tires.

4. What events led to Pat's calculator breaking?

＊ Pat woke up late and could not find his calculator cover. He was in a rush, so he did not let his dad repair his bike.

5. Could the calculator accident have been prevented?

＊ Yes. Pat could have been more organized or been on time.

Page 142

Name _____

Day 2 | Week 27

Language

Read the sentence. Complete it using a verb that agrees with the subject.

＊ 1. Marie and Tia ___write___ poems together.

＊ 2. Shelly ___loves___ oatmeal with maple syrup, raisins, and nuts.

＊ 3. Dad and I ___use___ the map to figure out which direction to travel in.

＊ 4. You often ___cry___ when your favorite sports team is winning.

＊ 5. Mr. and Mrs. Carter ___teach___ at the school that I attend.

Math

Answer the item.

6. Circle the letter that is backwards.

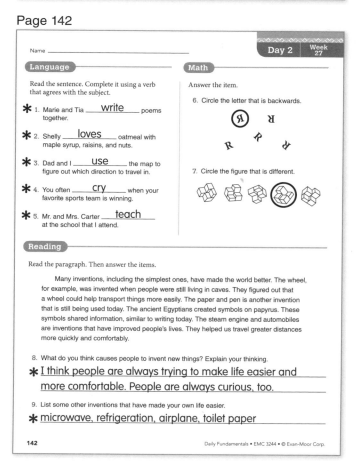

7. Circle the figure that is different.

Reading

Read the paragraph. Then answer the items.

Many inventions, including the simplest ones, have made the world better. The wheel, for example, was invented when people were still living in caves. They figured out that a wheel could help transport things more easily. The paper and pen is another invention that is still being used today. The ancient Egyptians created symbols on papyrus. These symbols shared information, similar to writing today. The steam engine and automobiles are inventions that have improved people's lives. They helped us travel greater distances more quickly and comfortably.

8. What do you think causes people to invent new things? Explain your thinking.

＊ I think people are always trying to make life easier and more comfortable. People are always curious, too.

9. List some other inventions that have made your own life easier.

＊ microwave, refrigeration, airplane, toilet paper

Page 143

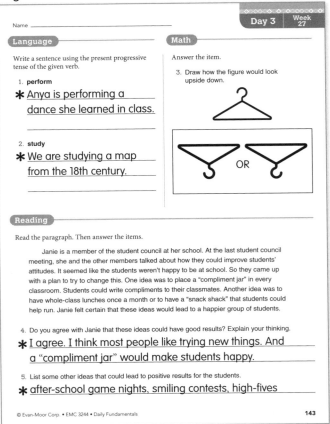

Name _____

Day 3 | **Week 27**

Language

Write a sentence using the present progressive tense of the given verb.

1. **perform**

✱ Anya is performing a dance she learned in class.

2. **study**

✱ We are studying a map from the 18th century.

Math

Answer the item.

3. Draw how the figure would look upside down.

Reading

Read the paragraph. Then answer the items.

Janie is a member of the student council at her school. At the last student council meeting, she and the other members talked about how they could improve students' attitudes. It seemed like the students weren't happy to change this. One idea was to place a "compliment jar" in every classroom. Students could write compliments to their classmates. Another idea was to have whole-class lunches once a month or to have a "snack shack" that students could help run. Janie felt certain that these ideas would lead to a happier group of students.

4. Do you agree with Janie that these ideas could have good results? Explain your thinking.

✱ I agree. I think most people like trying new things. And a "compliment jar" would make students happy.

5. List some other ideas that could lead to positive results for the students.

✱ after-school game nights, smiling contests, high-fives

© Evan-Moor Corp. • EMC 3244 • Daily Fundamentals 143

Page 144

Name _____

Day 4 | **Week 27**

Language

Write a sentence using the past progressive tense of the given verb.

1. **smile**

✱ Tawana was smiling when she found her lost pencil.

2. **swim**

✱ Trey was swimming in the pool a few hours ago.

Math

Answer the item.

3. How many ◺ s will fit in the rectangle?

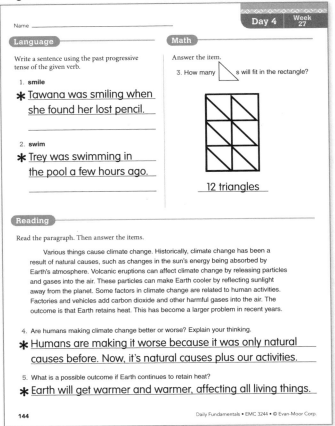

12 triangles

Reading

Read the paragraph. Then answer the items.

Various things cause climate change. Historically, climate change has been a result of natural causes, such as changes in the sun's energy being absorbed by Earth's atmosphere. Volcanic eruptions can affect climate change by releasing particles and gases into the air. These particles can make Earth cooler by reflecting sunlight away from the planet. Some factors in climate change are related to human activities. Factories and vehicles add carbon dioxide and other harmful gases into the air. The outcome is that Earth retains heat. This has become a larger problem in recent years.

4. Are humans making climate change better or worse? Explain your thinking.

✱ Humans are making it worse because it was only natural causes before. Now, it's natural causes plus our activities.

5. What is a possible outcome if Earth continues to retain heat?

✱ Earth will get warmer and warmer, affecting all living things.

144 Daily Fundamentals • EMC 3244 • © Evan-Moor Corp.

Page 145

Name _____

Day 5 | **Week 27**

Language

Write a sentence using the future progressive tense of the given verb.

1. **grow**

✱ This plant will be growing by the end of April.

2. **find**

✱ Aziz will be finding a home for this kitten.

Math

Answer the item.

3. Is this figure symmetrical? Explain why or why not.

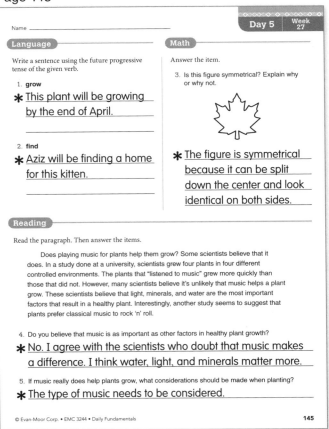

✱ The figure is symmetrical because it can be split down the center and look identical on both sides.

Reading

Read the paragraph. Then answer the items.

Does playing music for plants help them grow? Some scientists believe that it does. In a study done at a university, scientists grew four plants in four different controlled environments. The plants that "listened to music" grew more quickly than those that did not. However, many scientists believe it's unlikely that music helps a plant grow. These scientists believe that light, minerals, and water are the most important factors that result in a healthy plant. Interestingly, another study seems to suggest that plants prefer classical music to rock 'n' roll.

4. Do you believe that music is as important as other factors in healthy plant growth?

✱ No. I agree with the scientists who doubt that music makes a difference. I think water, light, and minerals matter more.

5. If music really does help plants grow, what considerations should be made when planting?

✱ The type of music needs to be considered.

© Evan-Moor Corp. • EMC 3244 • Daily Fundamentals 145

Page 146

Name _____

Day 1 | **Week 28**

Language

Read the sentence. Circle the simile.

1. Hua is (as strong as an ox.)

Write two sentences that each contain a simile.

✱ 2. Sheila's new horse is as big as an elephant.

✱ 3. The boy shot out of his seat like a rocket.

Math

Complete the tables by converting the measurements. The first one of each table has been done for you.

4.
Meters	Centimeters
1	100
2	200
3	300
4	400

5.
Centimeters	Millimeters
1	10
2	20
3	30
4	40

6.
Kilometers	Meters
1	1,000
2	2,000
3	3,000
4	4,000

Reading

Read the paragraph. Then answer the item.

The perfectly dressed lady held herself upright and tall, like a statue, as she walked to the counter at the bank. She wore fancy gloves, high-heeled shoes, a long coat, and shiny jewelry. She also wore a sour expression on her face. She didn't appear angry, but she seemed terribly unhappy. When she got to the counter, the clerk smiled at her. But she didn't return the smile. She squinted as if she was suspicious of the friendly employee.

7. Explain how the vocabulary in the text creates a strong image of the lady.

✱ The words suggest she's proud, unfriendly, and unhappy.

146 Daily Fundamentals • EMC 3244 • © Evan-Moor Corp.

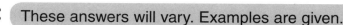
✲ These answers will vary. Examples are given.

Page 147

Language

Read the sentence. Circle the metaphor.

1. My family (is the sun in my sky.)

Write two sentences that each contain a metaphor.

✲ 2. Roxy's delicious chip dip is a party in my mouth.

✲ 3. Mom used a mountain of chocolate in these cookies.

Math

Complete the tables by converting the measurements. Then answer the item.

4.
Meters	Centimeters
5	500
7	700
8	800

5.
Centimeters	Millimeters
6	60
9	90
11	110

6.
Kilometers	Meters
2	2,000
5	5,000
7	7,000

7. Explain how you converted kilometers to meters.

✲ I used multiplication. A kilometer equals 1,000 meters.

Reading

Read the paragraph. Then answer the items.

Once upon a time in a land far away, three brothers lived in a magical kingdom ruled by animals. The animals were kind to the human brothers. A legend told of an evil wizard who would one day arrive at the kingdom and try to take over. But the brothers had a powerful family amulet that would protect the kingdom and all of the animals in it. And the brothers, although not originally from this kingdom, loved it with all their hearts.

8. What do you think is the genre of this story? Explain why.

✲ It's a fairy tale. It has fantasy genre words and theme.

✲ 9. Underline the words in the text that support your answer for number 8.

Page 148

Language

Write two sentences that each use a different meaning of the word *club*.

✲ 1. My mom joined a book club.

✲ 2. The man used a golf club to hit the ball.

List any other words you know that have more than one meaning.

✲ 3. bear, loop, weave, place, piece, puzzle

Math

Solve the problem.

4. Lia is collecting twigs to make a wreath. She found a twig that was 0.25 meter long. She found a branch that was 0.9 meter long. And she found another twig that was 30 millimeters long. Write the lengths in order from the shortest to the longest.

   30 mm , 0.25 m , 0.9 m

✲ Explain your thinking. The measure of 0.25 m equals 25 cm, 0.9 m equals 90 cm, and 30 mm equals only 3 cm.

Reading

Read the paragraph. Then answer the item.

Corbin was hanging out with his little sister, Cassie, who is in kindergarten. They were playing a board game, when Corbin said the phrase, "piece of cake." Cassie immediately thought there was cake in the house. Corbin laughed, and they kept playing. A short while later, Corbin said, "The ball is in your court, Cass." Cassie was confused, and she protested that this wasn't a game that had a ball in it.

5. Explain why Cassie was confused by the words Corbin was using.

✲ Corbin was using idioms, or figurative language. But Cassie was taking his words literally.

Page 149

Language

Explain what the idiom means in your own words.

1. Actions speak louder than words.

✲ What you do matters even more than what you say.

2. This is the best thing since sliced bread.

✲ This is a really cool idea or invention.

Math

Complete the table by converting the measurements. Then answer the item.

3.
Liters	Milliliters
5	5,000
7	7,000
8	8,000

4. Explain how you converted liters to milliliters.

✲ I used multiplication. A liter equals 1,000 milliliters.

Reading

Read the paragraph carefully. Then read it again. Answer the item.

A man walked up to the hotel counter and said to the clerk, "Ineida Frank." The hotel clerk politely told the man that nobody named "Frank" worked there. "No, Ineida Frank," the man said again. The clerk was confused. "Fine, try Ima Frank," said the man. The clerk then became very confused. The man tried again, "Kenya Dance"? Eventually, the man realized that he needed to explain to the clerk that these were names of hotel guests.

5. Explain why word choice plays an important role in this text.

✲ The names all sound like real words when read aloud, and their meanings added humor and confusion to the plot.

Page 150

Language

Read the proverb. Then explain what you think it means.

1. The early bird catches the worm.

✲ It means that it is worth it to wake up early and get an early start because it will be rewarding and will pay off.

Math

Solve the problem. Show your work.

1 liter = 1,000 milliliters

2. For a birthday party, Jody's mom bought 5 bottles that each contained 2 liters of lemonade. How many milliliters of lemonade were bought for the party?

   Work may vary.

   10,000 milliliters

Reading

Read the paragraph. Then answer the items.

Dr. Akers gave me the high honor of allowing me to introduce him at the Doctors and Medical Professionals' Conference last autumn. I was flattered that he asked me to perform this duty. He was the guest of honor at this respectable event.

3. Does the word choice used give this text a formal or informal tone? Explain your answer.

✲ It's formal because the words are high-level and adult.

4. Explain how different word choices could give it a different tone.

✲ The words used could be shorter and less professional.

These answers will vary. Examples are given.

Page 151

Language

Fix the run-on sentence by rewriting it as a compound sentence.

1. Hye Joon enjoys hiking she hasn't seen the trails here.

* Hye Joon enjoys hiking, but she hasn't seen the trails here.

2. Peter made a mess in the kitchen he's cleaning it now.

* Peter made a mess in the kitchen, but he's cleaning it now.

Math

Complete the tables by converting the measurements.

3.
Feet	Inches
1	12
2	24
3	36
4	48
5	60

4.
Yards	Feet
1	3
2	6
3	9
4	12
5	15

5.
Yards	Inches
1	36
2	72
3	108
4	144
5	180

Reading

Read the paragraph. Then answer the item.

Mount Kilimanjaro is a unique mountain. Known as the "roof of Africa," it's the highest point in Africa and the tallest lone mountain in the world. Kilimanjaro is 19,341 ft (5,895 m) high. Many people try to reach its summit every year. The mountain is known worldwide for its beauty and surrounding African wildlife. It contains different ecosystems: rainforest, heath, alpine desert, arctic summit, and more.

6. Circle the main idea of the text. Then write one detail that supports the main idea.

* The text states that Mount Kilimanjaro has many different ecosystems.

Page 152

Language

Fix the run-on sentence by rewriting it as two complete sentences.

1. Liza is learning American Sign Language she practices daily.

Liza is learning American Sign Language. She practices daily.

2. Dubaku is a fan of hockey he wants to go to a game.

Dubaku is a fan of hockey. He wants to go to a game.

Math

Complete the tables by converting the measurements. Then answer the item.

3.
Feet	Inches
2	24
5	60
10	120

4.
Yards	Feet
3	9
4	12
7	21

5.
Yards	Inches
4	144
5	180
6	216

6. Explain how you converted yards to inches.

* I used multiplication. A yard equals 36 inches.

Reading

Read the paragraph. Then answer the item.

Thomas Jefferson and John Adams were two U.S. presidents with some surprising similarities. Both of the men were patriots who helped gain independence during the American Revolution. They both helped to draft the U.S. Constitution, and both served as vice president before being elected as president. Astonishingly, they died on the same day, the 50th anniversary of the signing of the Declaration of Independence.

7. Circle the main idea of the text. Then explain how the details support the main idea.

* Both Jefferson and Adams were patriots. They both helped to write the Constitution and served as vice president.

Page 153

Language

Read the sentence. Write whether the sentence is a *run-on*, a *fragment*, or is *complete*.

1. Pedro and his family.   fragment

2. We joined a book club last month.   complete

3. The cat's collar is tight she needs a new one.   run-on

4. Our friends who live in Florida.   fragment

Math

Solve the problem.

5. Jedidiah can jump as high as 36 inches. Callie can jump as high as 2 feet. Manuel can jump as high as 0.5 yard. Write the heights in order from shortest to highest.

   0.5 yd   2 ft   36 in.

* Explain your thinking. The measure of 0.5 yd equals 18 in., and 2 ft equals 24 in., so 36 in. is the highest.

Reading

Read the paragraph. Then answer the item.

The blobfish is a rare species of fish that has an unusual appearance. Its features resemble a human face. It has no skeleton and very few muscles, so its face droops downward. It doesn't even have teeth to eat with! Many people consider the blobfish to be ugly because its body seems to have the texture of jelly. It lives deep in the ocean where the water pressure is very high.

6. Underline the details in the text. Then explain how they helped you better understand the main idea.

* The details helped me picture what the blobfish looks like, how its body might feel, and where it lives.

Page 154

Language

Circle *fragment* if the sentence is a fragment. Circle *complete* if it is a complete sentence. Then explain why you chose that answer.

1. When Bazul walks through the door.   (fragment) complete

* This is a dependent clause because of "when."

2. The new shopping mall will open next week.   fragment (complete)

* This is a complete thought with a subject and a verb.

Math

Complete the tables by converting the measurements.

3.
Pints	Cups
1	2
2	4
3	6
4	8

4.
Quarts	Cups
1	4
2	8
3	12
4	16

5.
Gallons	Quarts
1	4
2	8
3	12
4	16

Reading

Read the paragraph. Then answer the item.

Magnetism is at work all around us. When you use a compass, the needle shows you where north is by lining up with a magnetic force. But where is this force? It is in the middle of the planet—the center of Earth itself is actually a big magnet! Think of a giant bar magnet running from the North Pole to the South Pole. Its magnetic force extends through the poles thousands of kilometers into space, forming a barrier around Earth.

6. Explain the main idea of the text in your own words.

* Magnetism is all around us, and we are always affected by it because Earth basically has a giant magnet inside it.

These answers will vary. Examples are given.

Page 155

Name _____

Day 5 — Week 29

Language

Write four sentences. Circle the complete subject and underline the complete predicate.

* 1. (The palace) was extraordinary.
* 2. (I) am interested in ancient Egypt.
* 3. (Mexico) is a breathtaking country.
* 4. (The museum) is open every day of the week.

Math

Complete the tables by converting the measurements.

5.
Quarts	Pints
1	2
2	4
3	6
4	8

6.
Gallons	Cups
1	16
2	32
3	48
4	64

7.
Gallons	Pints
1	8
2	16
3	24
4	32

Reading

Read the paragraph. Then answer the item.

Objects make sounds by vibrating, or moving quickly back and forth. These vibrations produce sound waves that move just like ripples in water. The highness or lowness of a sound is called the *pitch*. The faster an object vibrates, the higher the pitch of the sound. The slower an object vibrates, the lower the pitch of the sound. People can hear a wide range of sounds—from a low, deep drum to a high-pitched whistle.

8. Explain the main idea of the text in your own words.

* Objects vibrate to make sound waves. People can hear high-pitched sounds and low-pitched sounds.

© Evan-Moor Corp. • EMC 3244 • Daily Fundamentals — 155

Page 156

Name _____

Day 1 — Week 30

Language

Read the sentence. Insert commas to correctly punctuate the series in the sentence.

1. Ashley got stickers, pens, and erasers as her birthday gifts.

2. Dharma enjoys math, English, and science.

3. Rafael has seen goats, cows, pigs, and horses.

4. Eleanor is afraid of mice, bugs, and reptiles.

5. Bruce's best friends are Carol, Gina, and Nat.

6. Chris collects rocks, stamps, coins, and books.

Math

Read the problem. Then plot the data from the table on the line plot.

7. The table shows how many plants a nursery sold at specific prices on a given day.

Prices of Plants Sold at Nursery		
$5.00	$10.00	$15.00
8	6	4

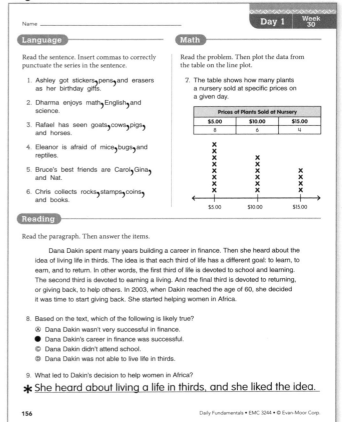

Reading

Read the paragraph. Then answer the items.

Dana Dakin spent many years building a career in finance. Then she heard about the idea of living life in thirds. The idea is that each third of life has a different goal: to learn, to earn, and to return. In other words, the first third of life is devoted to school and learning. The second third is devoted to earning a living. And the final third is devoted to returning, or giving back, to help others. In 2003, when Dakin reached the age of 60, she decided it was time to start giving back. She started helping women in Africa.

8. Based on the text, which of the following is likely true?
Ⓐ Dana Dakin wasn't very successful in finance.
● Dana Dakin's career in finance was successful.
Ⓒ Dana Dakin didn't attend school.
Ⓓ Dana Dakin was not able to live life in thirds.

9. What led to Dakin's decision to help women in Africa?
* She heard about living a life in thirds, and she liked the idea.

156 — Daily Fundamentals • EMC 3244 • © Evan-Moor Corp.

Page 157

Name _____

Day 2 — Week 30

Language

Write three sentences that each contain a series. Use correct punctuation.

1. Cheska has a dog, cat, bird, and lizard. *
2. Ross swims, jogs, and skates for exercise. *
3. James brought popcorn, juice, and nuts to the picnic. *

Math

Use the line plot to answer the items.

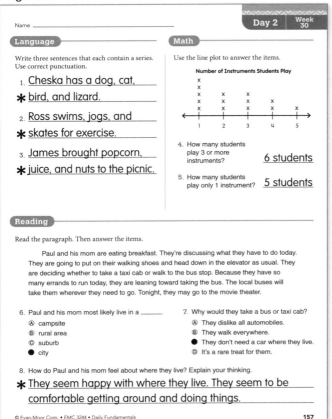

4. How many students play 3 or more instruments? **6 students**

5. How many students play only 1 instrument? **5 students**

Reading

Read the paragraph. Then answer the items.

Paul and his mom are eating breakfast. They're discussing what they have to do today. They are going to put on their walking shoes and head down in the elevator as usual. They are deciding whether to take a taxi cab or walk to the bus stop. Because they have so many errands to run today, they are leaning toward taking the bus. The local buses will take them wherever they need to go. Tonight, they may go to the movie theater.

6. Paul and his mom most likely live in a _____.
Ⓐ campsite
Ⓑ rural area
Ⓒ suburb
● city

7. Why would they take a bus or taxi cab?
Ⓐ They dislike all automobiles.
Ⓑ They walk everywhere.
● They don't need a car where they live.
Ⓓ It's a rare treat for them.

8. How do Paul and his mom feel about where they live? Explain your thinking.
* They seem happy with where they live. They seem to be comfortable getting around and doing things.

© Evan-Moor Corp. • EMC 3244 • Daily Fundamentals — 157

Page 158

Name _____

Day 3 — Week 30

Language

Read the letter. Insert commas to punctuate the letter correctly.

1. Dear Nyari,

Thank you for your interest in our school. We are always happy to hear from students at other schools. We like learning about how our schools are similar and different. Please write to us again in the future.

Sincerely,

Mrs. Delaney

Math

Use the line plot to solve the problem.

2. A health food store has 12 packages of granola left. Mr. Tomlin needs to buy 5 pounds of granola. The line plot shows how much the packages weigh in pounds. Write one way Mr. Tomlin can combine the packages to get how much he needs.

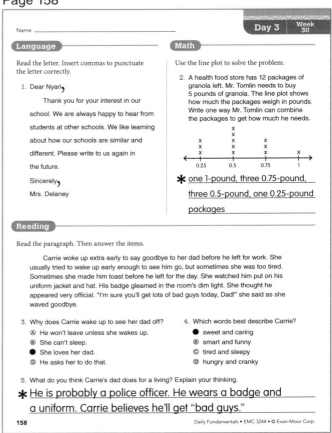

* one 1-pound, three 0.75-pound, three 0.5-pound, one 0.25-pound packages

Reading

Read the paragraph. Then answer the items.

Carrie woke up extra early to say goodbye to her dad before he left for work. She usually tried to wake up early enough to see him go, but sometimes she was too tired. Sometimes she made him toast before he left for the day. She watched him put on his uniform jacket and hat. His badge gleamed in the room's dim light. She thought he appeared very official. "I'm sure you'll get lots of bad guys today, Dad!" she said as she waved goodbye.

3. Why does Carrie wake up to see her dad off?
Ⓐ He won't leave unless she wakes up.
Ⓑ She can't sleep.
● She loves her dad.
Ⓓ He asks her to do that.

4. Which words best describe Carrie?
● sweet and caring
Ⓑ smart and funny
Ⓒ tired and sleepy
Ⓓ hungry and cranky

5. What do you think Carrie's dad does for a living? Explain your thinking.
* He is probably a police officer. He wears a badge and a uniform. Carrie believes he'll get "bad guys."

158 — Daily Fundamentals • EMC 3244 • © Evan-Moor Corp.

© Evan-Moor Corp. • EMC 3244 • Daily Fundamentals — **197**

Page 159

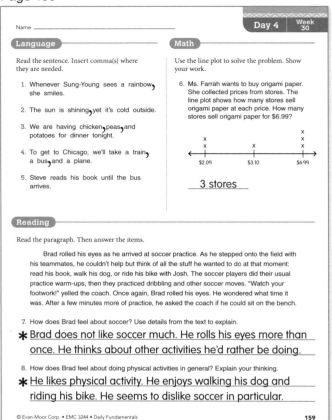

Name _____

Day 4 | Week 30

Language

Read the sentence. Insert comma(s) where they are needed.

1. Whenever Sung-Young sees a rainbow, she smiles.

2. The sun is shining, yet it's cold outside.

3. We are having chicken, peas, and potatoes for dinner tonight.

4. To get to Chicago, we'll take a train, a bus, and a plane.

5. Steve reads his book until the bus arrives.

Math

Use the line plot to solve the problem. Show your work.

6. Ms. Farrah wants to buy origami paper. She collected prices from stores. The line plot shows how many stores sell origami paper at each price. How many stores sell origami paper for $6.99?

$\underline{\text{3 stores}}$

Reading

Read the paragraph. Then answer the items.

Brad rolled his eyes as he arrived at soccer practice. As he stepped onto the field with his teammates, he couldn't help but think of all the stuff he wanted to do at that moment: read his book, walk his dog, or ride his bike with Josh. The soccer players did their usual practice warm-ups, then they practiced dribbling and other soccer moves. "Watch your footwork!" yelled the coach. Once again, Brad rolled his eyes. He wondered what time it was. After a few minutes more of practice, he asked the coach if he could sit on the bench.

7. How does Brad feel about soccer? Use details from the text to explain.

✳ Brad does not like soccer much. He rolls his eyes more than once. He thinks about other activities he'd rather be doing.

8. How does Brad feel about doing physical activities in general? Explain your thinking.

✳ He likes physical activity. He enjoys walking his dog and riding his bike. He seems to dislike soccer in particular.

© Evan-Moor Corp. • EMC 3244 • Daily Fundamentals   **159**

Page 160

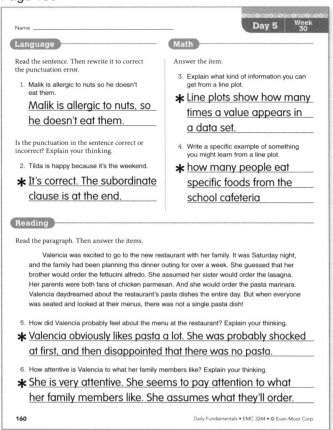

Name _____

Day 5 | Week 30

Language

Read the sentence. Then rewrite it to correct the punctuation error.

1. Malik is allergic to nuts so he doesn't eat them.

Malik is allergic to nuts, so he doesn't eat them.

Is the punctuation in the sentence correct or incorrect? Explain your thinking.

2. Tilda is happy because it's the weekend.

✳ It's correct. The subordinate clause is at the end.

Math

Answer the item.

3. Explain what kind of information you can get from a line plot.

✳ Line plots show how many times a value appears in a data set.

4. Write a specific example of something you might learn from a line plot.

✳ how many people eat specific foods from the school cafeteria

Reading

Read the paragraph. Then answer the items.

Valencia was excited to go to the new restaurant with her family. It was Saturday night, and the family had been planning this dinner outing for over a week. She guessed that her brother would order the fettucini alfredo. She assumed her sister would order the lasagna. Her parents were both fans of chicken parmesan. And she would order the pasta marinara. Valencia daydreamed about the restaurant's pasta dishes the entire day. But when everyone was seated and looked at their menus, there was not a single pasta dish!

5. How did Valencia probably feel about the menu at the restaurant? Explain your thinking.

✳ Valencia obviously likes pasta a lot. She was probably shocked at first, and then disappointed that there was no pasta.

6. How attentive is Valencia to what her family members like? Explain your thinking.

✳ She is very attentive. She seems to pay attention to what her family members like. She assumes what they'll order.

160   Daily Fundamentals • EMC 3244 • © Evan-Moor Corp.

Take It to Your Seat Centers
Math

Grades K–6

Independent practice, perfect for students at all levels.

Take It to Your Seat Centers: Math

Hands-on practice of core math skills! Each of the 12 centers focuses on key math concepts and presents skill practice in engaging visual and tactile activities. The easy-to-assemble centers include full-color cards and mats, directions, answer keys, and student record forms. Ideal for any classroom and to support RTI or ELLs. 160 full-color pages. Correlated to state standards and Common Core State Standards.

www.evan-moor.com/tmcent

	Teacher's Edition Print		Teacher's Edition E-book
GRADE	**EMC**	**GRADE**	**EMC**
K	3070	K	3070i
1	3071	1	3071i
2	3072	2	3072i
3	3073	3	3073i
4	3074	4	3074i
5	3075	5	3075i
6	3076	6	3076i

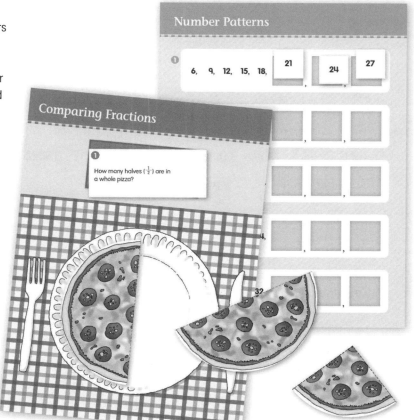

Daily Word Problems

Students' problem-solving skills improve day by day as they take part in meaningful, real-life math practice!

Grades 1–6

- Students learn to persevere in solving 180 word problems through engaging practice of meaningful, theme-based problems.

- The 36 weeks of practice activities address grade-level math concepts such as addition, fractions, logic, algebra, and more.

- Monday through Thursday activities present students with a one- or two-step word problem, while Friday's format is more extensive and requires multiple steps.

Correlated to state standards and Common Core State Standards.

www.evan-moor.com/dwp

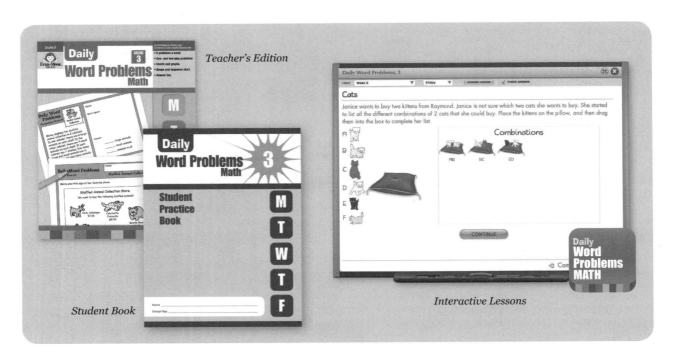

Teacher's Edition

Student Book

Interactive Lessons

Order the format right for you

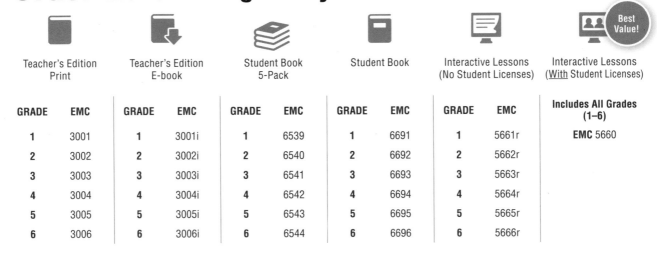

Teacher's Edition Print		Teacher's Edition E-book		Student Book 5-Pack		Student Book		Interactive Lessons (No Student Licenses)		Interactive Lessons (With Student Licenses)
GRADE	EMC	GRADE	EMC	GRADE	EMC	GRADE	EMC	GRADE	EMC	Includes All Grades (1–6)
1	3001	1	3001i	1	6539	1	6691	1	5661r	EMC 5660
2	3002	2	3002i	2	6540	2	6692	2	5662r	
3	3003	3	3003i	3	6541	3	6693	3	5663r	
4	3004	4	3004i	4	6542	4	6694	4	5664r	
5	3005	5	3005i	5	6543	5	6695	5	5665r	
6	3006	6	3006i	6	6544	6	6696	6	5666r	